RENÉ DESCARTES
A Biography

RENÉ DESCARTES

A Biography

BY

JACK ROCHFORD VROOMAN

G. P. Putnam's Sons

New York

Copyright © 1970 by Jack R. Vrooman

Library of Congress Catalog Card Number: 68-25463

To Andrew

ACKNOWLEDGMENTS

I am indebted, for the kind assistance they gave me in the preparation of this work, to Miss Sandra Flitterman, Miss Jean Muramoto, and Miss Joan Piurek, who all three labored as typists and research assistants. I should also like to express my thanks to Professor Jean Boorsch of Yale University for his reading of the manuscript in its early stages and his helpful suggestions and encouragement. Similarly Professor Gilbert Gadoffre of the University of Manchester gave me very useful direction and incentive by both his work and his conversation. To my colleagues, especially Professors Basil Guy and Walter Rex, I owe thanks for their continued interest and invaluable criticism.

J. R. V.

Contents

Illustrations

Following page 156

It was the mission of Descartes, and the bent of his nature, both to discover truth and to proclaim it. It was his misfortune that circumstances often set his two ambitions in mutual antagonism.

A. BOYCE GIBSON,
The Philosophy of Descartes

Introduction

MORE has been written about Descartes in the past sixty years than in the two and a half centuries following his death in 1650. Recent Cartesian scholarship is largely concerned with interpreting his work, with a reevaluation of both his philosophical and his scientific writings. There is also an interest in his correspondence, of which the definitive edition by Adam and Milhaud was completed in 1963. Biography, too, has played an important role in the study of the philosopher who, perhaps better than any other, demonstrates the close relationship between one's life and one's work. Since Charles Adam's monumental study, *Vie et Oeuvres de Descartes—Étude historique* in 1910, there have appeared no less than fifty books and articles that are biographically orientated. Another life of the philosopher is justified, however, particularly for English readers, because the only biography in English, Elizabeth Haldane's *Descartes, His Life and Times*, was published in 1905. Although age is no criterion for a book's authenticity or completeness— Baillet's seventeenth-century work will always remain essential for any study of Descartes' life—recent scholarship, particularly in French, has added much to our appreciation and knowledge of that country's most influential philosopher.

The author has tried to focus on six periods in the philosopher's life that were crucially important for his personal development and for the works he produced. The chapters are intended to present a series of portraits, each of which displays a different aspect of his many-faceted genius. Although references to his work are not only unavoidable, but imperative for any understanding of the man, the present work remains essentially a biography rather than a critical study.

Often Descartes speaks for himself through his letters. The *Correspondance*, with its invaluable notes by Adam and Milhaud, has been quoted extensively. Many of the letters appear here for the first time in English. All the translations are by the author, who has endeavored to make them as literal as possible without their appearing stilted. Descartes' style presents a rather unique problem to those accustomed to modern-day English. Often it is criticized for its Latinisms, as being overly complicated, and many of the letters and works were originally written in Latin. If occasionally the sentence structure seems awkward, it is because the author has preferred to keep as close to the original as possible, believing that the style reveals the man. Descartes was never awkward, whether writing in French, Latin, or Dutch; yet to transform his prose into the most current English usage would make him speak in a false voice.

The immensity of the works devoted to Descartes is evidenced by Gregor Sebba's *Bibliographia Cartesiana*, which contains some 3,612 entries. Many of these are articles written by and for specialists. Descartes wanted to be known by the public at large, *le grand public*, and therefore the more technical aspects of his work and the large portions of his correspondence concerning scientific experiments have been virtually ignored. That part of twentieth-century scholarship which has added to our knowledge of the man's life since Adam's *Vie* and Gustave Cohen's *Ecrivains français en Hollande* has been included insofar as possible. Noteworthy among recent biographical works to which the author is indebted are those by Gouhier, Sirven, Poulet, Serrurier, and Lewis.

Every biography presents Descartes in a slightly different light, probably because each biographer has met his subject under different circumstances. Much of the philosopher's life remains a mystery. He was often secretive, and one will continue to question the true nature of this man who said he would appear behind a mask. It is hoped that the pages which follow will present him, if not in all his complexity, at least honestly and in such a way as to make the reader want to know him better.

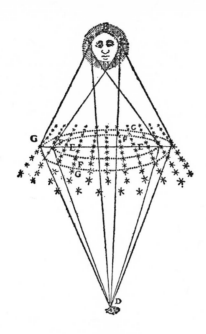

CHAPTER 1
The Formative Years

DESCARTES was no ivory-tower philosopher. His writings remain a monument to his genius, which encompassed both the sciences and the arts; yet the reflective scholar, so given to secluded meditation, was also an adventurer, a cavalier who danced, gambled, and was an excellent swordsman. A gifted mathematician and physicist, Descartes was simultaneously the well-bred gentleman given to intellectual pursuits and the impetuous traveler who by his daring could outwit a band of mariners plotting against his life. The philosopher, although he frequently retreated into solitude, was very much a man of action. He was continually searching for truth, not in

19

the abstract, but as it could be applied to his own existence and made to serve as a guide to future generations. He was, for example, one of the first to experiment with the use of wheel-chairs for the handicapped and, toward the end of his life, was fascinated with ways to prevent his hair from turning gray. His writings, which reflect his life both public and private, are filled with paradoxes, with passages that alternate between hope and despair, between denial and affirmation. Yet in the man himself there lies an essential unity which resolves these seeming con-tradictions. One has only to follow him through the various stages of his quest, which at times resembles a labyrinth of en-tangled paths, in order to discover the reality of Descartes: a great thinker, but also a human being who still speaks to man-kind as a friend eager to help us endure and, hopefully, improve our fate.

From the moment of his birth Descartes seemed destined for an early grave. His mother, Jeanne Brochard, who had married Joachim Descartes in 1589, was suffering from a disease of the lungs when René was born on March 31, 1596 in the little town of La Haye in Touraine. It was from her that the future phi-losopher said he inherited a slight cough and a pale complexion. His delicate health was to remain with him through adolescence and was an important factor in determining the kind of education he was to receive; but by the time he was twenty Descartes had overcome this obstacle to the point of becoming an accom-plished horseman, and by the time he was in his forties he con-fessed that he never felt farther from death.

Very little is known about Descartes' mother. The daughter of a lieutenant general, she came from Poitiers, where Descartes would eventually study law. He was her fourth child; the first, a boy named Pierre, died at birth; the second, also called Pierre, was born in 1591 and later took the name of Sieur de la Bretaillière; the third, Descartes' older sister, was christened Jeanne after her mother and grandmother. The exact date of her birth is unknown; some accounts place it in 1593, while others record it as early as 1590. Descartes' own birth date would be uncertain were it not for an inscription on a portrait by Frans van Schooten for the second edition of the Latin translation of his *Geometry*, published in Holland in 1659. Descartes had refused to let the date of his birth appear in the first edition or, for that matter, during his lifetime, because he feared it might give rise to speculation by those who cast horoscopes. He believed that such matters belonged properly to family archives and church records, and he was always to remain circumspect where his private life was concerned. Legends sprang up regarding even the place and circumstances of his birth, some contending that he was born not in his grandmother's house in La Haye but rather beside a ditch when his mother was taken by labor pains and could not continue her journey. If this were true, he would have been a native of Poitou rather than of Touraine; the quarrel still continues between the two provinces, each wanting to claim Descartes as its own.[1] At any rate, Descartes never mentions these conflicting accounts, and one might assume that he remained ignorant of them. Whereas La Haye's claim appears more valid, usually Descartes referred to himself as a gentleman from Poitou, for he was certainly aware of strong ancestral ties with that province.

His mother died in childbirth on May 13, 1597, and three days later her fifth and last child followed her to the grave. Her death occurred when René was about fourteen months old, and thus it seems strange that in his only reference to her Descartes could make so serious a blunder as to write that his mother died "a few days after my birth from a lung ailment caused by some sort of grief."[2] Although this reminiscence was given many years later in a letter to Princess Elizabeth, it remains a mystery that Descartes should have been ignorant of the circumstances and time of his mother's death. One thing is certain, and that is his mother exerted virtually no influence on Descartes' child-

hood, unless it was through her absence—psychologists, for
example, are tempted to explain Descartes' early behavior as an
effort to find the kind of security which was never afforded him
by a mother—and from the cradle until he was old enough and
strong enough to enter school, Descartes was cared for by his
maternal grandmother and a nurse whom he was never to forget.

But of these two women, again there is scarcely a word. His
grandmother is mentioned only in terms of family inheritance
or baptismal registers, and the name of his nurse, whom he was
to remember on his deathbed, is never given. In all extant letters
of his immense correspondence, there is not one addressed to
his sister who, along with his older brother Pierre, was reared in
their grandmother's house. Descartes did occasionally write to
his brother, but the tone is always cool, the subject is usually
business, and one has the impression that there was friction between the two. If any of his immediate relatives did influence
his childhood, it probably was his father.

Joachim Descartes (Des Cartes, Des Quartes, or Des Quartis,
as the name was originally spelled) held the post of councilor
at the *parlement* of Rennes in Brittany. These provincial courts
were similar in structure to the Paris *parlement*, although less influential. They were composed of magistrates who constituted
the highest court of law. Princes of the blood were frequently
among their members, and the king himself sometimes presided
over their activities. Joachim's duties at court required his attendance for no more than six months out of the year at Rennes;
consequently, most of his family life was spent at La Haye
until his second marriage, which took place around 1600, when
he bought property and moved to the town of Rennes. The
Descartes family was one of the most respected in the whole
region. Most of Joachim's ancestors had served in the army and
later retired to live as country gentlemen. Although not of noble
origin, they could lay claim to being members of the *petite
noblesse* and were thus exempt from taxation. Rather than follow

the profession of arms, Joachim chose the practice of law, as had his father and as would his eldest son. René was therefore born into a family that assured him both a certain amount of financial security and a privileged position in society. His father, aware of the child's fragile health, was at first most concerned with the development of the boy's body and resolved to postpone his studies until he was strong enough to withstand the rigors of a formal education, which in the seventeenth century was more demanding and began earlier than most today. The lad, left almost exclusively in the care of women—his grandmother, his faithful nurse, and perhaps his sister—must have led a relatively lonely life at first, but his father soon became aware of his extraordinary curiosity and used to refer to him as his "little philosopher." Once, many years later, in a joking mood, when comparing his two sons, the father said that René was "good for nothing except getting himself bound in leather." [3] That the philosopher was not particularly ambitious to have his thoughts published is borne out by a note to his friend Marin Mersenne, which might be considered a direct retort to his father's comment: "I am more careful and I think it is more important to learn what is useful for the conduct of my own life than it is for me to publish the little that I have learned." [4]

Because of René's natural inclination toward study, Joachim Descartes decided to choose the best school he could find for his younger son's education. His choice of the Collège de la Flèche was probably the most important act in the relationship between father and son. Although Joachim undoubtedly enjoyed the pleasures of the countryside, there is little reason to believe that he spent much time introducing his son to them. By the time René was ten years old, his father had remarried and had taken up permanent residence at Rennes. Fond as he was of the child, theirs was never that close relationship which ideally unites father and son. Descartes' letters to his father, like those to his other relatives, are few and speak almost exclusively of money matters. And yet at his father's death in 1640, the philosopher appears to have been seriously affected. "I am not one of those," he writes the following year to a friend who was suffering from the loss of his brother, "who believe that tears and sadness belong only to women and that in order to appear a true man one must always feel obliged to present a tranquil countenance. I felt [experienced] not long ago the loss of two people who were very close [to me]." [5] One of these two people was certainly his father; the other could have been either his sister or his daughter. But just how many tears Descartes shed is impossible to ascertain, for he was by then the mature philosopher, long separated from his family. His brother did not bother to inform him of their father's death, which could mean that they had never been particularly close or could be interpreted as a sign of Pierre's disdain for anyone who would adopt a literary profession. If Descartes was grieved by the loss of his father, he was also able to rationalize his unhappiness and attempt to remedy it as quickly as possible. In the same letter, after speaking of his own father's death, he counsels his friend to rid himself of his sadness:

> Besides, it would be too cowardly to abandon oneself entirely to unhappiness; and it would be a miscalculation not to try with all one's strength to rid oneself of such a troublesome passion. The profession of arms, in which you grew up, accustoms men to see their best friends die without a second thought; and there is nothing in this world so annoying that custom doesn't make it bearable. [6]

He continues by comparing the loss of a hand (his friend had lost an arm in battle) to the loss of a brother and says that since his friend never seemed particularly bothered by the loss of one, why should he be afflicted by the loss of the other. This stoicism, if not cynicism, occurring where and when it does, only serves to add support to the theory that Descartes and his father were not on very close terms. Joachim was an amiable man but, like the rest of Descartes' relatives, not very distinguished.

Family ties seemed to have little direct bearing upon Descartes' life up to the time he entered school. Perhaps the place of his childhood left a stronger impression on the boy than did the people who surrounded him. He came from one of the most beautiful parts of France, a fruitful region whose streams kept it green all summer long. Feudal castles dotted the countryside and may well have inspired memories of chivalry or of the most recent devastation caused by religious wars. The routes were not always safe for travelers, and this sometimes enabled his father to absent himself from attendance at the *parlement* in Rennes. Just how much time René spent in the country is impossible to determine, for he makes few direct references to it, but his writings abound in comparisons and descriptions which could well have been prompted by memories of childhood days of Touraine. Since it was a region of vineyards, it is not surprising that Descartes should speak of apples and grapes and compare things to new wine and to the harvests. No matter where he traveled later, he was always to feel the need of open air and greenery about him. He may well have been thinking of the delights of his birthplace in the garden of France when he hesitated, a year before his death, to go to that "country of bears, between rocks and ice" [7]—Sweden.

One of the most memorable passages in which Descartes recalls the early years of his life concerns neither his family nor his native province. Writing in answer to a friend's question about the cause of love and what makes us love one person rather than another to give substance to a rather complicated theory of psychology and physiology, Descartes draws the following example from his own youth:

> When I was a child, I was in love with a girl of my own age who was slightly cross-eyed; because of this, whenever I looked at her unfocused eyes, the impression which the sight [of her] produced on my brain was so joined to that which awakened the passion of love, that for a long time afterward, whenever I saw cross-eyed people, I felt more inclined to love them than others, simply because they had this fault; and yet I didn't know the reason.[8]

Like so many other episodes in Descartes' life, the cross-eyed girl remains a mystery. It is almost as if he had deliberately tried to veil in his later writings any details which would elucidate his innermost feelings. Although he was not eager to increase his personal reputation, he was ever mindful of the image he would create of himself in his works. One of the mottoes he would claim as his lifetime guide was that the good life is the secret life: *Bene qui latuit, bene vixit.*[9] But the roots of the man who would later have to defend himself against charges of atheism are undecipherable in the young Descartes. His real formation as the man who was to revolutionize thought began when he was ten years old. In 1606 René's father placed him in the Collège de la Flèche. He could not have made a better choice for the future education of his son than this school, newly founded by the king.

Henry IV was one of France's most ambitious and also most amiable kings. Today schoolchildren remember him for his promise of a chicken in every pot, but at the time of Descartes' entering La Flèche the situation both at home and abroad was far from the affluent or peaceful society of which the peasantry might dream. Henry was then in the twelfth year of his reign, and France was passing through a time of intellectual depression, of dogma and intolerance. It was a period of transition from the Renaissance to the future achievements of the age of classicism. France had been torn apart by political and religious upheavals and now wanted rest and order. Henry's immediate predecessor on the throne had been assassinated, and his own marriage with Marguerite de Valois in 1572 marked the same date as the St. Bartholomew's Day Massacre. It was Henry's task to put an end to the civil wars which set Huguenot against Catholic, nobleman against commoner (and often against the king), and in every case Frenchman against Frenchman. As father of his country, he was faced with the necessity of uniting its warring factions and subjugating private interests to the good of the state. There can be no doubt that he had the welfare of his country at heart. Out of political anarchy Henry strove to establish absolute monarchy. He became in the eyes of his subjects not only a symbol of freedom from oppression, but also a living witness to God's presence in their kingdom. In times of plague or when receiving the scrofulous poor in public ceremonies, the king was considered a direct link with divine power when he uttered the words, *"Le roi te touche, Dieu te guérisse."* Henry can be credited with restoring law and order to a nation in desperate need of security. And in 1598, with the signing of the Edict of Nantes, religious warfare came to an end.

Henry's dealings with the Jesuits had been many. In 1594 he banished them, for it was rumored that they were connected with an attempt on his life. In 1603, however, they were recalled, despite the protests of the king's principal minister, the Duc de Sully. Henry even chose a member of the Society of Jesus as his personal confessor. The king was impressed by the work that the Jesuit order had been doing elsewhere, and he realized that the destiny of France would be guided by the education of her future leaders. He allocated large sums of money for the conversion of the royal palace at La Flèche into a school specially designed for the training of gentlemen commoners such as Descartes. The site particularly appealed to the king, for his mother had lived there at the time of his birth, and he had often returned to visit. In detailed instructions written in his own hand, the king requested that his heart and that of his queen be laid to rest in the college chapel. One of Henry's most trusted counselors, the Marquis de la Varenne, who was a native of La Flèche, urged the king to spare no expense. Varenne was also influential in dispelling any earlier distrust concerning the Jesuits. The terms in which Henry speaks of them in the contract for the founding of the school show that his admiration and trust of the order were by now limitless. The conditions Henry imposed upon the establishment of the school [10] are not only detailed in matters of buildings and grounds, but also reveal a concern for the caliber of scholarship that might well make a college administrator smile if it were to appear in a handbook of university regulations today:

> Because His Majesty wants to remedy as much as possible the abuses which are being committed in his kingdom, having recognized that confusion has spread among letters as well as the other arts, professors granting indifferently the degrees of *licenciés, bacheliers,* and *docteurs* to all those who appear providing they have money, His Majesty orders that there will be eight professors at the college, each of whom shall be paid by said college five hundred écus yearly, four of whom will be in medicine and four in jurisprudence, and who, having judged the students and others who present themselves before them as worthy of the above-mentioned degrees, shall pass them without taking anything from them; and so that there be no fraud committed, these professors may not admit anyone to said degrees without his having taken a public examination which four of the fathers shall attend and who will sign with the professors the degree which the student shall receive.[11]

Henry wanted La Flèche to be the best school of its kind, not only in France, but in the world. Even though many of his grandiose projects were never completed, the college quickly earned a reputation as the most illustrious institution a student could enter. And whenever a gentleman at court asked the king where he should send his son to school, the immediate reply was always, "To La Flèche."

René was ten years old when he arrived in the spring of 1606[12] to begin his studies. This first experience away from home must have left a deep impression on the boy whose delicate health had prevented him from starting in the winter months. He could not help but be awed by the magnificence of the buildings, the charm of the surroundings, and most especially by the challenge of starting a new life amid the bustle of activity created by approximately 1,200 schoolboys and their masters. News of the school's excellence traveled rapidly, so that as the enrollment increased, so did the staff. In 1606 there were forty-two teachers; by 1611 there were eighty-three! The Jesuit fathers had gained the well-deserved reputation of having the most modern and most effective educational methods. They quickly established themselves not only as the best, but also as the most sympathetic instructors for the youth of France. The Collège de la Flèche was far removed from the kind of institution which Montaigne ridiculed as "jails for captive youth." The Jesuits tried hard to rid their instruction of everything which smacked of dogmatism and pedantry. Classes were enlivened by open discussions and competitions for prizes, and the priests lived with their students as mentors, confessors, and friends. There was nothing somber or oppressive about their school. Religious it was, but religion was oriented toward life, which was viewed as something joyous rather than one long act of penitence. Being a relatively new order, the Jesuits were open to new ideas. In addition to their learning in theology, they were interested in literature and the sciences. It was particularly because of the promulgation of new scientific ideas that their program of study was superior to that in comparable schools. The library, for example, could boast of one of the most complete collections of scientific works, and the fathers strived to incorporate this new knowledge into their courses.

The young Descartes was not lost in this academic atmosphere, nor was he unduly burdened by his studies. His natural curiosity and his keen mind made him seek additional readings and lessons, and it soon became apparent that he was no ordinary student. He occupied a very special place in the school, not only because he was able to surpass his contemporaries in the intellectual exercises of the classroom, but also because of the rather unusual privileges that were granted him by the fathers. Upon his arrival René's father had entrusted his son to the care of Père Charlet. Undoubtedly he told him of the boy's fragile health and unusual precociousness. The rector, who was distantly related to the Descartes family, took to the boy immediately. He assumed the role of father and friend, one of the many with whom Descartes would correspond years after he had left school. Père Charlet, in addition to guiding the boy's intellectual growth, was particularly anxious to improve his physical development.

The youth might have been entitled to certain privileges, for he had been entered as one of the twenty-four *gentils-hommes* in the school.[13] Distinctions of class, however, were of little importance within the confines of La Flèche, and sons of the nobility were treated with the same equanimity as their bourgeois counterparts. The result was a broader education and a basis for many lasting friendships. Descartes was one of the few boys who had his own room and did not live in the dormitory. Père Charlet, taking into consideration his charge's frail constitution and his meditative nature, allowed him to stay in bed late in the morning, long after the other boys were at their studies. This favor permitted René to conserve and increase his strength, and it also gave him time to reflect. The habit was never lost. To the end of his life he preferred to stay in bed as late as possible. He found these early morning hours best for reflection, and often, in later life he would wake, spend several hours in meditation, and write his thoughts while still in bed.

Although his intelligence marked him as superior to his classmates, Descartes, unlike so many precocious children, was no problem to either his teachers or other students. He was good-natured and eager to please. Rather than considering him a showoff, the boys could only admire his talents and share the respect his teachers had for him. His quick mind at times must have astounded if not embarrassed his instructors. Often, for example, he would question them about their definitions of terms, taxing their vocabularies if not their patience, and he was quick to point out that if the first principle of an argument was not accepted as true, then obviously all of the reasoning which followed was useless. But the Jesuits were, after all, both knowledgeable and urbane. The discipline which reigned in the school derived from the boys' admiration for their masters, whose learning and especially whose manners they strove to emulate. Naturally, René wanted to be the first in his class, and because he was so gifted, his teachers exempted him from regular attendance and from many of the routine assignments.

When not in class or involved either in physical exercises or meditation, he used this extra time afforded him by the fathers to read books that were forbidden to other students. He was fascinated by works on occultism. His schoolmates were also intrigued by tales of black magic and were sometimes duped by village charlatans. One of the professors, Père François, was making a study of the occult with the intention of refuting what were then termed the curious sciences. These included that portion of optics which produced strange effects with mirrors and glasses, astrology, cabal, magic in general, and chemistry.[14] The freedom with which Descartes was allowed to choose his own reading showed great tolerance on the part of the Jesuit fathers. Others were not so free from prejudice. A few years later a man was condemned as a sorcerer and executed for possessing a book on occult philosophy—the same book which Descartes had been reading at La Flèche.[15] But of far more importance than these tangential readings to the formation of Descartes' character and mode of thought was the regular curriculum.

His formal education began with the study of what he called fables and histories. By fables were meant the *Metamorphoses* of Ovid, and histories signified biographies of the great men of Greece and Rome. The first five and a half years were devoted to language and literature. He learned Greek and Latin grammar thoroughly. For him Latin was not a dead language, but one that he could both write and speak fluently. He corresponded and composed verses in Latin. Later he was to write three important works in Latin: *Meditationes, Epistola ad celeberrimum Voetium,* and *Principia philosophiae.* Latin authors such as Cicero, Vergil, Horace, and Seneca influenced his style and his thought. It was from them that he inherited his facility in rhetoric and his concept of the humanities. Study was not an arduous task for him; instead he considered his readings to be like conversations with the most respectable and well-bred men of the past—very special conversations in which they revealed only the best of their thoughts.[16] Long after Descartes had left La Flèche the words of the poet Ausonius were to return to him in a dream: *Quod vitae sectabor iter?*—"What path shall I follow in life?" [17] And in 1646, when disillusioned and discouraged by accusations of skepticism and atheism, he turned to Seneca, the Stoic philosopher he had studied in his youth, for a motto he could accept as his own:

> *Illi mors gravis incubat*
> *Qui, notus nimis omnibus,*
> *Ignotus moritur sibi.** [18]

After literature came the study of philosophy. The final three years of the program consisted of courses in logic, mathe-

* A sad death awaits the one
Who, too well known by others,
Dies unknown to himself.

matics, and physics. For this type of study René's enthusiasm knew no bounds. His interest in science verged on a passion, and he appeared a born mathematician. Nothing was more useful than this part of his education, for therein lay the key, he believed, to all the other sciences, indeed to all knowledge. At that time the teaching of physics and the other sciences was not divorced from that of metaphysics. Certainly it is not surprising that in the seventeenth-century Jesuit school, the sciences should be taught on a theological basis. A course in physics, for example, was based on Aristotle's philosophy transformed by the writings of Saint Thomas Aquinas, and in the classroom the *Summa theologica* was placed on a table next to the Bible. Descartes was later to take these two books with him when he traveled to Holland. The relationship of theology, more specifically ethics, to the sciences was not emphasized by his teachers.

René delighted in mathematics because of the certainty and logical reasoning he found there, but he still had not discovered their true use. The spheres to which mathematics could be applied appeared to him far too restricted, being limited almost exclusively to the mechanical arts. Even at this early age, he was interested in making his own education as practical as possible. The Jesuits, too, were aware of the necessity of teaching their students how to apply their knowledge to their present needs and future professions. Since the majority of the boys enrolled at La Flèche would enter military careers, any practical application of mathematics was geared toward the study of fortifications, navigation, and surveying. Descartes would eventually revolutionize the teaching of mathematics and effect a reform in the entire educational process.

During his stay at La Flèche two events occurred that stand out above all the others for their lasting impact not only on Descartes but on the world at large. The first took place on May 14, 1610, when Henry IV was assassinated by a fanatic named François Ravaillac. Ironically the king was stabbed as his carriage, halted momentarily by traffic, was passing by the Cemetery of the Innocents. All France mourned his death, but nowhere was the loss felt more deeply than at La Flèche, the school he had founded and in which he had taken such interest. The Jesuits had lost their most influential benefactor, and France without a strong king fell prey to all the incipient forces of feudal disorder. There were soon to be fresh revolts by nobles and Huguenots while Marie de Médicis acted as regent for the nine-year-old Louis XIII. Royal authority still rested upon insecure foundations, and the religious and political struggles that Henry IV had sought to end quickly revived. The day after the king's death, the Marquis de la Varenne reminded the queen of Henry's wish that his heart be sent to La Flèche. It was publicly displayed in Paris until June 1 when a procession of churchmen, princes, and nobles followed by an immense crowd set out for La Flèche, where they arrived three days later.

The entire school was draped in black. A 27-foot triumphal arch covered with mourning cloth and illuminated by candles stood in the courtyard. Everywhere were seen coats of arms, death masks, and tableaux depicting the king being carried by angels to heaven. Amid this funeral decor a herald ascended the platform in front of the altar, where he received the king's heart from the Duc de Montbazon. Three times he repeated, *"Le Roi est mort; priez pour son âme."* The herald placed the heart in a gilded urn and then, turning to the silent audience, said again three times, *"Vive le Roi! Vive Louis Treize, très chrétien roi de France et de Navarre!"* The ceremony was over, but so that the memory of their benefactor might be perpetuated, the Jesuits declared June 4 of every year be set aside for the solemn celebration of the anniversary of the king's death.[19]

The funeral service must have created a deep impression on the mind of the young Descartes. He had been chosen as one of twenty-four selected pupils to participate in the elaborate ceremony of the burial of the king's heart.[20] Of even more significance for Descartes were the events of the following year when the college celebrated the first *Henriade*. The Jesuits wanted this first anniversary of Henry's death to be marked with as much pomp and circumstance as they deemed appropriate. The affair turned out to be the most elaborate in the history of La Flèche. It lasted three days, and neither students nor those who came in droves from neighboring towns had seen anything comparable. From the first year of its founding the college had attracted curious villagers to an annual literary competition. This created a strong academic rivalry among the students, for the best compositions were read to the public. This tradition was now incorporated into the other festivities which began on June 4, 1611. A gigantic effigy of the king's heart was erected, and once again the students decorated the entire school with symbols and inscriptions which they delighted in explaining to visitors. On the first day there was a procession from the Church of Saint-Thomas to the school chapel. Two funeral orations were given, the first in French in the morning, and the second that evening in Latin, pronounced by Descartes' protector and friend Père Charlet. The second day was devoted to philosophic dissertations and literary exercises—all in honor of the dead king. These were followed by the reading of compositions in Latin, Greek, and French—both in prose and in verse. On the third day, as was customary in practically all celebrations at La Flèche, a play was presented by the students.[21] These theatrical allegories were extremely popular, and it was perhaps a distant memory of these activities which formed part of his inspiration when, two months before his death, Descartes composed verses on the birth of Peace and even wrote a comedy ballet—a mixture of prose and poetry.

It is impossible to determine the exact extent of the impact of this celebration on the fifteen-year-old René. If he wrote verses to the dead king (and surely he did, for his enthusiasm for poetry at the time is well known), they have either been lost or exist unsigned and unidentifiable among the thousands of lines collected in what Rochemonteix refers to as the *Larmes du Collège de la Flèche*, an account of the proceedings published in Latin in 1611 bearing the title *In anniversarium Henrici Magni obitus diem lacrymae Collegii Flexiensis Regii S. J.* Descartes never once mentions Henry IV in his correspondence; but this omission should not belie the importance of the first *Henriade*. One thing is certain: His sense of patriotism and belief in the monarchy were closely associated with his religious faith. The king and the school, like the king and the chapel, become inseparable.

Descartes had participated in the transferal of Henry's heart and in the pageant of the *Henriade*; in addition, he attended chapel, where every day mass was said in honor of the benefactor of La Flèche. These ceremonies combined to produce in Descartes a lasting respect for his king and for his Church. These religious and commemorative activities also instilled a love of pageantry in René's mind. Ritual and pomp seemed to hold a special fascination for him, and later he will be found attending such diverse spectacles as the coronation of the Emperor Ferdinand II in Frankfort, the doge's traditional marriage with the sea in Venice at carnival time, and a papal jubilee for Urban VIII in Rome.

The year 1611 was important in Descartes' life for another reason, one which was to have a more direct influence upon both the schoolboy and the future scientist. Among the sonnets recited in memory of the king, there was one which bore the title "On the Death of King Henry the Great and on the Discovery of Some New Planets or Stars Moving Around Jupiter, Made This Year by Galileo, Celebrated Mathematician of the Grand Duke of Florence." [22] The verses are dull and virtually devoid of any literary merit, yet they are historically significant to anyone interested in the intellectual climate in which Descartes grew up. By a curious combination the popular conception of astronomy is linked to that of the Church and the state. The anonymous poet speaks of France as threatened by a second deluge because of the tears shed for Henry IV. Then the sun appears to offer solace to the grieving nation:

> *Lorsque l'astre du jour, qui va faisant la ronde*
> *Autour de l'Univers, meu des proches malheurs*
> *Qui hastaient devers nous leur course vagabonde*
> *Lui parla de la sorte, au fort de ses douleurs:*

> *"France de qui les pleurs, pour l'amour de ton Prince,*
> *Nuisent par leur excès à toute autre province,*
> *Cesse de t'affliger sur son vide tombeau;*

> *Car Dieu l'ayant tiré tout entier de la terre,*
> *Au ciel de Jupiter maintenant il esclaire*
> *Pour servir aux mortels de céleste flambeau."* * 2³

In the eyes of the schoolboy-poet, the sun, revolving around the earth, now had in the heavens a second celestial body which was to serve as a guide to humanity. For the enlightenment of mankind, God had raised Henry IV to the sky and placed him in the form of a star next to Jupiter. The author of the sonnet was obviously blind to the importance of Galileo's discovery, but for Descartes it was to prove of lasting consequence.

The recently invented telescope was then the talk of the day. Galileo constructed his first *lunettes d'approche*, those which bear his name, in 1609. The same year shops along the Seine were selling them to curious Parisians. The Italian scientist

---

*Then the star of the day, making its rounds
About the universe, moved by the approaching misfortunes
That were quickening their vagabond course toward us,
Spoke thus in the midst of the country's griefs:

"France, your excessive tears for the love
Of your Prince are harming every other province.
Stop grieving over his empty tomb;

For God having taken him bodily from the earth,
He now shines in the heavens
And serves as a celestial torch for mortals."

continued to perfect his devices until on January 7, 1610, he was able to observe four satellites of Jupiter. These stars were connected not only with the dead king, as in the case of the sonnet, but were also called the *Astres de Médicis,* a name which paid homage to the family of the queen mother, then regent of France. All of Galileo's discoveries corroborated the Copernican explanation of the universe rather than the Ptolemaic system. Galileo, however, did not declare his acceptance of Copernican theory until 1613. Some twenty years later he was to be condemned as a heretic, but on the first anniversary of Henry IV's death the Jesuits at La Flèche, like the rest of Europe, were too fascinated by the discovery of this new world in the sky to be critical of any possible consequences.

Descartes shared this enthusiasm. The telescope enlarged man's vision of the universe, and it was soon to change his entire conception of the world about him. As a schoolboy Descartes heard talk of the four satellites and also of different phases of Venus as well as spots on the sun—all brought into view by the telescope. In 1611 the Jesuit fathers saw no danger in teaching their students about these newfound discoveries; on the contrary, even their college in Rome had that very year supported theses in favor of Galileo's observations. What for many others turned out to be a passing fad, the curiosity of the moment, became for Descartes a lasting interest. In later writings he would attempt to explain such phenomena by the application of new principles. In all of these discoveries, he was less interested in the facts than in the theory which lay behind them. He hoped for a scientific explanation of the uses to which the telescope might be put. This was one of the tasks he set for himself in the *Dioptrique,* the application of geometry to the world of physics. Descartes was forever searching for the practical effect, and if the telescope were constructed scientifically, would not its powers of observation be limitless?

In a lengthy and extremely technical letter on the subject

of convex and concave lenses that he wrote in 1629 to Jean
Ferrier, a French artisan known for his skill in the making of
optical instruments, Descartes shows that his faith in scientific
progress was highly optimistic:

> Besides, don't expect to work miracles on the first try with
> these new machines; I warn you so that you won't get your
> hopes up and so that you don't begin working unless you are
> resolved to spend a lot of time; but if you had a year or two to
> equip yourself with everything necessary, I would wager that
> we'll see . . . if there are animals on the moon.[24]

The impact of his Jesuit education was great upon the mind
of René. It was also lifelong, for he continued to write both to
and about his teachers at La Flèche. But it is impossible to tell
what his thoughts were while he was actually there. Everything
he wrote about La Flèche was penned long after he had left
the college, and when viewed in retrospect, one's thoughts are
often tempered by feelings that occurred later. It is necessary,
therefore, to examine with extreme care Descartes' appraisal of
his years at La Flèche and remember that his evaluation is not
that of an adolescent schoolboy, but of one who had long since
graduated. His most complete account is given in the *Discourse*,
which appeared twenty-three years after he had left the school.
He begins: "From my childhood I was nourished on letters, and
since I was led to believe that by their study one could acquire
a clear and certain knowledge of all that is useful in life, I had
a great desire to learn them." [25] This attitude corresponds with
all that has been said about Descartes as a student, the nature of
his studies, his enthusiasm, and particularly his desire to put
knowledge to a practical use. He has nothing but praise for his
teachers who undoubtedly were responsible for instilling in him
this respect for the study of the humanities and, more specifically,
the Greek and Roman classics. It comes as a surprise, therefore,
when in the next sentence he confesses that as soon as he had

finished his course of studies, he changed his mind completely. At some time between his life as a student and the writing of the *Discourse*, his initial optimism concerning the value of this kind of education turned to disillusionment. Why? "Because," he continues, "I found myself involved in so many doubts and errors that it seemed to me in trying to educate myself I had done nothing more than discover my own ignorance at every turn." [26]

What follows is an indictment of almost every aspect of his education. Granted that La Flèche was the best school in Europe and that he was one of its best pupils (the young scholar was far from modest when he came to evaluate his own talents), Descartes found that every discipline was either useless or in need of drastic change. After giving a modicum of credit to certain studies, the *Discourse* then proceeds to point out their faults. A knowledge of Latin and Greek is necessary if one is to read the classics, but too much time spent in the study of the past often makes us ignorant of our own times. Literature is frequently far removed from reality, and one who tries to model his actions on those of legendary heroes will find himself ill adapted to life as it exists. The young philosopher admits that he was at first enraptured by poetry, but true poets are born such—no amount of study will produce what comes to them through inspiration. The language of "agreeable fancies" and the art of rhetoric are unnecessary to the man who would convince another of the truth of his statement. In reviewing the curriculum, he is pleased by the study of mathematics, because of the certainty and evidence of its reasoning, but he notes that its application is far too restricted and that it should have been the basis for far greater knowledge. The writings of the moralists he compares to "very magnificent palaces which were built on nothing but sand and mud." Theology, based as it is upon faith, must remain above our comprehension without some special help from heaven. Philosophy continues to dispute the same questions without ever resolving a single one of them. Since so many learned men have upheld such conflicting opinions, he doesn't hope for any better results. The other sciences (and by these Descartes means physics, medicine, and law) fare no better in his estimation. They are all based on rather shaky foundations, that is to say, Aristotelian principles, and offer neither sufficient glory nor profit to tempt him to continue their study.

What Descartes was condemning was not his teachers, nor even their methods, but rather the whole humanistic orientation of education. The Jesuits, like many other educators, had praised the study of Greek and Roman classics for their ultimate and very practical utility. Descartes found that the impression of life they had instilled in him was at odds with the life he was experiencing. Even the sciences were of very little use, for they were taught in a manner that was devoid of unity and which offered only certain formulas that exercised one's memory rather than one's intelligence.

René was only an obscure schoolboy when he left La Flèche in 1614. His formal education was virtually complete, for although he later studied law at Poitiers, that institution left no significant mark on his temperament or intellectual development. He refers again and again to La Flèche, but in his entire correspondence there is not one reference to his legal studies. Descartes at eighteen was ready to face the world. It was not a question of his having to earn a living, for his family had enough money to make his future profession of no immediate concern: "I did not feel, thank God," he tells us, "in a state which would oblige me to make a trade of science in order to increase my fortune." [27] La Flèche had given him the manners of a young gentleman and the knowledge considered appropriate for one of his station. By most modern standards his education would be deemed seriously lacking, for it included no real study of history, no chemistry or biology, and no physics except that of

Aristotle. But in addition to his training in philosophy and letters, the Jesuits had taught him not only how to ride, fence, and dance, but also how to walk, stand, and even how to move his eyes in a socially correct fashion. As their product he had what might be termed an elegant *savoir-faire*. He possessed, to use his own words, a spirit far above pedantry, for which he duly thanked his instructors: "And I must give this honor to my masters and say that there is no place in the world where philosophy is better taught than at La Flèche." [28]

Despite his later criticism of the curriculum, at eighteen Descartes was far from being a young iconoclast. On the contrary, his opinions were extremely orthodox, particularly in matters concerning politics and religion. The principal aim of the Jesuit fathers was to instill in their students a respect for their king, for many of them would become public administrators or enter military careers, and a respect for ecclesiastical authority. In short, education at La Flèche was designed to produce loyal subjects of the crown and faithful members of the Church. Even though he never officially studied theology, for it was not taught to lay students, he regarded it with a certain amount of awe, as a science unto itself which possessed mysteries that no layman could comprehend. The Jesuits encouraged their students in logical arguments, in the art of debate, and in the methods and application of reasoned questioning. This spirit of free investigation, however, was strictly severed from theological matters. Descartes could therefore remain extremely orthodox in his faith and express skepticism in his secular inquiries, for he was a sincere Catholic. His political views, however, were also extremely orthodox and closely linked with his religious ones. His love of ceremony, whether attending mass or witnessing a coronation, can be traced to his days at La Flèche, and his deep respect for nobility and particularly sovereigns verged on the passionate if not the religious.

But the most important effect of his schooling was the taste for method in all things, which the Jesuits had instilled in him. The young René was inordinately curious. His desire to learn the truth coupled with the dialectical methodology he had learned produced an obsession for certainty. He had found some satisfaction in his study of mathematics because of the solidity of the proofs; their application, however, was far too trivial. In his other studies he rapidly became dissatisfied. His precocious nature was unable to find answers to his questions by using the methods he had been taught. He felt that he must, therefore, turn from the world of books to the book of the world. The time had come for him to break away from the precepts of his teachers, from what he considered the empty maxims of the ancients, and strike out on his own.

It is impossible to pinpoint the exact date of his change in attitude from tacit acceptance of traditional knowledge to an ever-increasing skepticism. The change was undoubtedly gradual, but it occurred at some time during his last years at La Flèche and his first years in the outside world, once free from the close supervision of his tutors. Perhaps without realizing it, he began to feel that his studies were more concerned with method than with matter, with arbitrary reasonings than with truth, with the known than with the unknown. In a sense his dissatisfaction was that of his entire age, one that would be voiced with increasing urgency as the century progressed and exploded in the Enlightenment. Medieval modes of thought were no longer sufficient to explain man rationally to himself. Descartes had learned one very important lesson at La Flèche, perhaps in spite of his teachers, for it was the lesson of Montaigne: *"Que sais-je?"* With his eight years' course of study completed, he was becoming aware of his own ignorance and that of others. The only way by which he could seek to explain himself and his relationship to the world surrounding him was to start afresh where others had failed. His search for truth, to be obtained methodically and therefore rationally, did not begin so ambitiously or so naïvely as an effort to explain all the mysteries of the universe. In his studies he had been struck by the lack of unity in the various fields of knowledge, one discipline being completely separate from another. From his study of mathematics and geometry he was impressed by the difficult conclusions that were reached by means of a long series of very simple reasonings. Why, then, should not all knowledge be connected in a similar way? This is what he came to believe, at least insofar as the sciences were concerned, in the *Discourse*: "There is nothing so far removed from us as to be beyond our reach, or so hidden that we cannot discover it, provided only we abstain from accepting the false for the true, and always preserve in our thoughts the order necessary for the deduction of one truth from another." [29]

The young Descartes was not seeking to revolutionize the world but rather to form a life for himself. For the moment he had enough of book learning. What his preceptors had been unable to teach him he could perhaps find for himself through exposure to the world and meditation upon his experiences. He need not have been conscious of any specific goal other than to know that the proper one would give him the kind of certainty that had been lacking thus far in his career. The quest for truth, whether his own or the world's outside him, had begun.

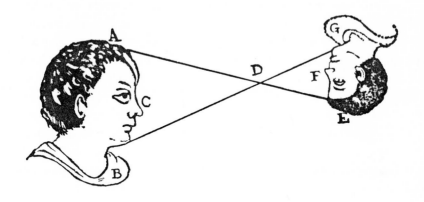

CHAPTER 2
Three Dreams—A Turning Point

IN trying to follow what Descartes did for the next four years, one is faced with either a virtual blank or a web of pseudo-historical hypotheses. Between 1614 and 1618 he left almost no trace of his activities that can be authentically documented. There are certificates showing that he was godfather to a tailor's child, received his law diploma, and served as a witness to several baptisms; but these are hardly sufficient enough to establish the authenticity of the many rather romantic accounts of his adventures and misadventures. Supposition therefore, remains the basis for this interval, and although his first biographer's "facts" may not always be verifiable, most of them are at least plausible if tempered by more contemporary and less prejudiced commentaries.

Now that he was free from the discipline of the Jesuits at La Flèche, René spent some time at Rennes and in the country with his family, riding and fencing in an effort to improve his still rather delicate health. Although too young for either the army or the priesthood (the two most logical careers for a young man of his background), he yearned to escape from the narrow and rather idle life of relatives who had little to offer his active intelligence. He sought adventure and succeeded in persuading his father to let him go to Paris. There he soon made the acquaintance of some rather frivolous, not to say debauched, companions, although there is no reason to believe that he was overly tempted by the more worldly pleasures that the capital had to offer. He did develop a taste for gambling and was quite successful probably because his interest in mathematics made him try to reduce the role of chance to a system. His calculations pleased him as much as his winning. He met Marin Mersenne, a former friend from school days, who had just recently been ordained. Mersenne was seven years his senior and soon rekindled his interest in study. Another acquaintance made at this time was Claude Mydorge, the famous mathematician. The three remained close friends until death.[1]

The diversions of Paris soon palled, however, and even his studies proved insufficient reward. The satisfaction he sought could not be found either in amusements or scholarship. He found social activity too empty, and the isolation required for meditation was difficult to find in the city. Paris was but a rather disappointing sojourn, and he decided to begin his travels in earnest. Descartes was now twenty-two, and even though he had studied law at Poitiers, he had no desire to follow the profession of his father and elder brother. Early in 1618, determined to explore more fully the book of the world, he set out for Holland to join the army of Prince Maurice of Nassau.

This decision was not tempted by military ambition, for he had neither the strength nor the inclination for a successful career in the army. He had enlisted, as had many other Frenchmen his age, as a volunteer in the Protestant cause against France's and Holland's mutual enemy, the Spanish-Austrian monarchy. The war with Spain was at a temporary halt, however, and he arrived at Breda to find a state of armed peace. His life turned out to be more that of a tourist than of a soldier. For him the army was a means of traveling, of becoming acquainted with a different way of life (that he was later to criticize), where he could play the spectator's role. It is doubtful that he ever participated in battle, and he received no pay. Only once did he accept remuneration in the form of a coin which he kept as a memento. Nor did he have any particular political involvement, for the following year he left Holland and joined the opposing forces of Maximilian I, Duke of Bavaria. His military "career" in any case was short-lived. He found the idleness, crudeness, and debauchery of barracks life extremely distasteful. The only advantage that he derived from his two years in the army was the time afforded him to devote to his scientific pursuits.[2] His being in the army, however, had little connection with the three momentous events that were to prove decisive in his future career. All three occurred on November 10 in successive years. The first was his meeting with Isaac Beeckman.

Descartes had been in Breda for approximately a year and was undoubtedly beginning to feel a certain amount of ennui. The army was idle, Prince Maurice was away, and for the religious disputes between the Arminians and the Gomarists, that were affecting political as well as ecclesiastical affairs, he showed no interest. He was in need of something or someone to keep him from succumbing to apathy or indolence. Such a person appeared on November 10, 1618, when he was looking at a mathematical problem which had been posted on a wall. Prince Maurice took an active interest in mathematics, and such problems were often posted about the city as a kind of challenge to the savants. Descartes, who had not yet learned sufficient Dutch, asked a stranger standing nearby to translate the puzzle into either Latin or French. The man who complied was Isaac Beeckman, a young doctor from Middelburg, who had come to town but a few weeks earlier in order to help his uncle in his butcher business and ostensibly to look for a wife, as he noted in his diary. Beeckman gave the inquisitive soldier his address so that he might bring him the solution the next day. The exact nature of the problem is not known, or even if Descartes succeeded in solving it, but their mutual interest and talent in mathematics sparked a friendship which from the start made the two almost inseparable. This chance meeting was to have an immense impact upon the future philosopher's life. Beeckman noted their meeting and from then kept a meticulous account of their conversations and letters in a journal, not found until 1905, that furnishes most of the details of their relationship.[3]

Beeckman was eight years older than his new friend, which sometimes made him somewhat condescending, for later he was to boast that he was the teacher, Descartes the pupil. Yet at the beginning, their friendship could not have been warmer. The older man compared the "Seigneur du Perron," a title that Descartes was not adverse to using, to a child's top which remains upright while spinning. "René," he wrote, "makes me think that a man could hold himself straight in space."[4] And Beeckman certainly captured the admiration of René, the man from Poitou ("Renatus Picto," as he called him), who wrote that he had never known anyone except Beeckman who used the method of study he preferred and who combined so carefully physics with mathematics. Beeckman directed him in the study of falling bodies, liquid pressures, and various geometrical and mechanical problems. The first tangible result of their friendship was a treatise on music, the *Compendium musicae*, which Descartes completed at his friend's request and which he dedicated to him with the stipulation that the work be kept secret. As the end of the treatise declares, he sent it only "on condition that it remain eternally hidden in your study. Others would not overlook its imperfections, as I know you will, and would concentrate on the passages where I have set forth candidly a few of my thoughts. They would not know that it was composed in haste for you alone by an idler who finds himself faced with the ignorance of soldiers and subjected to a kind of life entirely different from his thinking." [5]

The work, which was dated at Breda, December 31, 1618, was not to be published until after his death. Descartes' interest in music was more mathematical than aesthetic. He knew something of harmony and may even have played an instrument, yet had difficulty hearing the difference between an octave and a fifth. The *Compendium* treats music as a science. Harmonies and discords are discussed as well as certain methods of composition that should be followed to produce pleasurable effects. He also discovered how the vibration of a string varies inversely with its length. In itself the treatise is not particularly noteworthy, but it shows that Beeckman proved to be the catalyst necessary to reawaken Descartes' enthusiasm and encourage him to undertake new enterprises. Several months later he expressed his gratitude thus: "To speak truthfully, you alone have drawn me from my idleness and made me remember what I had learned and almost forgotten; when my mind was wandering from serious occupations, you brought it back to the right path. If I produce anything of merit, you will be entitled to claim it entirely for yourself." [6]

Twelve years later, in 1630, he would have reason to regret such an expression of indebtedness, for Beeckman bragged to

Mersenne and others of being the originator of his ideas. Descartes became infuriated, asked for the return of his manuscript, and told his former mentor, "When you boast of such things in front of people who know me, it injures your own reputation. . . . And you have shown my letters as testimony for naught because one knows that I am accustomed to instructing myself even with ants and worms, and one will think that is how I used you." [7] The invectives which he hurled in the guise of friendship, for he claimed to be telling Beeckman this for his own good, are unworthy of him. Rarely did he reveal such a bad temper, but he was overly sensitive whenever the originality of his works was questioned. The storm passed rather quickly, however, and the two were reconciled by 1631.

It was their mutual love of mathematics and particularly their desire to explore the relationship between mathematics and physics that brought Beeckman and Descartes into such close association. The latter, once encouraged by his Flemish friend, began to produce works at an amazing rate, even though he constantly referred to his laziness and most of what he wrote was left in fragmentary form. He kept a notebook, entitled *Parnassus*, in which he jotted his observations, his discoveries (such as how to divide an angle into as many equal parts as one wished), and his future projects. Beeckman left Breda for Middelburg on January 2, 1619, taking the *Compendium musicae* with him. The two now continued their conversations by letter, always in Latin. Although they probably spoke French, for Beeckman had traveled and studied in France, Descartes was accustomed since his days at La Flèche to expressing his scientific and literary ideas in the language of his Jesuit teachers. Yet even in Latin, his style reveals the warmth and sincerity of his friendship, which went beyond the purely intellectual:

> Your letter, which I waited for so impatiently, has arrived, and at first glance I was delighted to see the notes of music. You could not have shown me more clearly that you have not

forgotten me. I was expecting something else besides: some details about where you are and what you are doing, about your health. Do not think that I am interested only in your studies and not in you, in your mind and not in your entire person.[8]

Descartes was now overcome with a passion for creativity. He had dedicated himself to his muses, the sciences which had brought them together, but even these he would forsake sooner than the eternal friendship which bound them together. In addition to his scientific pursuits, he was studying design, military architecture, and Flemish. In mid-March he went to Middelburg to visit his friend, who was away at the time, apparently still in search of "the wife of his dreams." [9] Upon his return to Breda on March 20, he spent six days with his compass working out problems of square roots, cubes, and the like. He became so enthusiastic about his discoveries that he announced his plan to his confidant: "And so as not to hide anything from you about the nature of my work, I would like to give to the public not an *Ars brevis*[10] but a completely new science which would resolve generally all questions of quantity, continuous or discontinuous." [11] His project was still rather vague, nonetheless, with the "completely new science" limited largely to matters of algebra and geometry; but it is obvious that he was on the verge of a discovery he intended to publish. His grandiose scheme, however, needed further fermentation. It would not take precise form until the following November 10, exactly one year from his meeting with Beeckman, when another decisive event occurred, one which was to be the turning point in his career.

In the same letter announcing his enthusiasm for his recent studies and his plans for a new work, Descartes informed his friend that he was leaving Breda. Despite his newly found passion for discovery and invention, he was undoubtedly bored by the garrison life of an inactive army and decided to seek new adventures, this time in the service of the Catholic cause. Trouble had broken out in Germany, and the news of the disturbances which were to result in the Thirty Years' War determined him to join the forces of Duke Maximilian of Bavaria. Shaken from his intellectual torpor by his friend and filled with great expectations, he set off for Germany on April 24, 1619. The day before, he sent one last letter of farewell to Beeckman:

> I do not want to leave without renewing once more in writing a friendship between us which must not expire. Do not expect anything, however, from my muse. I am making preparations to leave tomorrow, and my mind has already begun to travel. I am still in a state of uncertainty. "Where will destiny lead me? Where shall I come to rest?" [12] These rumors of war are still not certain enough for me to stay in Germany, and I suspect that there will be gatherings of troops but no battle.[13]

As it turned out, the crisis that was waiting for him did not take place in combat.

Before assuming his new post, he planned a rather leisurely itinerary which would take him by way of Denmark, Poland, and Hungary. If he found sufficient time in route, he promised his friend that he would continue to work on his treatises on mechanics and geometry. By midsummer, he was in Frankfurt. There he saw the preparations for the election of Ferdinand II as emperor and was present at his coronation on September 9, one of the most magnificent spectacles Europe had to offer. The Bohemians, however, were opposed to Ferdinand and even before his coronation had proclaimed Frederick V as their king. Conflict thus seemed inevitable; not only was the Bohemian throne at stake but also the very existence of Protestantism. When Descartes subsequently learned that if he continued in Maximilian's service he would be forced to fight against the Protestant cause, he took another post. Upon his arrival, however, the campaigns had been temporarily interrupted by diplomatic negotiations, and Descartes was to spend the winter on the outskirts of Ulm at Neuburg on the Danube.

Undoubtedly he must have felt some of the same deception he had experienced at Breda; yet this time he found a welcome solitude. Feeling himself destined, as it were, to create great things, he devoted himself wholeheartedly to his studies. This time he was not subjected to barracks life; instead he rented a heated room, his famous *poêle*, where he spent long hours in meditation. It was here, locked up in his "stove," as he called it, that he experienced the major crisis of his life, one which can be compared to those great mystical revelations that change the lives of saints and wise men. Descartes was not yet a philosopher. He walked, as it were, with a mask, playing alternately the role of soldier, tourist, and scientist. He was still in search of a career and his interests were divided, although Beeckman had been strongly instrumental in keeping him from becoming a dilettante. Later, in his *Olympica*, he devoted a dozen pages to the details of his "illumination."

Situated strategically on the road leading from Frankfurt to Vienna, Ulm was at this period a center for mathematical studies and had a school for engineers. Both of these were important to the army for the construction of fortifications and the organization of their camps. In this imperial city Descartes met Johann Faulhaber, the most famous mathematician of the country, who introduced him to the work of Peter Roth, *Arithmetica philosophica* (1604). Both men are mentioned in the *Olympica*, and with the former he carried on discussions pertinent to both their works. Faulhaber was a member of the Rosicrucians, and many biographers believe that he initiated his French acquaintance into some of the secrets of that society; yet despite Descartes' avowed interest in the occult ever since his days at La Flèche, there is no reason to believe that he ever became part of the group in which membership was considered a crime both in Holland and France.[14]

It was not in the city, however, that Descartes was to find what he was looking for, but in the solitude of his heated room. Doubts had been pursuing him—doubts which had followed him from his school days, which had made him seek seclusion when in Paris, and which his conversations with Beeckman had made him all the more eager to dispel. Locked up in his *poêle*, he began to review systematically and skeptically all the knowledge he had accumulated. In the arts as well as in the sciences he was struck by disunity and uncertainty. He noted the imperfection of works composed by several authors, and in the sciences he found treatises based upon suppositions rather than demonstrable proofs. Only in mathematics did he discover the certainty he sought, and yet this did not make the other branches of learning any clearer. Men, he felt, had let themselves be guided by their appetites rather than their reason, and the scholars' solutions were often equally as unacceptable as those of children. What was needed was a fresh start, one that would sweep away all systems which had become encumbered with false logic or, at best, half-truths. The task that gradually took shape in his mind during these long hours of self-confinement was how to arrive at the certainty of mathematics in other fields which, like philosophy, appeared in a state of chaos. This riddle not only plagued him, but left him with feelings of impotence. Its solution would require a revision of herculean proportions, one that he would have to accomplish slowly and for himself before it could be given to the public. Perhaps all his efforts would prove useless. Could he destroy the old theories without having some idea of what would replace them?

It was in this state of mental crisis and intense intellectual effort that he faced the events of November 10, perhaps the most memorable day and night of his life. His search had put him into a state of great excitement. He had been in the process of ridding himself of all his former "prejudices," or preconceived ideas. How was he to rebuild, to use his own image, the house he had just burned? Feeling that he was on the verge of discovering the truth such as it had never before been stated, he denied himself any diversion. Scorning company and even solitary walks, he isolated himself with his thoughts. After many hours of taxing his mind to its utmost, he finally found the method he had been seeking. He was left both exhilarated by his discovery and exhausted almost to the point of delirium. The joy he felt was greater than he had ever experienced, for he had succeeded in solving more than a particular problem—he had discovered more than the principles of a single science. What he now realized, as if in a blinding flash, was the unity of all the sciences, indeed, of all knowledge. Years later he expressed his discovery thus:

> Those long chains of simple and easy reasonings which the geometers use to arrive at their most difficult conclusions made me believe that all things which are the objects of human knowledge are similarly interdependent, and that if one will only abstain from assuming something to be true which is not, and always follow the necessary order in deducing one thing from another, there is nothing so remote that one cannot reach it, nothing so hidden than one cannot uncover it.[15]

At the age of twenty-three, he felt he had made the supreme discovery of his life. He was now in possession of "everything at once," the "foundations of a marvelous science" which would replace current confusion and disparity with the unity of an architectural monument. The enthusiasm of his discovery was followed by a night of anguish. His brain, as if it had been seized by fire, was now left in a state of exhaustion, of nervous collapse, and that evening, after the joy he had experienced during the day, he had three consecutive dreams. So extraordinary were they that he felt they had been divinely inspired. His mind was undoubtedly in a state receptive to visions or hallucinations. It was St. Martin's Eve, a time when it was customary to indulge rather heavily in drink, but Descartes, as if foreseeing that others might attribute his experience to intoxication, was careful to note that not only was he completely sober but for the past three months he had drunk no wine. The manuscript of his narration and interpretation of the dreams has been lost, but the substance of his account has been preserved by Baillet and later verified by Leibniz, who transcribed passages from it.[16]

His first dream, or nightmare, he felt was the work of some evil genius. Phantoms appeared before him and so terrified him that as he walked through the streets, he was forced to turn over to his left side in order to reach the place he wanted, for he felt a great weakness in his right side which kept him from leaning on it. Ashamed of walking in that way, he tried to straighten himself but was suddenly caught up in a kind of whirlwind which made him revolve three or four times on his left foot. What frightened him most, however, was that the difficulty he had in dragging himself along gave him the impression he was falling at every step. Finally he noticed a college with an open gate which he entered, hoping to find a refuge. He tried to reach the church of the school in order to pray, but perceiving he had passed a man whom he knew without greeting him, he tried to retrace his steps to make amends and was thrown violently against the church by the wind. At this time he saw in the courtyard another person who called him by name and told him that if would go in search of a Monsieur N., he would receive something. He imagined that it was a melon which had come from a foreign country. People began to gather around him, and he was surprised to see that they stood straight and steady whereas he was still bent over and staggering. Then he noticed that the wind, which had almost upset him, had become less violent.

At this point he awoke. He turned over to his right side, for he had gone to sleep on his left, and prayed that he might be protected from any evil effect of his dream. He feared punishment for his sins. His life might have been irreproachable in the eyes of men, but perhaps he had erred in the eyes of God. For nearly two hours he meditated on the various kinds of good and evil in the world, and then he fell asleep again. Almost immediately he was visited by a second dream, which consisted solely of his hearing a piercing noise, like a clap of thunder. Frightened, he opened his eyes to see a great number of sparks all around his room. This had happened to him before. Often he would awake to find his eyes sparkling to such an extent that he could perceive only the objects closest to him. Thus, after blinking his eyes several times, he dissipated his fear and a few moments later fell asleep again.

His third dream, unlike the first two, had nothing terrifying in it and was much more complicated. This time he noticed a book on his table. Who had placed it there he did not know. Opening it, he was delighted to find that it was a dictionary he thought might prove useful. At the same moment he discovered another book, as surprising as the first, for he had no idea who could have put it there. It was a collection of poems entitled *Corpus poetarum.* Prompted by curiosity, he opened the volume and chanced upon the line *Quod vitae sectabor iter?* As he was reading, a stranger appeared and gave him some verses beginning with the words *Est et non.* Descartes told the man, who insisted on the excellence of the poem, that he knew the work well, that it came from the *Idylls* of Ausonius, one of the authors in a bulky anthology that he had on the table. Wanting to show it to the visitor, he began thumbing through the volume, and as he was looking for the place, the man asked him where he had obtained the book. He was unable to tell him, and then he noticed that the book he had been looking at just a moment before had mysteriously disappeared. No sooner had he said so than he saw it reappear at the other end of the table. This dictionary, however, was slightly different from the one he had seen earlier.

Meanwhile he found the poems of Ausonius that he had been looking for but could not locate the one beginning with the words *Est et non*. He told the man he knew of an even better passage beginning with the words *Quod vitae sectabor iter?* At this point both the man and the books disappeared, and yet he did not awaken. He began to doubt whether what he had seen was a fantasy or if he had actually experienced it. While still dreaming, he proceeded to interpret the significance of what had just happened. He judged that the dictionary represented all of the sciences gathered together, and that the *Corpus poetarum* signified the union of philosophy with wisdom. He felt that poets, even triflers, often say more profound things and say them better than the philosophers because of the divine nature of their inspiration. The words *Quod vitae sectabor iter?* he interpreted as the counsel of a wise man or possibly even of moral theology. Then, doubting whether he was dreaming or meditating, he awoke and continued the interpretation of his dream along the same lines.

The collection of poets he understood to represent revelation and inspiration and hoped to see himself favored by both. The poem "Est et Non," the "Yes and the No" of Pythagoras, stood for truth and error in human knowledge. Since all the elements of his dream seemed to lend themselves to a logical interpretation, he felt that it had been sent to him by the spirit of truth which had deigned to enlighten him as to the future. The two earlier dreams he believed to be admonitions touching his past life. The melon offered in his first dream symbolized the charms of solitude. The wind and the pain in his right side were connected with an evil genius which was trying to force him into a place where he intended to go on his own accord. This was why God would not allow him to be carried by a spirit not of His sending, even though the place was a holy one. The terror he had experienced in the second dream showed his remorse for sins he might have committed during the course of his previous life. And the thunder he understood to be a signal of the spirit of truth descending on him.

The following day he reflected upon what course he should take. Still troubled by the previous night's visions, he prayed to God to guide him in the search for truth. Next he implored the Holy Virgin that she might enlighten him on this matter, and he vowed to make a pilgrimage to Notre-Dame-de-Lorette, to travel there by foot from Venice, and if his strength were not sufficient, he would at least wear the most devout and poorest clothing he could find. As it turned out, the voyage, which he intended for November, was postponed. In a few days his enthusiasm left him, but even though he was restored to a state of relative calm, he still did not know exactly what his future actions would be.[17]

Descartes' own words in the *Olympica* for his crucial discovery on November 10, 1619, are these: "*mirabilis scientiae fundamenta*"—"the foundations of a marvelous science." He neglected, unfortunately, to specify the exact nature of this "marvelous science" and thus gave rise to numerous conjectures concerning his revelation. Since he himself stated that he had yet to find a way of utilizing his discovery, it is obvious that at this date he had not formulated the method which was to become codified eighteen years later in the *Discourse*. Nor was the new science that of a universal mathematics which he would formulate at a still later date. Most probably his revelation was more in the nature of an intuition, one foreshadowed in his letter to Beeckman when he spoke of a completely new science that would enable one to solve difficulties in a variety of disciplines.[18]

One modern critic has expressed Descartes' discovery in terms of a two-sided proposition in which the analogy between the events of his daytime activity and those of his dreams becomes apparent:

> The principle of science must be looked for *within ourselves*, because it exists in us like fire within flint; and it must be sought not by the reasonings of philosophers but by the inspiration of poets, that is to say, by intuition which engenders these thoughts by its use of the natural correlation between tangible objects and spiritual things. On the other hand, the truth of this type of knowledge is guaranteed by God, who alone protects us from the illusions prompted by our "evil genius" and assures our inspiration of its validity both for science and for wisdom.[19]

Descartes had thus discovered on that memorable night, perhaps not so much from his studies and experiments concerning the external world as from within himself, a new relationship between his self-knowledge and his knowledge of God. He was certain that his intuition, which suggested the possibility of the unity of all the sciences, had been divinely inspired. God had shown him his mission, that of revealing the unity of all truth, a universal science which had been symbolized by the dictionary in his dream; but how he could discover and express that unity remained uncertain. In answer to the question *Quod vitae sectabor iter?* he now knew that the path he must follow, the one which had been pointed out to him from on high, would lead to knowledge. With the zeal of a religiously inspired young poet, he was ready to set out on the mission of building a new scientific philosophy.

The accuracy of Descartes' interpretation of his own dreams, long before the advent of psychoanalysis, will always be open to question. Some critics have even doubted that he dreamed at all and attribute the whole episode to his desire to express himself metaphorically. Even his contemporaries were amused at his explanation that the melon symbolized the "charms of solitude," although at that period the expression was the equivalent of saying "charms of nature," including sensuous nature marked by its fecundity and succulence as represented by this fruit.[20] The eighteenth century was quick to seize upon a more sexual interpretation and tended to laugh at Descartes' "naïveté." Today psychiatrists are still puzzling over the possible meaning of his dream and attribute its events to such diverse causes as a desire to reconstruct a mother image, a conflict between his superego (his teachers) and his appetites (his id), and an inability to meet the demands of adult life stemming from a basic insecurity if not from latent homosexuality.[21]

Yet no less an authority than Sigmund Freud, when asked to express his opinion of the dreamer's interpretation, replied that dreams of this kind, the *"von oben"* type, consist of ideas that are prompted by what has been happening in the preceding waking-consciousness and draw only a small portion of their substance from the more deeply hidden states of mind. A patient can, therefore, quite easily interpret them at once, according to Freud, except for those portions which are deeply rooted in the subconscious. Aside from some of the very bizarre incidents, he seems to admit that Descartes' own explanation of his dreams was correct, at least insofar as their main outlines are concerned.[22]

Another more recent interpreter of the three dreams is Georges Poulet, who compares the events of November 10 to a drama in two acts: The first, the result of his discovery during the day, ended in triumph and joy; the second, his experiences during the night, brought him terror, anguish, and eventually calm. Poulet believes that while concentrating on his "marvelous science," Descartes had succeeded in raising himself up into a world of law and harmony where one is completely cut off from the past, where time has no part at all. But in his dreams he is forced to return from this zone of light into a world of darkness and sorrow. His first dream is one of discovery, the discovery that he is an unhappy man. Poulet interprets the various images of the dream as symbols of life divided in two, and Descartes' unhappiness stems from the rupture between that part of the mind which dwells in timelessness and the rest which is situated in an obscure and confused duration. His first two dreams were "menacing admonitions concerning his past life." In the third he found reconciliation, for, as Poulet explains it, "the past has now lost its venom; the present, on the other hand, exists by virtue of the power of divine grace; the latter is more than a prop for the present; it is a kind of guarantee for the future. Who knows if it will not renew itself with each new step, provided this step is taken in the direction of the light?" [23] This last dream is thus a kind of reconstruction of duration, and like Descartes, Poulet interprets its symbols as pertaining to the orientation of his future activity. The dictionary again represents all the sciences gathered together and reflects the *"mirabilis scientiae fundamenta"* he had discovered during the day. This image disappears almost immediately, however, for it is insufficient, to be replaced by another image, that of the anthology of poetry. This represents a higher form of knowledge in which philosophy and wisdom are joined together. The encyclopedic science of which Descartes had dreamed but a moment earlier has been supplanted by an Olympian science, one which is sparked by poetic enthusiasm, one which will shine as if by divine grace. "Such," concludes Poulet, "is the science of innate ideas, which are called innate only because at every moment God permits them to be born in the soul so that natural light may shine there: a new assurance of the endless repetition of the creative act." [24]

Poulet's analysis is both the most detailed and the most imaginative of any modern critic's. Whether or not it is correct is another matter. Descartes began the interpretation of his visions while still asleep and continued it in the *Olympica* and in random notes later collected under the title *Cogitationes privatae*, of which only five fragments remain. He has been accused of misinterpreting his visions, of giving them an order which they lacked at the time, because he was viewing them in retrospect. Even Baillet's abridged transcription is suspect, for his admiration for his subject could have led him to omit or even change certain passages. Poulet looks at them from a distance of more than 300 years and has at his disposal, but perhaps not to his advantage, a knowledge of psychoanalytical techniques and an image of Descartes based upon his total life and work. He rediscovers all the elements of the philosopher's mature writings in the dreams of his youth. He believes that "all that is most subterranean and most exhalted, most secret and most luminous in Descartes appears at one stroke in this episode of his youth." [25] All the bases of what would later be called Cartesianism are contained within these early visions; namely, the determinist mechanism of a nature in perpetual movement, the transcendental reality of the mind, guaranteed by natural light and free will, and the absolute reality of God, conceived as a simple and instantaneous activity.[26] During the span of a few brief hours Descartes had moved from the discovery of the unity of the sciences, passed through varying stages of enthusiasm and anguish, experienced the intuition of God, and begun the elaboration of a philosophy.

Whereas Poulet recounts the event with obvious skill and admiration, another contemporary French critic does not share his enthusiasm. On the contrary, Jacques Maritain sees in Descartes' *"mirabilis scientiae fundamenta"* the seeds of a philosophical reform which was to change the course of intellectual endeavor for three centuries. Descartes, he believes, is responsible for what the modern world will call The Science with all the hopeful reverence which such a term evokes. This is not, according to Maritain, the true science, but one which promised everything and yet led men astray from the eternal verities. Far from being a divinely inspired panacea for human ills, it has resulted in eventual disillusionment. "It is," says Maritain, "the

Mid-Autumnal Night's Dream conjured up by a mischievous genius in a philosopher's brain—it is the dream of Descartes." [27] It must be added, however, that it is not so much Descartes whom Maritain is criticizing as the Cartesian spirit which has been for him the "French sin" in modern history.

The revelation that Descartes experienced on November 10, 1619, and which he referred to as the most significant event in his life, would have remained but a vision had it not been for his continuing efforts to find some means whereby he could decipher the enigma of nature and remove the veil that covered the secrets of science. In realizing that all the sciences are one, he perceived also that the statement of that unity must be the work of a single person. The order and clarity which he sought would be a task of creation comparable in its coherence to the state of true religion, where God alone made all the ordinances. He was now in search of a method, one which would be applicable to much more than his immediate investigations and which would encompass all branches of research.

For the next few months, probably until February, 1620, without renouncing either his military career or his travels, he set to work studying the different sciences, including astronomy, music, and optics, in an effort to distinguish certain general characteristics. Having established certain principles in one field, he would then test their validity in other disciplines. He was searching for certainty, not probability. He would need to make a *tabula rasa* of all his earlier beliefs which were not demonstrable to the same extent as the proofs he found in the mathematical sciences. He began undoubtedly with the simpler and more concrete studies of geometry and algebra, and it was most probably at this time that he worked on the *Thesaurus mathematicus*. He worked and then reflected upon his method of work, noting his observations which today exist in an extremely fragmentary form under such titles as the *Cogitationes privatae*, *Opuscules, Studium bonae mentis, Éclaircissements sur les ovales*

—all of which are extremely difficult to date with any precision. And at this period, in order to introduce the true, he would have to destroy the false. He therefore reviewed alchemy, astrology, and magic to show that their scientific claims were nil. Yet despite his advances, he could not remain in the solitude of his "stove," and by spring he was ready to renew his travels. His preparations for the discovery of truth, for the reform of science, and for the eventual reconstruction of the whole of human knowledge could not be completed in isolation. He would reenter the activity of the outside world. On this new stage, nonetheless, he would pursue his still secret mission like an actor. Behind the uniform of a soldier was a young man whose interest was in something far greater than military maneuvers. At the beginning of his notebook entitled *Cogitationes privatae,* he wrote: "As an actor, ready to appear on the stage, dons a mask to hide the blush on his face, in the same manner I shall go forward in this theater of the world where until now I have been only a spectator." [28]

It may have been the news that a delegation of French ambassadors was being sent to Ulm which prompted him to return to the city. There he would have the pleasure of seeing some of his countrymen and also of witnessing the spectacle of opposing troops, approximately 40,000 men, encamped at such a close distance that the slightest incident could have provoked all-out warfare. Any such melee was averted, for peace was declared on July 3, 1620, after negotiations which had lasted a little less than a month; and the treaty was duly signed by Maximilian, as head of the Catholic League, and the Duke of Anspach, as Frederick's representative. The truce, however, was short-lived, and by fall the Catholic troops marched against Frederick, who lost his crown at the battle of the White Mountain, at Prague, on November 8. It is doubtful that Descartes took part in the siege, for he makes no mention of it. He may even have left the army by this time, although he had not completely abandoned the idea of a military career. Two days later, however, again on November 10,[29] he notes for the third successive time a significant event.

On the first anniversary of the day of his discovery of a "marvelous science" and of the night of his three dreams, he made an entry in the *Olympica* which remains even more cryptic than his earlier mention of the *"mirabilis scientiae fundamenta."* Instead of a "marvelous science" he now speaks of a "marvelous invention"—*"coepi intelligere fundamentum inventi mirabilis."* Again commentators are reduced to conjecture. Some believe the "invention" referred simply to the solution of a geometrical problem. Others state that Descartes must have meant the discovery of optical lenses used for observing the stars, not that he had invented them, but that he had established the principle which lay behind their operation. A more plausible theory, and one which has the advantage of lending a coherent chronological sequence to his activities, is this: November 10 in the years 1618, 1619, and 1620 represents three stages of development in the same direction. The first was his meeting with Beeckman, which initiated a new enthusiasm for intellectual inquiry, especially for mathematics and physics. The second was marked by his realization of the possibility of the unity of all sciences and his three dreams which gave him the impression that God had inspired him. The third, in November of 1620, was an intuition of the method he would later use to discover and prove the unity of which the previous year's visions had assured him. He had been working steadily, and now a year after the experience of the *poêle*, there came to him a new light. His goal had been set in 1619; there remained the discovery of the means to accomplish it. On November 10, 1620, he would seem to indicate by the term "marvelous invention" that he was finally in at least partial possession of a method that would enable him to accomplish his mission. He would still have to elaborate its various steps and test it in various fields—a task, as it turned out, which would take him many more years. But he was headed in the right direction. Having moved from the world of books to the book of the world, he was discovering new truths and falsehoods both within and without. It may appear strange that his observations at a time when he was surrounded by political upheaval have almost no bearing on the events that were occurring around him. He was in the world but scarcely of it. From behind his mask he would continue to observe, but he may well have been learning more about himself than about the spectacle to which he was a witness. The real drama that was taking place was an interior one, but Descartes was to wait another seventeen years and to experience much more before giving the world the record of how he arrived at the method he was to use for the rest of his life, the method that would be adapted by virtually the entire civilized world, the method that would be accepted as a monument in the history of Western thought.

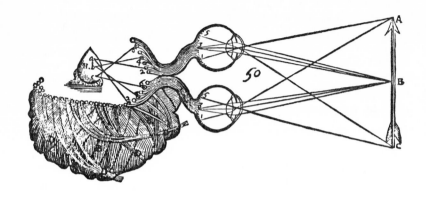

CHAPTER 3
A Revolution in Thought

ALTHOUGH his experience in the *poêle* had given him the assurance that he had a definite mission and he knew that he now had to work out a method for accomplishing that mission, his next nine years were spent not in the quiet of a study but in almost perpetual travels. There was still something of the *Wanderlust* in him, and after his apprenticeship as a soldier, he now entered what could be termed the social or *mondaine* period of his life. "I did nothing but roll from one place to another," he was to write in retrospect. "I was ridding my mind of all the errors which had crept in earlier." [1] He would visit polite society and some not so polite, that of the *libertins*. He would observe the difference between pleasures and vices, employ every divertisement, and perhaps in this rather patternless fashion learn more about the truth than from studying books. "At any rate," he concluded, "these nine years slipped by before I had taken any definite stand on matters usually disputed by the learned, nor had I begun to look for the foundation of any philosophy more certain than that commonly accepted." [2]

In March, 1622, he visited his father at Rennes. He had not seen him for more than nine years, and yet his return home seems to have been prompted less by any filial affection than by the desire to settle financial matters pertaining to his inheritance from his mother. The property he received, one-third of his mother's estate, he sold almost immediately and then, at the age of twenty-six, set off for Switzerland and Italy. Only a few details remain about this trip, reminiscences of the climate, which was not to his liking, and his impression of the snows on the mountains, for he was curious about the strange phenomena called avalanches, as he passed through the Alps. It is not even certain that he ever made the pilgrimage to Notre-Dame-de-Lorette, which he had vowed to undertake during the night of his dreams. By the summer of 1625 he was back in Paris, where he set up headquarters at the house of a family friend, Monsieur Levasseur d'Étoiles, and where he was to remain, except for occasional visits to the provinces, until the fall of 1628.

Far more mature than on his first visit to the capital, he was now introduced into Parisian society, not that of court life but that of the learned and occasionally the pleasure-loving. Although Baillet observes perhaps incorrectly that he had lost his passion for gambling, there is no reason to believe that his life was devoid of the more earthy pastimes. Years later, when he was accused of having led a debauched existence, in fact, of begetting illegitimate children, he replied, "Oh, if I had, I would not deny it. I was young. . . . I never took a vow of chastity nor have I wanted to pass for a saint; but the fact is I never had any." [3] His success, or lack of it, with women has always been a subject of conjecture. At this period he still had not chosen a career, and it seems probable that his father was pressing him both to decide upon an occupation and to find a wife. He had enough money to live where he wanted, and the idea of settling down in the country was repugnant to his ideal of freedom. Routine, either in a career or in marriage, was equally repellent. Of the many anecdotes concerning his relations with the opposite sex, two are consistent with his character, even if their authenticity is somewhat doubtful. To one young lady of high birth, the future Madame du Rosay, he presumably said in a rather uncavalier manner that he could find no beauty equal to that of the truth. And yet to this same lady is attributed an adventure in which he is said to have fought a duel and, having disarmed his opponent, returned his sword with the words that he owed his life to this maiden for whom he had just braved his own. [4] He was later to have a child, but that he was ever capable of a deep and lasting love is doubtful. His relationships with women seem to have been almost entirely platonic. He was more interested in devoting himself to his quest for truth, and his position might be summarized, at least for this period of his life in Paris, by the remark he made to a group of young gallants. He was astonished that so many of them could have been made dupes by the fairer sex, whereas he was able to remain aloof. "His own experience—not to say his refinement of taste—led him to declare that a beautiful woman, a good book, and a perfect preacher were, of all the things in the world, the most difficult to find." [5]

Shortly after his arrival in Paris, Descartes visited the court at Fontainebleau to pay his respects to the papal legate. As far as is known, however, he never met Richelieu, who had been named a cardinal in 1622 and who began his ministry the year before Descartes' return to Paris; nor is there any evidence that he came into contact with the famous Corneille, whose plays were soon to dominate the French stage, although there are many similarities in their philosophies.[6] Neither the court nor the fashionable salons, such as the Hôtel Rambouillet, held much attraction for him, and he preferred to live as simply as possible. His servants were few, and at a time when people of high birth or means usually traveled about with a train of attendants, he walked alone in the streets, dressed in a suit of simple green taffeta, carrying a plumed hat and his sword as "marks of quality which a gentleman of that day could not dispense with." [7] During his three-year stay in Paris, most of his time was spent with former acquaintances, who in turn introduced him to men of similar intellectual interests.

He renewed his friendship with Mersenne, who was to remain one of his most faithful admirers. A mutual interest in science was the basis for their close relationship, and Mersenne, unlike most clerics of his day, had no fear that scientific truth might conflict with religious dogma. On the contrary, he hoped that science would be instrumental in combating atheism. He had even written a treatise on mathematics designed specifically for use by the clergy and developed his ideas in two other works, the second of which, *The Truth of the Sciences Against the Skeptics*, appeared in 1625.

Besides churchmen, such as Mersenne and Picot, and scientists, such as Mydorge and Desargues, Descartes also met Claude Hardy, the mathematician and language scholar who, at the age of twenty, had just published an edition of Euclid in the original Greek accompanied by his own Latin translation and notes. Another friend was Jean Louis Guez de Balzac, the celebrated *épistolier* whose dissertations, written in the form of letters, appealed greatly to him. He admired Balzac's eloquent style and was especially careful to polish his own letters when writing to him, although Descartes, unlike many other philosophers, was always conscious of the necessity of expressing his thoughts in a style characterized by the utmost clarity and without the affectation which was to develop into the *préciosité* of seventeenth-century salons and literature.

In addition to his many friends there were endless acquaintances, many of whom proved annoying. His study, intended for a retreat, soon became a meeting place not only for his scholarly associates but also for secretaries, booksellers, and the merely curious, who were attracted by his growing reputation. He was beginning to feel increasingly inconvenienced by this intrusion on his privacy and the lack of peace required for meditation. Before changing his residence a second time, for he had already moved once from Monsieur Levasseur's house in an effort to find seclusion in the Faubourg-St.-Germain, he attended a curious meeting which was to have important consequences both for his personal ambition and for his reputation.

The Papal Nuncio, Monsieur de Baigné, who was later to be named a cardinal, had invited a group of scholars to listen to a lecture by Chandoux, a doctor extremely well versed in chemistry, who was to speak against the current methods of teaching philosophy. He was against not merely the methods used but against the entire Aristotelian system. The subject of such a lecture might appear dry and overly pedantic to a modern reader, but to an audience in 1628 it was a daring enterprise. This was a period of extreme repression, and any new ideas that questioned the authority or orthodoxy of the established institutions were severely censured. As recently as 1624, three men had undertaken to discuss publicly, in one of the finest halls in Paris and before an audience of some thousand spectators, forty propositions that contradicted the Aristotelian school. The hall was evacuated by official order even before they could begin their speeches, their books were condemned, and the three authors were exiled. In addition, it was decreed illegal to teach any doctrine that ran contrary to the "ancient authors," and the penalty for so doing was death. Such was the dominion of Aristotle, who had at his service both the Church and the state.[8]

Chandoux spoke with conviction and considerable charm in opposition to what he termed "the yoke of Scholasticism." His aversion to Aristotle was evident from the beginning, and he discoursed at great length, developing a system that he claimed should replace the one taught in the schools. His remarks received enthusiastic applause from everyone except Descartes. Among those present was the Cardinal de Bérulle, who observed Descartes' reaction and asked why he obviously disapproved. When he replied politely that he could say nothing against a speech which had received the commendation of so many who were more competent to judge than he, the cardinal, seconded by the nuncio, urged him so strongly to voice his opinion publicly that he could not refuse. Addressing the assembly, he first praised Chandoux's eloquence and his effort to draw philosophy away from the stilted rule of the Scholastics. Next he pointed out the power of the merely plausible or probable to masquerade as truth, which, it appeared to him, was what had happened on this occasion. In other words, he considered that the audience had been too eager to accept Chandoux's proposals, which were indeed plausible, for irrefutable truths. In order to prove his point, he asked that someone in the assembly submit a truth he considered absolute and, therefore, incontestable. This was done, and Descartes displayed, through a series of arguments which were all plausible, that the proposition was false. Next he asked for a false proposition, one which was commonly accepted as such, and then in a similar fashion proceeded to prove that it could be recognized as true. His audience was astonished at the keenness of his intellect and even more so by their own former willingness to be duped by the merely probable. They wanted to know if he knew of some infallible means of avoiding such sophisms. This gave him a brilliant opportunity to expose his own method and to impress the gathering by its correctness and its novelty. Long before developing its details in print, Descartes presented before this distinguished assembly the rudiments of the most celebrated part of his philosophy. "It was there," he recalled several years later, "that I made the entire company acknowledge the effect which the art of sound reasoning can have on the minds of moderately learned people, and the extent to which my principles are better grounded, truer, and more natural than any of those currently employed by the studious." [9]

It was not his intention to reveal Chandoux as a charlatan, although unfortunately the latter was to be hanged three years hence for having turned his knowledge of chemistry into making counterfeit coins. He agreed with Chandoux that Aristotle should be replaced, and he genuinely admired his dexterity; but the system he would advance suffered from many of the same defects as that currently taught. Clearer and more certain principles were needed which would make it possible to account for the total complexity of nature's happenings. Of all those in the audience, none was more impressed than the Cardinal de Bérulle, who asked that Descartes visit him in private so that he might learn more about the young man's proposed method. This he did a few days later and pointed out the practical advantages which his principles would have if applied to medicine and mechanics. Mankind might hope to see its health restored and conserved and its labors diminished. The cardinal grasped the importance of such a plan and, speaking both as friend and spiritual director, urged him to undertake the task. He emphasized that this was in fact an obligation of conscience, that God had given him an insight far greater than that of other men, and that he would be responsible to the Supreme Being for the wrong he would commit if he deprived mankind of the fruit of his meditations. God, the cardinal assured him, would not fail to reward his efforts. This meeting with Chandoux and the subsequent conversations with Bérulle served to rekindle the enthusiasm and sense of mission he had received from his earlier friendship with Beeckman and the revelation of his dreams.[10]

The cardinal was not alone in pressing him to pursue and reveal his knowledge. His other friends began to clamor for a public statement of his method and wanted him to publish the results of his research. But this he was still reticent to do, and the crowded and fashionable world of Paris was not the place for him to put his thoughts into their definitive form. He needed now to withdraw to a more solitary life and in a country where he would be relatively unknown. For this reason he left the French capital at the end of 1628 to begin an exile which was to last, with few interruptions, for more than twenty years.

His decision to settle in Holland was a crucial one. Various interpretations have been given as to his choice, one of the most current and probably most erroneous being that Holland was a land of religious tolerance. What need was there for a Catholic in France to fear persecution? And the Dutch, contrary to popular belief, were not always receptive to the practice of the Catholic religion. The only reason Descartes himself gave for his choice was the need for peace and isolation necessary for his work, although his "isolation," as will be seen, was far from complete. He was obviously disillusioned with Parisian society and felt that if he were ever to accomplish his mission, to give definite shape to the ideas that were simmering within him and up to this point had remained only in sketchy form, he needed to withdraw from the life of the capital and find the solitude for reflection elsewhere. He was already acquainted with Holland. He had many friends there, and certainly the chance of seeing Beeckman again would have been a strong attraction. Holland was also the home of many other French exiles besides being a center of learning, for in the future he would never be far from a university. There is also the possibility that his choice was partially determined by his finances. He had enough means to live without the necessity of working, but could he not live more comfortably in Holland, granted that his tastes were simple, than in Paris?[11] He was going to a land where trade prospered. The details of how he invested his money, despite his repeated references to family affairs, are largely unknown. Another incentive was that besides knowing the language of his newly adopted country, he preferred it to either Italy or Paris because of its climate. But the final and most important reason for his choice of Holland would seem to be not so much his need for solitude as his desire for independence, both for his person and for the works which he was yet to publish. While remaining a faithful subject of the Church, he knew that Holland would be far less strict in its censorship than a country which was under papal jurisdiction. He was not seeking titles or honors that either his king or his Church might bestow, and his move was calculated at least in part to enable him to publish his thoughts without offending either. Certainly he wanted acceptance, but not at the cost of compromising his integrity.

What was his reaction to Holland upon his return? From the letters he wrote to Balzac, it would seem that he found the tranquillity he had been searching for, which for the time being was more important to him than increasing his reputation: "Here I sleep ten hours every night without being disturbed by any care. And after my mind has wandered in sleep through woods, gardens, and enchanted palaces where I experience every pleasure imaginable, I awake to mingle the reveries of the night with those of the day." [12] Even amid the noisy activity of Amsterdam, he had acquired a philosophic detachment which enabled him to view men in such a way that they did not intrude upon his inner peace. He could pass among them assured of his anonymity:

> In this great city, where everyone except me is engaged in business, each is so worried about his own profit that I could

remain here my entire life without ever being seen. I go for walks every day in the confusion of great crowds with as much freedom and repose as you would find in your parks; and I consider the men whom I see just like the trees or the animals in your forests. Even their noise interrupts my reveries no more than the rustle of a brook. . . . What other place in the world could one choose where all the commodities of life and all the diversions one could wish are so easy to find as here? In what other country could one enjoy such complete liberty and sleep with less anxiety than here where there are always armies ready to guard us and where poisonings, betrayals, and slander are less known? Where else could one find more of what remains of the innocence of our forefathers?[13]

These two letters to Balzac show that Descartes had found the relative peace he was seeking. His wanderings were at an end, although he was to make frequent changes from one small town to another. In the letter just quoted, he was referring to Amsterdam, but he preferred the smaller towns and houses situated in the country. Often, when writing to friends, he would falsify the place from where he was sending his letters in order to make sure that he would not be disturbed by inopportune visits. After his nine years of traveling, he was ready to settle down to what may be termed the constructive period of his life. The period of his works was yet to come, for he was still in no hurry to publish. In this, as Beeckman wisely observed, he differed from so many of the would-be savants of his day:

I believe that the reason why there are so few really learned men is that those who are gifted for the sciences, as soon as they have made a discovery, are so eager to publish that they mingle their recent research with the scientific discoveries of the past to such an extent that their work is completely lacking in originality. . . . This man Descartes, on the contrary, has still written nothing, but by meditating until the age of thirty-three, he seems to have found what he was looking for better than the others. This should be said so that one will imitate him rather than the host of scribblers.[14]

Beeckman's *Journal* furnishes many valuable insights into the philosopher's preoccupations at this time. When his friend visited him at Dordrecht on October 8, 1628, Beeckman made the following entry about their reunion:

> He told me that insofar as arithmetic and geometry were concerned, he had nothing more to discover, for in these branches during the past nine years he had made as much progress as was possible for the human mind. He gave me decisive proofs of this affirmation and promised to send me shortly his *Algebra*, which he said was finished and by which not only had he arrived at a perfect knowledge of geometry but also he claimed to embrace the whole of human knowledge. Perhaps he will come here to perfect and publish it so that together we may complete the study of what remains to be discovered in the sciences.[14]

Descartes had thus completed writing the major portion of the section on geometry which was later to accompany the *Discourse*. While not neglecting his mathematical studies completely, he was now more interested in his research on lenses, later to become the *Dioptrique*, which would also be published with the *Discourse*. And it is probable also that his method was already in a preliminary draft. But there was another interest which is not mentioned in his letters to Beeckman, one which would gradually overshadow, at least momentarily, his scientific pursuits, although he continued to experiment with optics and spent an increasing amount of time in the study of anatomy through the dissection of animal parts obtained from local butchers.

Prior to his move to Holland, he had studied primarily as a scientist, but now that he had chosen to retreat from society, his interests broadened. He became less desirous of solving a particular problem than of finding the universal principle which lay behind all such problems. Gradually he was becoming a philosopher, in the true sense of the word. In order to do so, he would have to reconcile his physics with his religious beliefs. Metaphysics, then, was to have an increasingly important place in his thinking. He had thus a double preoccupation during these first years in Holland: The first was to continue to elaborate his scientific method, the mission revealed to him on that memorable night of November 10, 1619; the second was to integrate his system with a religious metaphysic, a task that was obviously required if his findings were to gain acceptance by the Church.

Descartes' new interest in metaphysics was first announced in a letter to Père Gibieuf, the Oratorian vicar whom he had known in Paris.[15] In this letter he tells that he is working on a treatise on the subject, now lost, which will take two to three years to finish and which he hopes his friend will correct. It is with extreme caution that he approaches this field of thought, for he adds that he may decide to burn the treatise, or at least make certain that it is very carefully thought out, before showing it to any but his close friends. A year later he wrote to Mersenne, with whom he was always in correspondence on both scientific and religious matters (and even a project for a universal language), that for the past nine months he had been working almost exclusively on proving that the truths of metaphysics are even more demonstrable than those of mathematics. The truth of all his discoveries would eventually be based upon God—upon His existence, His laws, His gifts. The rapport between the scientist, the philosopher, and his Creator became evident when Descartes observed: "I believe that all those to whom God has given the use of reason are obliged to use it mainly to know Him and to know themselves. That is how I tried to begin my studies, and I would not have been able to find the basis for my physics if I had not looked for it along these lines." [16] He continued by saying that when writing on physics, he would treat many metaphysical questions; namely, that mathematical truths, which are called eternal, were established by God and depend entirely on Him as do the rest of His creatures. He concluded:

> Do not be afraid to proclaim everywhere that God established these laws in nature just as a sovereign establishes laws in his kingdom. . . . And just as a king has more majesty when he is less familiarly known by his subjects, we judge God's greatness as incomprehensible and do not think that we are without a king. One will tell you that if God established these truths, He would be able to change them just as a king changes his laws; to which one should reply that it is possible if His will can change. But I understand these truths as eternal and unvarying in the same way that I judge God. His power is beyond comprehension, and generally we assure ourselves that God can do everything we are capable of understanding but not that He cannot do what we are incapable of understanding, for it would be presumptuous to think that our imagination has as much magnitude as His power. I hope to write all this within the next two weeks in my *Physics*; but I do not ask that you keep it a secret; on the contrary, I urge you to speak of it as often as the occasion presents itself, provided of course that you do not mention me by name.[17]

This last word of caution emphasizes how eager he was to safeguard his anonymity while at the same time promulgating his ideas. He feared lest the theologians find his mathematical writings in conflict with the teachings of the Church and was therefore careful to point out, as in his next letter to Mersenne, that he was speaking as a scientist and philosopher but not as a religious critic: "I do not want to get mixed up with theology, and I am even afraid that you may consider my philosophy as too emancipated in daring to voice its opinion about such elevated matters." [18] His correspondent, because of his position in the Church and his association with the Parisian scholars, was ideally placed to provide the sounding board he needed before making his views public and acknowledging their authorship. Descartes' insistence upon secrecy during this period was based upon his desire to retain his privacy. He would not publish his thoughts if they were likely to arouse controversy, and for the time being he was more interested in instructing himself than in sharing his discoveries with the world at large. As he told Mersenne: "I have a thousand different things to consider altogether so as to find an easy way of telling the truth without surprising anyone's imagination or shocking commonly accepted opinions." [19]

After several visits with Beeckman at Dordrecht and a short stay in Amsterdam, Descartes' first major residence in Holland was at Franeker, where in April of 1629 he enrolled at the university and rented a small château on the outskirts of town. Here life would be simple enough, and despite his attendance at the university, where his name was inscribed as "RENATUS DES CARTES GALLUS, PHILOSOPHUS," he would have sufficient time for his meditations. In addition to metaphysics, he continued his research in optics and even invited his friend Ferrier to join him from Paris so that they might carry on their studies together. Ferrier never accepted his offer, although the philosopher had made rather elaborate plans to set up comfortable lodgings where they could work without being deprived of the amenities of life. "If he had come," he wrote to Mersenne, "I would have bought some furniture and set part of the château aside for our own apartments. I had already contacted a young man who knew how to cook in the French manner." [20] In a letter to Ferrier he stated:

If you have some furniture which you are planning to leave in Paris, it would be better to bring it, at least the most useful pieces; for if you come, I shall rent an apartment exclusively for you and me where we can live as we please. I would ask

you to bring me a camp bed, for the beds here are very un-
comfortable and have no mattresses, but spending money in
Paris would mean inquiries about my whereabouts, and that I
do not want.[21]

Even to Ferrier, he gave his address as Amsterdam in order to
remain incognito at Franeker.

Even though he seemed well content with his life at Franeker,
so much so that he told Ferrier he proposed to remain there for
three years, in less than six months he returned to Amsterdam,
where he was to stay until the spring of 1635 except for occasional journeys such as the one to Denmark in 1631 and to
Deventer in 1632. During this period of study in Holland, his
intellectual activity increased both in depth and in breadth, for
despite his intention to outline his theory of the interrelation-
ships of all knowledge, his research was divided by many rival
interests. All of these, he hoped, would one day explode into a
coherent form, so that what might appear as lack of direction
or laziness would be contradicted by the product of years of
inward, almost unconscious, reflection. By the spring of 1630,
his treatise, *Le Monde*, was still far from finished, and he told
Mersenne that it would probably take him another three years
to bring it to completion:

> I am now studying chemistry and anatomy together, and I
> learn something every day which I could not find in books.
> . . . Furthermore, I pass the time so pleasantly instructing my-
> self that I never write anything in my treatise except out of
> constraint so that I can fulfill the resolution I have made to
> send it to you, if I do not die beforehand, by the beginning of
> 1633. I mention the date in order to engage myself more fully
> and so that you can reproach me if I fail. You will be sur-
> prised that I am taking such a long time to write a discourse
> which will be so short that one can read it in a few hours;
> but that is because I believe it is more important for me to

learn what is necessary for the conduct of my life than to amuse myself in publishing the little that I have learned.[22]

In the summer of 1630, Descartes temporarily left his house in Amsterdam to enroll at the University of Leiden, where his name appears on the register as "RENATUS DESCARTES PICTO, STUDIOSUS MATHESEOS"—a significant change from the wording of his status at the University of Franeker the previous year. At Leiden he continued his studies in mathematics with Jacob Golius, who had replaced Snellius at the University, and met the astronomer Martinus Hortensius, who had carried on solar observations with Beeckman. This was the time of Descartes' quarrel with Beeckman and also of a brief visit to Holland by his loyal correspondent, Mersenne. In the fall the philosopher was back again in Amsterdam and continued to keep his friend informed about the progress of his work, which was slow, for he wanted perfection. His letters show almost a mania for secrecy, for both his work and his person: "If they ask you where I am, I beg you to say that you are uncertain, for I had planned to go to England. . . . If they ask you what I am doing, tell them, please, that I enjoy studying for my own instruction, but that given my frame of mind, you doubt that I will ever publish my findings." [23] He had found a certain peace of mind in his study, and this he guarded most jealously. Even to Balzac, he was reticent to explain the exact nature of his projects: "Please do not ask me what that occupation could be which I consider so important, for I should be ashamed to tell you. I have become such a philosopher that I disdain most things which are ordinarily esteemed and value others which are commonly held to be of little value." [24]

The correspondence from 1630–1633, the three years which Descartes had set for the completion of his treatise, is filled with references to his slow progress and his aversion to publication.

Finally, in July, 1633 he told Mersenne that the work was almost finished, that he had only to correct certain sections and then recopy it. He would keep his promise and send the manuscript before the end of the year. Then, just when all was ready, he learned that Galileo's *Dialogue on the Two Chief Systems*, published the previous year, had been condemned by the Church. The news made him discard any thought of sending his own work to his friend as a New Year's gift. So alarmed was he that the Italian scientist had been forced to sign a formal abjuration of his belief in the Copernican doctrine, that his book had been publicly burned, and that he had been sentenced to an indefinite term of imprisonment by the Inquisition that he wrote Mersenne to tell him he had now had a complete change of heart:

> I was so astounded that I have quasi resolved to burn all my papers or at least not to show them to anyone. I cannot imagine that an Italian, and especially one well thought of by the Pope from what I have heard, could have been labeled a criminal for nothing other than wanting to establish the movement of the earth. I know that this had been censured formerly by a few cardinals, but I thought that since that time one was allowed to teach it publicly even in Rome. I confess that if this is false, then all the principles of my philosophy are false also. . . . And because I would not want for anything in the world to be the author of a work where there was the slightest word of which the Church might disapprove, I would rather suppress it altogether than have it appear incomplete—"crippled," as it were.[25]

The reversal of his project, although temporary, has led some critics to accuse him of moral weakness. Certainly he shared Galileo's views that the earth did indeed move and that it was not the center of the universe. And living in a Protestant country, he need not have feared his Italian contemporary's fate, which was first strict confinement and later, while still under surveillance, weekly recitation of the seven penitential psalms for a period of three years. Descartes would continue to believe in the earth's motion, but unlike Galileo, he would not publish the fact. The truths he had discovered in his studies could not rationally be discarded, and yet he saw the necessity of upholding the Church's teachings—at least for the time being. He would await a more propitious moment, for it was not in Holland that he wanted acceptance of his theories—Beeckman, Golius, Gassendi, in fact almost all of the Dutch and the French scholars living in Holland accepted Galileo's views and taught them. Descartes wanted universal acceptance and, in particular, the support of both the Church and the Sorbonne. In his next letter to Mersenne, he again states his reasons for failing to keep his promise:

> You shall have an even better opinion of me in knowing that I have decided to suppress my treatise entirely and thus lose almost all of my labor during the past four years in order to render entire obedience to the Church. . . . I am seeking only rest and tranquillity of spirit which are gifts which cannot be had by those who harbor either animosity or ambition. I do not however, remain idle but now I think only of teaching myself and consider that I am scarcely capable of instructing others.[26]

Intermingled with exaggerated threats of burning his papers and renouncing forever the role of missionary or reformer, there are also protestations of friendship and perhaps hints that his present failure to keep his promise will soon be remedied. After telling Mersenne that if his writings cannot be approved without controversy, he would prefer never to publish them, he adds: "At any rate, since I would be impolite after having given you so many promises and over so long a period of time, I shall not hesitate to show you what I have done as soon as possible; but I beg you for yet another year's delay in order to revise and polish it."[27] Mersenne never did receive the long-awaited *Le*

Monde. Like the *Rules for the Direction of the Mind,* it was not to be published until after the philosopher's death. But despite the individual merit of the posthumous works composed during Descartes' first five years in Holland, the ideas expressed therein were to find their definitive form in yet another work for which they serve as the genesis and which the general public to this day considers the most significant of his writings: *The Discourse on Method.*

Even though he was intimidated, not so much for his personal safety as for the future of his work, by the Church's condemnation of Galileo, Descartes' resolve not to publish did not last long. His apparent resignation to papal authority did not prevent him from beginning three new treatises as soon as the initial shock was past. By the spring of 1635, when he was at Utrecht, visiting his friend Henricus Reneri, a professor of philosophy at the University, his new work was in its final stage except for minor revisions and the preface which had yet to be added. In 1636 he returned to Leiden shortly after the epidemic of plague that had taken the lives of 14,000 victims the previous year. It was here that he at length announced his decision to publish and began looking for a printer, for he wanted someone close at hand so that he would be able to supervise the book's progress and correct the proofs as they were completed. He might have arranged to have the work published in Paris through the intermediary of Mersenne, but he hesitated to send him his original copy, for the handwriting was negligent, there were errors in spelling and punctuation, and most important of all, the drawings, which he had sketched himself, needed to be redone by a professional artist. Obviously he needed to be in contact with the printer so that he could interpret any obscurities which might cause difficulty and remove any imperfections. He wanted his first work to be not only free from any printer's mistakes, but in addition he insisted upon its being a handsome volume, one which used attractive type and high-quality paper.[28]

His decision to publish for the first time at the age of forty, after so many years of hesitation, was prompted by many reasons. If his first reaction to Galileo's condemnation was one of resignation, he now felt that the time for action rather than tacit consent had arrived. The Church's ban on the *Dialogue on the Two Chief Systems* still prevented him from publishing his *Le Monde*, for, as he said earlier, if Galileo were wrong, then all of the principles he had stated therein were wrong also. But his new work, while not overtly contradicting the Church's stand, could at least pave the way for the eventual publication of his earlier treatise. He could thus begin to sound public opinion and simultaneously, by indirect references to the system he had expounded in *Le Monde*, pique his readers' curiosity to know more about his theories. He must have realized that if the condemnation of Galileo were allowed to remain, then any hope for reform in the sciences and in philosophy would be impossible. In a sense, this first published work was propagandistic, a maneuver to reverse the Church's judgment concerning the movement of the earth.

Another reason for his choosing to appear in print was the double debt he owed to both his friends and the public. So many reiterated promises made in letters had to be fulfilled if his friends were not to think him incapable of the great projects of which he had continually spoken. And he had acquired a reputation not only in Paris but also in Holland as a man of great learning; yet to date the only proof of his discoveries was in his letters, his conversations, and his appearances at a few public gatherings, such as the encounter with Chandoux. He had, therefore, to prove to his friends, as well as to his unknown admirers, that he was indeed the man to reveal the truths upon which he had been meditating for so many years. Although he claimed to dislike the career of "bookmaking," as he called it, and had been more interested in learning for himself than in sharing his discoveries with others, he must have felt something of an author's pride in introducing the public to the kind of accomplishment which would distinguish him as a superior intellect, augment his reputation, and further his chances of eventually revealing the entirety of his system.

One final reason, while perhaps less apparent from a cursory reading of the *Discourse* than the two already given, should not be overlooked. It was a practical, or pragmatic, one both for him and for society. As he continued his research, he became increasingly aware of the immensity of his task, and that if he were to complete his system, innumerable experiments would be necessary. These would take both time, which could be shortened were he to have the collaboration of others, and money, which his own private resources could not adequately finance: "I see that they [my experiments] are of such a nature and so numerous that neither my hands nor my revenue, even if I had a thousand times more than I do, would suffice for all of them." [29] He asked, therefore, that those who took a genuine interest in the public's well-being communicate their discoveries so as to help in continuing the research which remained to be done. For himself he wanted information and assistance from other scientists; and he also wanted the necessary funds. His appeal for the latter was not directed toward possible wealthy patrons but toward the public in general in the hope that its interest might result in some kind of state assistance. In order to elicit society's approval and eventually its participation in his scheme, he had to offer some practical advantage. This he did by pointing out that his discoveries in physics as in other realms would one day have an immense influence upon improving all the material conditions of human life, including even that of prolonging it. He would not talk of politics or theology. He would avoid, as he stated in reference to Galileo, any opinion that might appear as prejudicial to either the state or religion. But he could emphasize that his method and its applications for the discovery of nature's laws would not only help to explain the universe but also to transform human existence. He was thinking less of a technical science by which engineers might profit or artisans might perfect their crafts, although both were to be eventually aided by his work, than of the benefit in general terms to the whole of humanity:

> As soon as I had acquired certain general notions concerning physics and applied them to problems in other fields, I became aware of just how far they might lead and how much they differ from those used up until now. I thought that I could not keep them hidden without committing a grave sin against the law which obliges us to work to our utmost toward the common good of all men.[30]

Instead of the speculative philosophy taught in the schools he proposed one that would enable man to do more than contemplate nature. His aim was to master it and, particularly, to preserve life through the study of medicine. Descartes' final reason for deciding to publish his three treatises and the accompanying outline of his method was thus a desire to be of immediate and practical value to mankind—a humanitarian ideal which gave him faith in the possibility of progress through enlightenment, an optimistic belief that man could rid himself of the errors and evils of the past.

When he first announced his new work to Mersenne, Descartes gave as its tentative title: *Project for a Universal Science Which Might Raise Our Nature to Its Highest Degree of Perfection. Next the Dioptric, the Meteors, and the Geometry, Where the Most Curious Matters Which the Author Could Find to Give Proof of the Universal Science He Proposes Are Explained in Such a Manner That Even Those Who Have Never Studied Can Understand Them.* He noted that in the first section he had explained a part of his method and tried to demonstrate the existence of God and the separation of the soul from the body, and that he had added other things which he believed the reader would not find "disagreeable."[31] In the *Dioptric*, besides refractions and the invention of lenses, he spoke particularly about the nature of the eye, of light, of vision, and of everything concerning optics. The section entitled *Meteors* dealt primarily with the causes of winds and thunder, the composition of snow, and the colors of the rainbow. Here he had tried to show the nature of each color and explain the phenomenon of parhelia, or mock suns, which had been seen in Rome in 1629. The latter had fascinated him to such an extent that even five years later while working on his *Meditationes* he had corresponded on the subject with Mersenne, Reneri, and Gassendi. In the final section, the *Geometry*, he proposed to give a general method for treating all problems that remained unsolved in this area.

This was indeed a grandiose scheme. When the book was printed, however, it bore a far less comprehensive title. Instead of *Project for a Universal Science*, etc., which had promised to be all-encompassing, the final wording was altered to: *Discourse on the Method of Rightly Conducting the Reason and Seeking Truth in the Sciences. Next, the Dioptric, the Meteors, and the Geometry, Essays in This Method.* Mersenne objected to the new title and thought that the word "treatise" would be preferable to "discourse"; but Descartes replied that he had chosen the title with great care:

> I have not used *Treatise on Method* but *Discourse on Method*, which is the same as a preface or introduction concerning method, in order to show that I did not want to teach it but only to speak about it. As one can see from what I say, it is more practical than theoretical; and I call the sections which follow *Essays in This Method* because I believe that what they contain could not have been found without it. . . . Likewise, I have inserted a little bit of metaphysics, physics, and medicine to show that this method is applicable to all sorts of investigations.[32]

There are further restrictions stated in the *Discourse* itself which show that Descartes' intention was less didactic than narrative:

> My design here is not to teach the method which everyone ought to follow for the right conduct of his reason, but solely to show the way in which I have tried to conduct my own. Those who propose to give precepts must consider themselves more skillful than those whom they would teach, and if they err in the slightest, they are open to censure. But since I propose this work merely as a story, or if you prefer, a fable in which there will be found some examples worthy of imitation and others which it would be advisable not to follow, I hope that it will be useful to some without proving harmful to any, and that all will be pleased by my frankness.[33]

The two preceding quotations merit close analysis, for they give further insight not only into the author's intention but also the manner in which the work should be read. There is a certain ambiguity in his terminology. After protesting that he is not setting himself up as a preceptor but, on the contrary, desires only to tell how he arrived at his own method, he refers to his account as a history or fable. The difficulty lies in his deliberate use of the words *histoire* and *fable* which had several different meanings for his contemporaries and are still susceptible to various translations. Is he writing a history? If so, one would expect his account to be purely factual. Is he simply telling a story? If it is that of his own development, then one might underscore the autobiographical elements. Or is he relating a fable? If this is the case, then one could justly attribute his narrative to be largely fictitious. Surely the last was not his intention. Both *histoire* and *fable*, however, emphasize his desire that the work be read with the same ease as one would read a story—another reason for his choice of French rather than

Latin; and the two words also point to the fact that while the *Discourse* is personal, an account of his own progress in arriving at his method and not necessarily a lesson for others, it is also universal. As in a fable, there is a moral from which all men can profit. And although the *Discourse* will later overshadow the accompanying *Essays* to their virtual oblivion, it is clear from Descartes' correspondence with Mersenne, from his remarks in the work itself, and from the relative length he assigns to the different sections that the main interest of his book lies not in the *Discourse* but in the three essays which follow. He is less interested in expounding his method than in showing its value. Rather than show step by step in the three essays how he has applied his method, he gives only occasional references to his general theories.

Suffice it to say that the essays would never have been possible had he not been in possession of his method. They are designed, therefore, to show the merits of the method. Similarly, rather than state pedagogically in his preface the various constituents of his method, he is content to give a rapid narrative of his own intellectual development. Clearly his intention is apologetic, and again one senses his diplomacy in preparing the way for the eventual acceptance of the theories he had set forth earlier in his *Le Monde*.

Thus, in his first published work, Descartes gave his public something quite unique both in its form and content—a combination of science and philosophy, an apology and a polemic, an autobiography and a history not merely of his own development but of what in a few years was to be the method of the whole of Western thought. And the language which he chose reflected both the tenor of his ideas and the audience he wished to convince. Renouncing the traditional Latin of the Church and the schools, which was customary for such learned subjects, he explained:

If I write in French, which is the language of my country, rather than in Latin, which is that of my preceptors, it is because I hope that those who use only their natural reason will be better judges of my ideas than those who believe only in ancient texts; and as for those who join good sense with study, those alone whom I desire as judges, they will not be so partial toward Latin that they will refuse to understand my reasoning just because I explain things in the vulgar tongue.[34]

His work was not intended exclusively for the learned but for anyone who had wit enough to understand plain meanings and was thus accessible "even to women." His experiment of writing in French was to have far-reaching consequences, for scholars and the general public alike became aware that the French language was capable of expressing highly complex philosophical and scientific thoughts with a simplicity and clarity which made it worthy of careful cultivation. Descartes' style, despite certain Latinisms, still ranks with that of the greatest seventeenth-century prose writers.

For his printer he had chosen a man named Jan Maire, and the contract was signed before witnesses in the presence of a notary in Leiden on December 2, 1636. As publisher, Maire was to have the rights for the first two editions, the second to be printed either in Holland or France, and the number of copies would be limited to 3,000. In one of his letters, the author had said that his preface would probably run to about 60 pages. His estimate proved to be a close one, for the preface to the first edition of the *Discourse* had 78 pages,[35] roughly a sixth of the entire work, for the essays took 413 pages. The printing was not completed until June 8, 1637, a delay probably occasioned by the wait for Mersenne to obtain permission for the work to be printed in France. The title page bore no name of the author, and this at Descartes' explicit request. As he had told Mersenne: "Following my former resolution, I do not want to set my name to it, and I beg you not to tell anyone about it." [36] He must have been extremely annoyed, therefore, when his friend, while waiting for the French censors to give their approval, wrote a very elaborate preface in which he not only betrayed the author's anonymity but spoke of other works which could be expected in the near future. Another annoyance must have come from the fact that no sooner had the work appeared in Paris than people began asking Mersenne if he knew the author's religion. But, in general, the work was quite favorably received, both in France and in Holland, where it was incorporated the following year by Reneri into his courses at the University of Utrecht. A year later his friend and colleague Henricus Regius, who was an even more enthusiastic disciple, wrote Descartes that teaching his doctrines had augmented not only the author's reputation but his own as well, for the new theories had drawn increasing numbers of students to attend his lectures. [37]

Before examining the general plan and importance of the *Discourse*, mention should be made of two rather curious facts connected with its initial printing. The first concerns the many errors which ran throughout it. These Descartes sought to explain by having Maire insert the following note after an entire page of errata: "One will find a great number of minor mistakes which can be easily excused when one realizes that the author is not a professional grammarian and that the typesetter does not understand a single word of French." [38] The second concerns the author's payment. Instead of royalties, which went to the printer, Descartes had asked that he be given 200 copies of the new work so that he might distribute them to friends. This he set about doing at once, sending the first few to persons in high places. Naturally, as a French subject, he offered copies to Louis XIII, Richelieu, and the French ambassador at The Hague. In recognition of the favors he had received in his adopted country, he also remembered his host, Frederick Henry: "Having enjoyed perfect rest and peace under his protection, I am deeply obligated to him and believe that this book, which contains the fruits of that tranquillity, should be offered more appropriately to him than to any other person." [39]

Descartes' original intention was to sound public opinion by publishing his *Dioptric* first and, if it proved successful, to follow it with his *Treatise on Metaphysics.* The finished *Discourse* with the accompanying *Essays* reveals a change of tactic. Instead of science followed by metaphysics, there is a happy combination of the two. By establishing beyond a doubt the principles of his physics, he made the acceptance of his entire system inevitable. The metaphysics included in the *Discourse* are intended to help overcome prejudice and influence the public to accept his whole system before it realizes some of its more controversial implications. Mersenne and others complained that his proofs of the existence of God were far from conclusive, that they were in fact the weakest section of his work. Descartes replied that he had deliberately omitted certain parts of his reasoning, partly because he was writing in French rather than Latin and partly because he wanted to prevent certain "weak minds" from falling into error had he proposed all the doubts which would have been necessary in order to remove them subsequently and thus show the entire complexity of his reasoning.[40] The main reason, however, for the rather slender treatment was that he wanted to give only that portion of his metaphysics which would help his audience to realize the unity of his science and to show that the *Essays* were indeed really models and not merely fragments of scientific research.[41]

To the uninitiated a first reading of the *Discourse* may come as a surprise. From its title one would expect to find a clear outline, a logical explanation, of the method, followed by specific examples of its application. Instead only a very short section, Part II, is devoted to method, and the reader is struck by a seeming confusion of reminiscences about the author's past life, anecdotes concerning his travels, random observations on morality, biology, skepticism, Stoicism, physics, and the future of the sciences. Each of the six parts of the *Discourse* treats a different realm of thought. After a short introduction, Part I relates the story of his education at La Flèche, his subsequent disillusionment with his studies, and ends with an account of his travels. Part II tells of his illumination in November, 1619, the idea of the unity of all the sciences, and then proceeds to state the four principal rules of his method. The next section gives certain moral maxims that should be held provisionally in order to live as happily as possible. Part IV treats metaphysical questions, and it is here that occurs his famous "*Je pense, donc je suis,*" which in itself has been the subject of literally thousands of commentaries. In Part V he exposes his theory of physics and some of the general traits of his biology. Part VI serves as both a conclusion and an introduction. In it Descartes tells why he decided to publish fragments of his research and ends with a kind of appeal to the public summoning all to contribute toward the advancement of the sciences—a transition, as it were, to the *Essays* which follow.

How is one to find unity in such diversity, not to say incoherence, when, in addition to the multiplicity of subjects treated in the different parts, one section seemingly contradicts another? The morality, proposed in Part III, for example, and based largely on conformism and resignation (even though he had previously condemned Stoicism), is in apparent conflict with the ideal set forth in Part VI for man's eventual technical domination of the world. The promised method is at best only fragmentary and stated in the most general of terms; and only one of the *Essays*, the *Geometry*, demonstrates a fairly direct or easily recognizable application of that method. This lack of homogeneity can be explained in part by the work's chronology, the fact that it was composed over a period of years, and its various sections often reflect several revisions. Rather than a synthesis of his thinking, the *Discourse* offers a series of reconstructions of the author's past thought and emotions at various stages of his development. Its unity is the same as that of Descartes' own life and can be best understood when viewed not as the exposition of a system but rather as the story of how he came to be what he was. Written in the first person, it is the account of both his thinking and feeling self, a record of his progress from his early schooling, followed by disillusionment, to his quest for certainty and a partial revelation of his discoveries. To be sure, the *Discourse* had a didactic aim; indeed, it can be considered a work of propaganda. But its unity resides less in the philosophical or scientific aims contained therein than in its autobiographical structure.

Many critics have questioned the authenticity of certain passages, particularly the section which concerns his reaction to his schooling, claiming that they reveal the reactions of a man of forty rather than reconstruct the memories of an adolescent who had just finished his formal studies.[42] Yet such a criticism could be leveled against most autobiographies and certainly against many biographies where the temptation is often to interpret the thoughts and actions of the youth in the light of what is known about the adult. Rather than an exact and detailed account of his former life in all its complexity, Descartes presents a stylized portrait in which one can follow the alternating doubt and enthusiasm that led to his present state. Instead of a finished painting, the *Discourse* is better understood as a sketch that enables the reader to catch glimpses of the author and the atmosphere in which he moved during his quest for truth.

Coupled with his hostility toward Scholasticism and the principles of Aristotle was his almost naïve enthusiasm for what he believed were the limitless possibilities of science. Conjecture would be replaced by certitude, and here one feels no small measure of his daring self-confidence, of his idealistic faith in himself. Living in Holland, he could see evidence everywhere of man's progress in harnessing nature. In this land reclaimed from the sea, canals and windmills were but two examples of the strides that were possible in turning scientific knowledge into practical benefits. His dream of the creation of an earthly paradise through the application of his system of universal knowledge based on reason could be accomplished only if the sciences were removed from the purely theoretical sphere and given a utilitarian orientation and only if philosophy were freed from the rule of Aristotle and changed from the merely speculative to the truly practicable.

Such a gigantic enterprise would take time. Idealistically Descartes felt that eventually he would find the certainty of mathematics in every other branch of learning. Comparing himself to a man who walks alone and in darkness, he would proceed slowly to reconstruct all previously accepted precepts and ideologies by means of the four rules of his method outlined in Part II:

> The first was never to accept anything as true which I did not recognize as obviously being so; that is to say, to avoid carefully all hasty conclusions and prejudice and to accept only that which was presented so clearly and distinctly that I would have no occasion to doubt it. The second was to divide each of the difficulties which I was examining into as many parts as possible, as many as needed for its solution. The third was to conduct my thoughts in an orderly fashion, beginning with the simplest and the easiest to understand in order to ascend gradually to the knowledge of the more complex, assuming an order even in those thoughts which by their nature do not seem to have any sequence. And the last was to make such complete enumerations and reviews so general that I would be certain I had omitted nothing.[43]

Realistically Descartes knew that until he arrived at such knowledge, he would need, as would all men, certain rules of conduct, a moral science as well as a physical or mathematical one. At the beginning of Part III, he used another striking image to point out that it is not enough when one wants to rebuild one's house to tear it down and obtain the necessary architects and materials; one needs a temporary lodging where one can live until the new one is completed. Thus, in order to live as happily as possible while he was revising his opinions and so that he might act in a positive manner (for he had always dreaded irresolution in all things), he constructed a provisional moral code consisting of three or four general maxims:

The first was to obey the laws and customs of my country, adhering constantly to the religion in which God had graced me to be instructed since childhood, and to govern myself in all other matters according to the most moderate opinions, the most removed from extremes, which were commonly accepted by the most reasonable among those with whom I would have to live. . . . My second maxim was to be as firm and resolute in my actions as possible, and to follow faithfully as if they were certainties even the most dubious precepts once I had accepted them. In this I was imitating travelers lost in some forest who should not wander in one direction and then another or even less stop in one place but should always walk as straight as possible and not change their path for weak reasons, even if it were merely chance which directed them in the first place. In this way, if they do not go exactly where they want, they will at least arrive someplace where they will probably be better than in the middle of the forest. Thus, since our actions will often not allow any delay, it is certainly evident that when it is not in our power to distinguish the truest opinions, we should accept the most probable. . . . My third maxim was always to try to conquer myself rather than fortune and to change my desires rather than the outside world. In general I tried to accustom myself to the belief that there is nothing which is entirely within our power except our thoughts, so that after having done our best in regard to exterior things, all that we lack in order to succeed is absolutely impossible. This seemed sufficient to keep me from desiring anything in the future which I could not acquire, and thus I was content. . . . Finally as a conclusion to these moral maxims, I thought about reviewing all the different occupations which men have in this life in order to choose the best; and without wanting to say anything about those which others pursued, I thought that I could not do better than to continue in the one I presently had; namely, to employ my entire life in cultivating my reason and progressing as far as I could in the knowledge of truth, following the method I had established for myself. I had experienced so much satisfaction since I began using this method that I did not believe it possible to find anything sweeter or more innocent in this life.[44]

Neither the four rules enumerated in the *Discourse* nor the provisional moral maxims are sufficiently detailed to enable the reader to grasp the immensity of their implications. Descartes' entire philosophy was derived from his method, and yet the *Discourse*, it must be remembered, is not a formal philosophical treatise but rather a résumé of his own intellectual development. It was aimed at suggesting the merits of his method and not at elucidating or analyzing the complexity of its principles and application. His earlier work, the *Regulae ad directionem ingenii* (*Rules for the Direction of the Mind*), contains a far more systematic statement of his precepts as do his later works, the *Meditationes* and the *Principia*. The *Regulae* is invaluable for a clear understanding of Descartes' method and will be utilized later for that purpose. Some critics consider it not only a more significant work than the *Discourse* but also a more advanced treatment despite the date of composition. It was the *Discourse*, however, which as his first published work was to have the most revolutionary effect in convincing the world that here was a method superior to that of both ancients and moderns alike. Before examining some of its statements in more detail, it is important to note certain general characteristics.

From his account of his education it is clear that Descartes was dissatisfied with the state of learning in general and with Aristotelian logic in particular. Throughout the *Discourse* his remarks concerning Scholasticism are highly critical. He found that despite its prestige in both the Church and the schools, Scholasticism was more interested in teaching men how to talk than to think and more often than not was content with probabilities rather than truth. Its use of syllogism he considered fruitless, for it tended only to corroborate what was assumed from the start. In speaking of his own early studies, he condemned his instruction in logic because:

> . . . Its syllogisms and most of its other methods serve to explain to others what one knows or, as with the art of Lully, to speak irresponsibly about things of which one is ignorant rather than to understand them; and although it contains many precepts that are good and true, there are so many others that are either harmful or superfluous that it is almost as difficult to separate these as to draw a Diana or a Minerva from a block of marble not even roughly modeled.[45]

Descartes would replace the use of syllogism, in which the conclusion is already contained in its initial premise, by mathematical deduction, in which one's reasoning is dependent upon a series of reflections concerning each idea as it is perceived intuitively.

Besides the Scholastics, Descartes also attacked the skeptics. He realized that his own doctrine could easily evoke the criticism that he was himself skeptical, certainly in his evaluation of his schooling and his attitude toward the value of his classical heritage. Naturally he wanted to avoid such an accusation. Thus he was careful to point out that his use of methodical doubt led to a goal far different from that of the skeptics, who held that man was incapable of arriving at any general truth and that every proposition must remain speculative and no more probable than another. According to Descartes, they doubted for the sake of doubting and could never escape from a state of uncertainty. He, on the other hand, doubted in order to discard the false and discover the true. The kind of certainty he sought was comparable to that found in mathematics. Whereas all other disciplines seemed to him to be merely conjectural in their findings, mathematics alone held the key to true knowledge. As he wrote in the *Regulae*: "Those who are looking for the right path toward truth should not concern themselves with any object that cannot furnish them with a certainty equal to that of the demonstrations of arithmetic and geometry." [46] This did not mean that he would confine himself exclusively to mathematics but only that he would seek the same kind of certainty offered by its methodical proofs in other domains.

Another general characteristic of the *Discourse* is its insistence upon a metaphysical position that combines both realism and idealism. By use of methodical doubt the author rejects everything that he has learned heretofore, including even the evidence furnished by his senses. He thus hopes to arrive at a first principle of which there can be no doubt, and it is here that he establishes the *cogito* contained in his celebrated "*Je pense, donc je suis.*" From this he deduces three other propositions that appear equally self-evident and irrefutable: (1) that his entire nature consists in thought; (2) that all the things we conceive clearly and distinctly are true; (3) that a person who doubts is imperfect but contains within himself an idea of perfection. Here there occurs a reversal, for he moves from his previous state of doubting to the idea of God, and via the proofs of His existence, he reestablishes the reality of the exterior world and the validity of our sensory perceptions.

There is an apparent dichotomy in Descartes' explanation of the universe that can be described as being both mechanistic and spiritualistic. He conceived of all natural phenomena as being explicable in the same way as one might describe the working of a clock or a fountain, *i.e.*, by means of the movements of its parts. Even living matter, although more complex and more difficult to analyze, was no exception to his general rule that in the material world everything could be explained by the arrangement and movement of its parts. His mechanistic interpretation, however, was not totally materialistic, for when he came to speak of man, he refused to classify him as being merely matter and reserved a special category for the mind, which he kept distinct from the body and which he defined as a thinking substance rather than an extended substance. This dualism between mind and body or between spirit and matter later aroused great controversy, especially among his friends, and he took pains to try to resolve the seeming paradox.

He believed that man possesses a noncorporeal and immortal mind mysteriously injected somewhere into his body. The influence of one upon the other, he was later to state, occurred through a small gland at the base of the brain, the pineal body; yet he continued to underline their separateness. In 1642 he wrote in answer to objections to his *Meditationes*:

> All that we clearly perceive can be made by God in the manner in which we perceive it. But we clearly perceive mind, that is, thinking substance, without body, that is to say, without extended substance; and conversely, body without mind (as everyone will readily grant). Hence at least by the divine power the mind can exist without the body, and the body without the mind. Now substances that can exist one independently of the other are really distinct. Thus the mind and the body are substances that can exist independently of one another (as I have just proved). Therefore the mind and the body are really distinct.[47]

One final general characteristic of the *Discourse* that helps to elucidate the specific steps in Descartes' method is his concept of morality and its relationship to the rest of his philosophy. Throughout his life he was hesitant to make pronouncements in this realm and did so only in his later years at the insistence of one of his closest friends, Princess Elizabeth, for whom he wrote his *Treatise on the Passions*. In the *Discourse*, however, he was already on the way toward elucidating certain principles that were not to be codified until many years later. To Descartes morality represented the final stage of wisdom, the crowning discipline of all knowledge. Since he had not yet perfected the science that was to unveil all the mysteries of the universe, he needed a temporary set of moral standards that would enable him to act until he was in possession of the truths he sought. He set up, therefore, the provisional maxims. These reveal two constants in his moral philosophy: first, that happiness is the goal of mankind and morality but a practical tool toward its achievement; and second, that happiness is integrally connected with the strength of one's will. There is a great deal of caution as he proceeds through methodical doubt to reconstruct his own conception of knowledge, but while doing so, he is careful to avoid indecision by adhering steadfastly to his own provisional morality, pointing out that these maxims are for his own self-guidance. Through an effort of will, he believed, one could overcome one's passions and master oneself if not one's fortune. It is because of his insistence upon the importance of the will and his subsequent linking of happiness with generosity that many critics have drawn parallels between his philosophy and that of his contemporary, Pierre Corneille.

With these general characteristics in mind, one can now return to a brief review (not forgetting that the *Discourse* itself is but a brief review) of the four principal steps of Descartes' method. In answer to the question "What am I to believe?" he sought the same certainty in the natural sciences and in metaphysics as he had found in mathematics. His method, therefore, although inspired by the analytical procedures of the ancient geometers, contained his own modernization and extension. The first of the four precepts treats the rule of evidence: "never to accept anything as true that I did not clearly know to be such." By its very simplicity this first rule appears self-evident, a proclamation of the supremacy of human reason. Man has only to rid himself of any outside authority and rely upon his own judgment, freed from earlier misconceptions (perhaps the illusions sometimes created by the senses) and prejudices, in order to arrive at the truth. The wording that follows, however, requires a certain amount of explanation: "Carefully to avoid precipitancy and prejudice, and to comprise nothing more in my judgment than what was presented to my mind so clearly and distinctly as to exclude all ground for doubt." Descartes begins with doubting and accepts only that evidence that is beyond doubt. How then does he differentiate between acceptable and nonacceptable evidence? The answer lies in the words "clearly and distinctly." There is a parallel use of vocabulary in the third of his *Regulae ad directionem ingenii*, which states: "Concerning the objects we propose to study, we should investigate not what others have thought nor what we ourselves conjecture, but what we can intuit clearly and evidently or deduce with certainty, for there is no other way to acquire knowledge." [48]

There are, according to Descartes, only two mental acts that enable us to arrive at knowledge without any fear of error: intuition and deduction. These he proceeds to define in the passage that follows, another example of how the *Regulae* are virtually indispensable for any clear understanding of his method:

By *intuition* I understand not the unstable testimony of the senses, nor the deceptive judgment of the imagination with its useless constructions; but a conception of a pure and attentive mind so easy and so distinct that no doubt at all remains about that which we are understanding. Or, what amounts to the same thing, intuition is the undoubting conception of a pure and attentive mind, which comes from the light of reason alone and is more certain even than deduction because it is simpler; although, as we have noted above, the human mind cannot err in deduction, either. Thus everyone can see by intuition that he exists, that he thinks, that a triangle is bounded by only three lines, a sphere by a single surface, and other similar facts that are far more numerous than most people think because they scorn turning their minds toward such easy matters.[49]

Two paragraphs later he defines the second basic mode of thought, deduction, and compares it to intuition:

> One might wonder why we have added another mode of knowledge besides intuition, one that proceeds by *deduction,* by which we understand all that is necessarily concluded from certain other facts already known. This procedure was necessary, for many things are known with certainty that nevertheless are not evident in themselves, simply because they are deduced from true and known principles by the continuous and uninterrupted movement of a mind that clearly intuits each step. Thus we know that the last link of a long chain is connected with the first, even though we do not see at a single glance all the intermediate links on which the connection depends; it is enough that we examine them successively and remember that from first to last each was attached to the next. Therefore we here distinguish intellectual intuition from certain deduction by the fact that some movement or succession is conceived in the latter but not in the former. Besides, evidence is not necessarily present for deduction, as it is for intuition, but deduction acquires its certainty in some way from memory. From this we may conclude that those propositions that follow immediately from first principles are known, according to our point of view, sometimes by intuition, sometimes by deduction; but that the first principles themselves are known only by intuition, whereas the remote conclusions are known only by deduction.[50]

The final paragraph of his discussion of the third rule, although it summarizes what had been said earlier, reveals that characteristic caution with which Descartes expressed his belief in the limitless power of human reason. Here again one finds a dualism comparable to that of his distinction between mind and matter in his separation of scientific knowledge from religious faith and an effort to reconcile the two:

[Intuition and deduction] are thus the two most certain paths to knowledge. No others should be admitted by the mind, and all the rest are to be rejected as suspect and liable to error. This does not, however, prevent our believing those things that are divinely revealed to be more certain than all knowledge. For faith in these, although it concerns obscure matters, is not an act of intellect but of will, and if they have a basis in the intellect, they can and ought to be, more than all the rest, discovered by one of the two ways already mentioned.[51]

Thus Descartes establishes his general criteria for truth: those elements or principles that are so simple as to be at once irreducible and self-evident. These are usually perceived by the intuition as being so elementary as to contain nothing false and include both separate entities, such as God, the mind, and the body, and also the idea of relationships such as smaller, larger, equal, and the like. Another term used to describe this irreducible quality of truth in addition to the word "simple" so often employed by Descartes is the word "absolute." Elsewhere in the *Regulae* he wrote: "The secret of the entire method consists in discovering with great care what is most absolute in all things." [52] Scientific inquiry, like that in any branch of learning, thus starts from first principles that are evident in themselves and proceeds to the more complex via the deductive method described above, which reveals relationships that at first appeared nonexistent through a series of successive intuitions. Descartes' first rule, therefore, establishes the aim of knowledge, which is certainty arrived at through either intuition or deduction. The three rules that follow are concerned with the technique for attaining the general criterion stated in the first.

The second rule, "to divide each of the difficulties under examination into as many parts as possible and as might be necessary for its adequate solution," reveals a process that is analytical, and although derived from his training in algebra, it is capable of both a general and a specific application. Most of our knowledge or intuition, even from infancy, is concerned with objects or notions made up of several parts. In order for us to understand them, it is necessary to divide them into their components until one arrives at their simplest elements; thus, in a general manner, one can establish a certain number of irreducible principles that are the true constituents of any object of our investigation. In a more specific fashion, if one wants to solve a particular problem, one has only to reduce its difficulty by a series of simpler questions until one discovers its most elementary parts.

Descartes' third rule describes a procedure that is the inverse of the preceding one. Having arrived at first principles, one then moves to the more complex—from causes to effects. Stated thus: "To conduct my thoughts in such order that, by beginning with the simplest objects and the easiest to know, I might ascend little by little as by steps to the knowledge of the more complex, supposing order even among those objects that do not naturally follow one another," the third rule reverses the process of the second. Decomposition of the complex into the simple is followed by reconstruction from the simple into the complex. One thus moves from analysis, what Descartes here calls division, to synthesis or, again to use his vocabulary, deduction. The order of which he speaks is comparable to that followed by geometricians that places a notion after those upon which it is dependent and before those which are dependent upon it. If one examines a similar passage in the *Regulae*, one finds the order described in terms of absolute and relative:

> I call absolute everything that contains within itself the pure and simple nature that is in question; for example, all that is considered independent, cause, simple, universal, one, equal, similar, straight, or the like; and I call this the simplest and easiest of all, considering our use of it for resolving questions. The relative, on the other hand, is that which participates in

the same nature, or at least in something of it, in accordance with which it can be referred to the absolute and deduced from it through some sequence; but which, in addition, involves in its conception other things, which I call relationships. Such is all that is called dependent, effect, compounded, particular, multiple, unequal, dissimilar, oblique, etc. These relative terms are removed from absolutes in proportion to the number of mutually subordinate relationships they contain. And the present rule teaches us the necessity of distinguishing such relationships and the need of observing the pattern of interconnections between them and their natural order in such fashion that we can proceed from the last of them to the most absolute, passing through all the rest.[53]

The last of the four rules given in the *Discourse* appears disarmingly simple at first reading: "In every instance to make enumerations so complete and reviews so general that I might be assured that nothing was omitted." Descartes' meaning, however, is more complex than simply a desire to verify the results of his analysis by a rapid review that would insure that nothing had been omitted in his reasoning. Had this been his sole intention, as some have thought, he would not have given such importance to the formula as to rank it as one of the four major precepts of his method. Again one must examine the *Regulae* for elucidation. "In order to attain complete scientific knowledge," he states as his seventh rule, "it is necessary to run through, one by one, in a movement of thought that is continuous and nowhere interrupted, all those things that concern our investigation and include them in an enumeration that is both sufficient and ordered." [54] Several paragraphs later he describes what is meant by enumeration, a term that he uses synonymously with induction, and how it is related to deduction and intuition:

> This enumeration or induction is thus an inventory of everything related to a given question—an inventory so painstaking

and accurate that from it we can conclude with certainty and
evidence that we have omitted nothing by mistake. Thus every
time we use it, if the thing we are seeking escapes us, we are
at least wiser in this respect: We perceive with certainty that
it can be found by none of the ways known to us; and if, as
often happens, we have succeeded in reviewing all the ways
to it that are available to men, we may boldly declare that its
knowledge lies entirely beyond the reach of human intelligence.
It should also be noted that by sufficient enumeration or induction we understand only the means by which truth is more
certainly inferred than by any other kind of proof except
simple intuition. As often as an understanding cannot be reduced to intuition, since we have rejected all syllogistic bonds,
there remains only this one way to which we should give our
total confidence. For whatever single propositions we have
deduced from one thing to another have already been reduced
to a true intuition if the inference was evident. If, however,
we infer some one thing from many disconnected facts, the
capacity of our intellect is often insufficient to embrace them
all in a single intuition. In this case the certitude of the present
operation should suffice.[55]

Already in the third rule of his method Descartes had suggested that in some instances both intuition and deduction might
prove incapable of establishing a logical order of sequence between certain objects. There his wording, "supposing order
even among those objects that do not naturally follow one another," foreshadows his explanation in the fourth rule, as clarified
by the *Regulae*, of how enumeration or induction can serve to
establish a relationship of antecedence and sequence in those
objects where intuition and deduction fail. Thus the Cartesian
method, as summarized by the French philosopher Louis Liard,
"consists in dividing things into their simplest elements of
which the truth is recognized intuitively; next, by means of
these elements, to reconstruct things by a process of deduction
that proceeds from one evident proposition to another; and

finally, to fill up any lacunae in the alternating sequence of decomposition and composition by use of inductions."[56]

Descartes' life was consistent with both his method and his aims. The maxims stated in the *Discourse* were to remain constants in his thinking and actions even when he came to state his morality in definitive rather than provisional terms. In a letter written five years before his death, he recapitulated these same formulas in only slightly different terminology, but changing the first of his maxims to read: "One should always try to use one's mind to the best of one's ability in order to know what one should do or not do in every circumstance of life."[57] Having settled upon his vocation, he tried to adapt every detail of his material and spiritual life to his mission and to remain as aloof as possible from events over which he had no control.

Even before it was published, the *Discourse* drew enthusiastic praise from Descartes' admirers. One such was Constantijn Huygens, who wrote that it was the best structured, the most mature and highly knowledgeable book he had ever seen.[58] Other eulogies followed its appearance, but even Huygens foresaw difficulties among certain people, and it would be false to state that the *Discourse* enjoyed an overwhelming success. Many scientists remained skeptical or indifferent, and at Utrecht, where his friend Reneri had introduced his teachings, trouble was brewing that was to have long-lasting consequences for the author. The universities both in Holland and France remained generally hostile in their views, and the general public read the *Discourse* primarily as an introduction to the accompanying essays, which today have fallen into oblivion. His contemporaries would soon be given other works, the *Meditationes* (1641) and the *Principia* (1644), where his philosophy would be set forth more succinctly and more completely. But the *Discourse* gradually began to overshadow not only the essays but all his other writings, so that from the eighteenth century to the present it has been considered the manifesto of the Cartesian revolution. It heralds not only the coming supremacy of reason over centuries of blind acceptance but also a heroic ideal. Philosophy is presented not as an academic exercise but as an exciting adventure. When one reads the *Discourse* today, one can easily imagine its author as French writer Charles Péguy described him: "Descartes, in the history of thought, will always be the French cavalier who got off to such a good start." [59]

René Descartes is the hero of his own autobiography, but as the central figure of the *Discourse*, he is also a symbol of humanity. His words narrate his own career, and they reflect the search for truth, particularly in the sciences, which absorbed all of Western thought in its transition from medievalism to modernity. It is the story of a quest not only for certainty but also for utility. It is the account of man's thirst for both truth and liberty, for the latter is necessary for the former. If human reason is to reach its highest achievements, it must be free from all authority which is not sanctioned by reason alone. All other philosophers were but pygmies or dwarfs when compared to Descartes, declared the English philosopher Henry More. "He is a hero," wrote Hegel a century later. "He has reexamined things from their beginnings and has once again found the true field of philosophy from which it had strayed for [more than] a thousand years." [60] But the man who, according to La Fontaine, would have been made a god had he lived in pagan times was not to be deified. The *Discourse* produced many disciples, and the very fact that it was written in French won for its author a certain notoriety among the general reading public. Even though his name continued to be withheld from the title page, everyone soon knew that it was the work of Descartes and was eager, just as he had planned, to read more. But among scholars, it was less well received, and at the University of Utrecht, where it had first been introduced, quarrels arose between his supporters and the anti-Cartesians which rapidly turned the school into a hotbed of controversy. The longed-for peace which the philosopher sought in Holland was soon to be interrupted. He would be required in the near future to defend not only his work but his life.

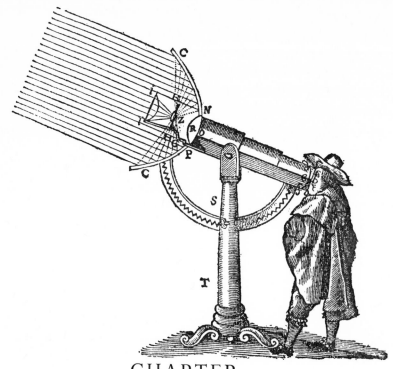

CHAPTER 4
Toward a Universal Science

VIEWED in retrospect, Descartes' interests during the nine years preceding the publication of the *Discourse* seem to have been largely scientific and particularly mathematical. Ever since his arrival in Holland, he never ceased experimenting and writing on algebra, geometry, physics, and optics. He pushed his mathematical interpretation of nature ever further, for his ultimate aim was to find the unity of all the sciences—the unity, in other words, of all knowledge. His universal science would be as rigorous as mathematics, not only analogous but mathematical in itself. His method, both in the *Discourse* with its accompanying *Essays* and in the earlier *Rules for the Direction of the Mind*, proclaimed a new kind of discipline which by its mathematical nature would be independent of the kind of material being measured. Mathematics was synonymous in his mind with science, with any discipline that sought to establish order and measurement. Thus astronomy, music, optics, and mechanics were all considered parts of mathematics, and whether one looked for order or measurement in the stars or sounds or figures or any other object, the principle was always the same.[1]

It was his desire to interpret nature in mathematical terms, to find a "universal mathesis," which led to his most celebrated discovery, analytical geometry. One of his first tasks was to apply numerical relations to figures in space. He could then proceed to transfer mathematical analysis as a whole to the study of moving bodies and thus encompass physics in his general scheme. Similar experiments were already being performed by Galileo, whose explanation of the laws of movement was later to be preferred to that of Descartes by Leibniz, who ridiculed many of the latter's geometric and mechanistic formulas. Descartes, however, was always rather disdainful of the accomplishments of others, especially those of his contemporaries. He preferred to find his truths for himself through his own experiments, and thus he had but little respect for Galileo's achievements. After a few quite perfunctory compliments to the Italian scientist, Descartes concludes one of his letters to Mersenne by saying:

> It seems to me that he, [Galileo], lacks a great deal in that he is continually disgressing and never stops to explain one topic completely, which demonstrates that he has not examined them in an orderly fashion and that, without having considered nature's first causes, he has sought only the reasons for a few particular effects, and thus he has built without a sure foundation.[2]

Another letter to Mersenne that shows Descartes' self-satisfaction with his own originality states that the *Dioptric* and the *Meteors* were intended merely to persuade his readers of the superiority of his method. He concludes by saying that the *Geometry* did more than that—it offered absolute proof: "I believe that one must not only think that I have done more than my predecessors but must also be persuaded that those who come after us will never find anything in this field that I could not have found as well as they if I had wanted to take the trouble to look for it." [3]

The three *Essays* offer an excellent opportunity for reviewing both Descartes' achievements and his originality as a scientist, both theoretical and practical. They reveal in microcosm his grandiose scheme for reducing all physical phenomena to a series of mechanical or mathematical formulas, and whereas a detailed examination lies beyond the scope of this work, a fairly rapid review of the *Essays'* contents and significance will enable the nonspecialist to appreciate the progress made by Descartes up to the time of their publication.

La Géométrie, although it was the last essay published, was probably the first to be conceived. Despite the author's statement that he had written and even invented parts of it while his *Meteors* was at the printers, the genesis of the work dates from a much earlier period. His enthusiasm and talent for mathematics were obvious while he was still a schoolboy, but no matter how precocious he may have been, it is difficult to accept the story propounded by Lipstortius that his great discovery in mathematics took place when he was only sixteen. [4] When answering the criticisms of Pierre de Fermat, the mathematician with whom he so often quarreled, Descartes affirmed the superiority of his own method and added that he had used this technique some twenty years earlier. [5] This would place his discovery in the years 1617–1618, when he was twenty-one. Some scholars interpret his dream of November 10, 1619 as the real beginning of this intuition concerning analytical geometry and the mathematical nature of the universe. His letters to Beeckman in 1619–1620 are filled with references to the correlation between numerical and spatial relationships. The summary given in the *Discourse* of his activities during this period describes the development of a method, but, as French mathematician Gaston Milhaud observes, the method is not identical to that of analytical geometry as stated in *La Géométrie*.[6] The methods are comparable, however, in that they both involve the correlation of algebra and geometry. No one can say for certain just what Descartes meant by his *science admirable* nor determine the exact date of his discovery. From his correspondence it is evident that as early as 1628 he had developed his method of drawing tangents to curves, and much earlier he was aware of the necessity of creating a new form of notation that would be applicable to both spatial and numerical relationships in order to arrive at a universal mathematical system.

One of Descartes' first steps toward the method he was to codify in the *Geometry* was the reform of algebraic notation. He found that the system then in use was confused and obscure. It used numbers which were never broken down into their most elementary roots; thus 225 was allowed to stand as 144 plus 81 without any mention that 144 was the square of 12; 81 of 9; and 225 was itself the square of 15. Another criticism that Descartes leveled against the existing system of notation was that the signs used to indicate powers (root, square, cube, etc.) were misleading. Sometimes capital letters were employed: *R* for the root (*racine*); *Q* for the square (*carré*); and *C* for the cube (*cube*). Sometimes symbols (*caractères cossiques*) were substituted to express these same powers: $\mathcal{X}$ for the root; $\mathcal{Y}$ for the square, and $\Gamma\mathcal{C}$ for the cube. What he sought was a system that would make immediately evident to the eye the function indicated by the symbol. What easier way than to substitute numbers for signs and letters? Whereas quantities, known and unknown, had been expressed by numbers, he chose to replace these by letters of the alphabet—those at the beginning to stand for known quantities, and those at the end for unknown ones. Thus what had previously been written as 1 R, plus 4 Q, minus 7 C, or as $P\ 1\mathcal{X}$ $\cdot P\ 4\ \mathcal{Y}\ \cdot M\ 7\mathcal{C}$, became in Descartes' new method of notation simply $x + 4\ x^2 - 7\ x^3$. It was thus a double reform that substituted letters for numbers to designate quantities and numbers for arbitrary signs and symbols to indicate powers.[7] Once this reform was accomplished, he proceeded to apply algebra to geometry and eventually to reduce all geometric problems to algebraic formulas.

La Géométrie is divided into three books, each containing a section on pure theory followed by the application of the theory to specific problems. In the first book the main principles of analytic geometry are set forth, and examples are given of problems that can be solved by the aid of circles and straight lines only. Here Descartes stated that every geometric problem could be reduced to a problem of straight lines which could be determined by nothing more advanced than the operations of arithmetic. To illustrate his point he took a problem already attempted by Euclid and partially solved by the Greek geometer Pappus and applied his own method.

The second book is the most difficult and also the most important, for here he treats the nature of curves. After classifying all curves into two kinds—geometric and mechanical—and then subdividing the geometric curves into different genres, he discusses his method of drawing tangents to curves. It is here that he describes the ovals which still bear his name.

The third book is almost exclusively algebraic. It discusses the nature of equations and contains his explanation of how to determine the number of positive and negative roots—a method that is known as Descartes' Rule of Signs.

The publication of the Geometry evoked a barrage of adverse criticism based mainly on two counts: Either the book was overly obscure, containing as it did many omissions, or it was an example of direct plagiarism, specifically of the ideas of the French mathematician François Viète. The author paid but little attention to the former; on the contrary, he had on several occasions stated that the omissions were deliberate.[8] He found it unnecessary to include all the steps of his reasoning, for he wanted to avoid restating what was already known. Writing with the desire to treat a diversity of highly technical matters as succinctly as possible, he foresaw that the number of readers who could appreciate his *Geometry* would be extremely limited. They would have to be specialists to begin with, and his work would demand very careful study. He wanted, therefore, to show only the originality of his research. "I can assure you," he wrote to his friend Florimond Debeaune, a mathematician whom he had known before leaving France, "that I have omitted nothing except on purpose. . . . I had foreseen that certain people who pride themselves on knowing everything would not have failed to say that I had written nothing that they did not know already if I had made myself totally intelligible for them, and I would not have had the pleasure of seeing the incongruity of their objections." [9]

Certainly no one could attribute his omissions to ignorance, for he had taken care to include the more difficult of his findings while skipping over the more elementary. As early as seven years prior to the publication of the work he had written to Mersenne that he was weary of mathematics. "As for problems," he told his friend, "I shall send you a million of them to propose to others if you like; but I am so tired of mathematics and now hold them in so little esteem that I can no longer take the trouble to solve them myself." [10] Descartes was not renouncing his interest in mathematics, but his correspondents had so beleaguered him with mathematical puzzles that he came to consider their solution a waste of time. So advanced was his own talent that he wanted to exercise his method in more complex fields. His words to

Mersenne also reveal his disdain for any intellectual occupation that was divorced from practical application. He explained in another letter that he had not given up the study of geometry entirely:

> I have resolved to abandon only abstract geometry; namely, the investigation of questions that serve only to exercise the mind; and this is in order to have even more time to cultivate another kind of geometry, which proposes the explanation of natural phenomena. If he [Gérard Desargues] would consider what I have written about salt, snow, the rainbow, etc., he would understand that my entire physics is nothing other than geometry.[11]

Descartes may have regretted the omissions and obscurities in the *Geometry*, for he later asked the mathematician and illustrator Frans van Schooten to add to his Latin translation of the work an introduction and the explanatory notes of Debeaune. With what was to become a characteristic dexterity at publicizing his own work, he had asked Père Derienne, who taught mathematics at La Flèche, for his comments on a copy of the *Geometry*. He not only wanted his work read but also suggested how it should be approached in terms which were far from self-effacing:

> I am not in the slightest hurry to receive your judgment, for I dare to hope that the later it arrives the more favorable it will be. I should especially like you to take the trouble to examine my *Géométrie*. It can only be done pen in hand and following all the calculations which may seem difficult at first, for one is not accustomed to them, but it takes only a few days for that; and if you pass from the first book to the third, before reading the second, you will find it easier than you thought. If I had wings to fly with, like Daedelus, I should come spend a week with you in order to make your beginning easier; but you can start on your own, and I am sure that afterward you will not in the least regret the time you spent on it.[12]

Adverse critics continued nonetheless to accentuate the work's obscurities, and Descartes continued to deprecate them, particularly his archrival Gille Personnier de Roberval, whose attacks he claimed to ignore as he would "the oaths of a parrot hanging in a window as I pass in the street."[13] Their quarrel lasted from 1638 to 1649, and Descartes' attitude is summed up by his remark: "I have never seen anything from him which could not serve to prove his incompetence."[14] Even more annoying than the charges of obscurity, however, were the accusations of plagiarism. He refused to acknowledge any indebtedness to Viète and, in his determination to prove his own originality, repeatedly stated that his work began where his predecessor had ended. That Jean de Beaugrand, the geometrician whom Descartes called the *géostatician*, should accuse him of borrowing from Viète was both "impertinent and ridiculous." Rarely did Descartes become so violent in his censure, and his own self-defense caused him to belittle often unjustly the achievements of others. He had read Viète's work, or at least glanced through it, but now that he reexamined it he found that he had nothing to learn from one who knew less than he had originally thought. He was justified in pointing out that Viète had given only a few specific examples whereas his own work discussed the number of roots in a given equation so that they could be applied generally to all equations.[15]

Despite its obscurities and in some cases its errors, *La Géométrie* was not only original but indeed revolutionary in its day. Now its main principles have been incorporated into every standard textbook. Probably its greatest innovation was the introduction of the notion of constant and variable into traditional geometry and the expression of the properties of curves by algebraic equations. Descartes took the first step toward a theory of invariants and through algebra saw the relationship between different geometrical problems which had previously seemed totally unrelated. His was the first systematic classification of curves, and he succeeded in elaborating "the transference of systematic structure from whole regions of algebra to whole regions of geometry." [16] Undoubtedly the most important aspect of his contributions to mathematics lies in the universal quality of his new method. As J. F. Scott has remarked:

> This is a momentous point. Not only are geometrical problems to be reduced to the questions anent the lengths of lines and so ultimately to algebraical problems, but it is hoped, by reducing all algebraical calculations to a few irreducible primitive ones, and all geometrical constructions to a few irreducible ones again, to detect fundamental parallelisms of structure between these two sciences and to exploit all the derived parallelism of structure for their inter-illumination. This magnificent plan is important philosophically also, for it breaks down the too rigid classification of the sciences by their formal objects. Therefore Descartes, wittingly or otherwise, took a decided step on the way to the arithmetisation and complete formalisation of mathematics as we know it today.[17]

La Géométrie does not represent the whole of its author's contributions to mathematics. Throughout his correspondence and other scattered writings one finds discoveries and theorems that prove he was a mathematician of genius; yet it was his unique talent for envisaging phenomena in general or universal terms, adequately demonstrated by his *Géométrie*, which placed his achievements above those of his contemporaries. Before Descartes mathematicians rarely looked for a general principle which would link the solution of one problem to that of another. His predecessors usually attacked each problem by separate *ad hoc* methods. His successors were quick to recognize the value of his method, so that by the end of the century his had become the normal mathematical procedure. Despite the originality and import of his accomplishments, today there are many who would tend to minimize his contribution. Auguste Nicolas, for example, has said that there is nothing new in

Descartes except his errors.[18] His work in geometry, nonetheless, when judged by its influence, is equal in importance to the discovery of infinitesimal calculus. Although he is often reproached for having failed to reach the later conclusions of Newton or Leibniz, recent scholars such as Jules Vuillemin have pointed out that his letters prove that he was in possession of many of the basic principles of calculus and that technically speaking he can be said to foreshadow the Newtonian discovery of fluxions.[19]

In *Les Météores*, the second essay accompanying the *Discourse*, Descartes seeks to apply his method to the realm of physics, to explain his theory of matter, and to demonstrate how all natural phenomena can be explained by natural causes. His investigations are not limited to meteors, although these were a striking example of what an ignorant people often attributed to supernatural causes. In a grandiose scheme for demystifying the universe, for dismissing the occult, and for establishing a mechanistic interpretation of cause and effect, he examines various subjects which had interested alchemists and scientists alike in order to show that man need not be frightened nor stand in awe of such things as thunder and lightning. "We have naturally more admiration for things that are above us than for those that are at the same height or lower." Thus begins his essay on meteors, and what follows shows that it is this very admiration or wonder that he seeks to dispel:

> And although clouds scarcely exceed the summits of some mountains and one sometimes even sees them lower than the tops of our bell towers, still, since one must turn his eyes toward heaven to look at them, we think of them as being so high that even poets and painters see them as the throne of God and pretend that He uses his own hands to open and close the doors to the winds, to sprinkle dew on the flowers, and to hurl lightning against the rocks. That makes me hope that if I explain their nature here so that one will no longer have occasion to admire anything about what is seen or descends

from above, one will easily believe that it is possible in some manner to find the causes of everything wonderful above the earth.[20]

Descartes had long been interested in meteorology, and besides his investigations into the nature of avalanches and the cause of thunder, he had been particularly fascinated by the parhelia, or false suns, observed near Rome in 1629. These formed the basis for his final chapter, which he completed in 1636 after sending many inquiries to Rome for additional information and which he attributed to a phenomenon of refraction. The treatise was a far cry from the accounts that were still being printed, such as the following in the *Le Mercure français:*

> During the Pentecostal celebrations in the principality of Anhalt there were seen in the air two knights mounted on horses covered with flames, one of them leading by the bridle a third horse also on fire. Two days earlier at Veneschav in Bohemia, two armies were seen in combat in the sky. And it rained a great quantity of blood or red water.[21]

Descartes admitted that he had never seen such phantoms and that stories told about them must be the result of superstition or ignorance. In the seventh section of the *Météores* he gives his explanation of such visions, attributing them to an optical illusion caused by the reflection of light on certain small cloud formations.

As early as October 8, 1629, Descartes confessed to his friend Mersenne that he was so engrossed in his research concerning meteors that he had no time for anything else. He asked the Minim friar to refrain from sending him any new questions in his letters, for:

> . . . My mind is not strong enough for me to concentrate on several different things at the same time. And since I never discover anything except by a long series of diverse considera-

tions, I have to devote myself completely to a subject whenever I want to examine one aspect of it. This is what I have experienced lately when searching for the cause of the phenomenon [the parhelia seen at Frascati on March 20, 1629] about which you write; for one of my friends showed me quite a detailed description more than two months ago, and having asked my opinion, I was forced to interrupt what I was doing in order to examine in turn all meteors before I could be satisfied. Now I believe I can reply fairly adequately, and I have resolved to write a short treatise that will contain the reasons for the colors of the rainbow (which gave me more difficulty than all the rest) and will discuss in general fashion all sublunar phenomena.[22]

Descartes' investigations were as thorough as possible with the result that *Les Météores* turned out to be one of his most carefully documented and logically constructed works. Its unity resides chiefly in his treatment of clouds, for these *nues*, as he called them, include all meteors. After discussing matter in general, he examines the nature of clouds, which are composed of vapors, and points out the differences between vapors and exhalations. Since clouds are moved by winds, he next examines why certain ones are stronger during the day than at night, and why some change their direction at specific times. The following sections describe how clouds are transformed into snow, rain, and hail. He discusses the formation of snow crystals and the size of raindrops. From clouds are also derived tempests, thunder, and lightning. He explains thunder as the result of a higher cloud falling upon a lower one, which creates a loud sound because of the resonance of the air. Lightning, which had always held a special fascination for him, is explained by a sudden exhalation from the space between two clouds as they come together. Descartes treats the two phenomena separately, for knowing nothing of electricity, he made no direct connection between the sight of lightning and the sound of thunder. He proceeds from effects to causes rather than inversely, and the resemblances that he notices between certain sounds or sights (the effects) he attributes often incorrectly to similar causes. He compares the sound of lightning, for example, to the sound of falling snow during an avalanche. From these similar sounds he concludes there must be similar causes and thus imagines the clouds which produce thunder to be filled with snow.

Descartes had documented his section on storms and tempests with accounts written by navigators and with information he had gathered from conversations with sailors. Much of his material was subsequently incorporated into Fournier's work on navigational theory, and his knowledge of meteorology, as will be seen later, astounded the captain of the vessel which was to take him on his last voyage.

After the chapter on storms, thunder, and lightning, he treats the phenomenon that so often appears after a tempest, the appearance of a rainbow. Although his explanation was incomplete, it marked a decided advance over all previous attempts. He was the first to account for the formation of the primary and secondary bow. From the time of Aristotle until the end of the sixteenth century, the explanation of the colors of the rainbow had been attributed to the principle of reflection. Descartes explains them via refraction and points out how the same colors may be produced by a prism or a triangular crystal. In some ways he foreshadows Newton's discovery of the composite nature of white light, although it was Newton's explanation of the formation of colors that in 1672 finally displaced that given by Descartes. And it is in the last discourse of *Les Météores* that he treats the subject that had served as the initial impetus for his essay, the appearance of the false suns seen near Rome in 1629, thus giving a parallel movement and similar logical development between his own investigations and the structure of his completed work.

Despite many of its merits *Les Météores* is less important than its author's work in mathematics or optics. Much of it is far too speculative; some of it is simply erroneous. Its chief claim to fame, however, lies in Descartes' making use of the most recent observations, and by modernizing the subject, he brought meteorology much closer to the realm of an exact science. He was soon followed by such men as Robert Hooke, who invented the now widely used barometer, and Edmund Halley, who in addition to encouraging Newton to complete his *Principia* alone directed the operations of the Greenwich Observatory for twenty years and in 1725 drew up his tables for computing the locations of the planets. His work, along with that of the French naturalist the Chevalier de Lamarck, prompted the development of a network of meteorological stations throughout Europe. It is perhaps not too great an exaggeration to say that the universality and the precision of present-day weather reports owe a debt of gratitude to Descartes for establishing the science of meteorology on a firm foundation and enabling men to view natural phenomena free of fear or consternation.

The enthusiasm that characterized Descartes' scientific discoveries often took the form of superlatives. His admiration for the geometrical method knew no bounds, and the excitement elicited by his research into astronomy is reflected in his words to Mersenne:

Although they [the stars] appear very irregularly scattered in the sky, I believe nonetheless that there is a natural order among them which is regular and fixed; and the knowledge of that order is the key and the foundation of the highest and the most perfect science that men can attain as regards material things; for by means of it one could understand *a priori* all the diverse forms and essences of terrestial bodies whereas without it we have to content ourselves with guessing at them *a posteriori*. . . . I believe it is a science which surpasses human understanding; and yet I am so foolish that I cannot refrain from dreaming about it.[23]

One of the results of his "dreams," or rather of his investigations, was *Les Météores*; but if astronomy was the key to the
physical sciences, Descartes' enthusiasm was still more exaggerated when he came to speak of optics, which he called the
"science of miracles." This was the most marvelous of the
sciences, for it enabled man to produce the same illusions that
magicians were to produce with the help of demons.[24]

La Dioptrique, like the other two essays accompanying the
Discourse, was imminently topical, but it was also the most
practical. The work combines speculation with concrete suggestions for the grinding of lenses. Descartes shows the relationship between geometry and physics not only in theory but also
in practice, for he states how his discoveries can be transformed
into useful inventions, specifically, a machine to produce tele-
scopic lenses. He wants to do more than explain the phenomenon of vision; he wants to improve it, and again his enthusiasm
for his project leads him into superlatives. "The entire conduct
of our lives," he wrote as the first sentence of the essay, "de-
pends upon our senses, among which that of sight being the
most universal and most noble, there is no doubt that inventions
which serve to augment its power are the most useful which
could exist."[25] The "marvelous glasses" of which he speaks
in the next sentence refer to the recent discovery of the telescope:

> And it is difficult to find any which increase it more than
> those marvelous glasses which, being in use only a short time,
> have discovered for us new stars in the sky and other new
> objects underneath the earth in greater number than those
> which we had seen before: So that by carrying our vision
> much farther than the imagination of our ancestors, they seem
> to have opened to us the way to attain a much greater and
> more perfect knowledge of nature.[26]

The study of optics dates back to antiquity. As early as the
fifth century B.C., Greek philosophers had proposed the doctrine

of ocular beams, a dual emission from the eye and from the object viewed. Both Plato and Aristotle wrote on the subject, and the latter opposed the emission theory, although with little success, for the doctrine of ocular beams was popular until the sixteenth century. As early as the thirteenth century artisans had made disks of transparent glass designed to correct man's vision, but these were usually regarded, especially by scholars, as serving only to distort reality and deceive the senses. Descartes wished to establish a scientific basis for the grinding of lenses, and it was his desire for precision which led him to decry the fact that the telescope should have been invented by chance, an invention that he attributed incorrectly to the Dutch inventor Jacobus Metius. Two other lensemakers, Jansen and Lipperhey, had both claimed the honor of being its inventor in the same year, 1608, and it appears that they had as their model a telescope constructed in Italy in 1590. But it was undoubtedly Galileo's experiments which brought the invention most into public notice, and Descartes had for several years, particularly in his correspondence with Huygens and in his dealing with Ferrier, been at work trying to perfect a means of making lenses which would completely eliminate any element of chance and bring the invention to its highest degree of precision. It must be remembered that although Galileo had provided the foundation of proof of the Copernican system with his instrument, the telescope that he had "perfected" was only slightly more powerful than present-day opera glasses.

The principal aim of *La Dioptrique* was a practical one, and as in *Les Météores* Descartes arranged its contents in a tightly organized sequence which moves from the general to the particular, from causes to effects. The essay begins with a discussion of the nature of light and colors. He finds that light is nothing other than a certain movement which exists in bodies which we call luminous. When he proceeds to examine the phenomenon of refraction, he compares the action of light to that of a bouncing ball. And in his explanation of color, which he attributes to the way bodies receive light and send it back to our eyes, many of his observations are deduced from his explanation of colors in the rainbow. His conclusions are sometimes wrong, and it is apparent that he was unable to abandon completely the emission theory; but his explanation is a step toward Newton's more complete and more correct explanation in the *Optics*. Descartes was among the first to propose that color was in some way connected with the various speeds of the actions meeting the eye.

After the statement of general laws pertaining to the nature of light and color, he next examined the eye, its nerves, and the formation of images upon the retina. In his account of the process of vision, the perception of distance, size, and shape, his own experiments with dissection furnished him with specific examples. Whereas he sought to find and state the truth for himself rather than point out where others had erred, his critics were preoccupied almost to the point of obsession with contradicting his writings in minute detail, seizing upon one minor point after another. When he was not moved to anger, as he certainly was whenever accused of plagiarism, Descartes usually considered their remarks with a lofty disdain which nonetheless contained a certain measure of abstract psychological truth. "I do not doubt," he wrote to Mersenne, "that you will hear many judgments, most of them adverse, of my writings; for those who are inclined to criticize can do so easily at first, especially when the works are little known by others." [27] Their misconceptions and inability to understand his work he attributed to their haste, for in order to judge fairly, one needs time to reflect.

One criticism which his contemporaries cited and which continues to this day is that he did not give enough weight to his experiments and that they were incomplete. Descartes was well aware of the importance of experiments and prided himself on his own accuracy. When, for example, Mersenne had the temerity to suggest that he was in error, Descartes replied rather brusquely: "I dare to assure you that none is false because I did them all myself, and in particular the one you cite concerning *hot* water which freezes more quickly than *cold*. I did not say *hot* and *cold*, but rather that water which has been kept over fire for a long time freezes more quickly than that which has not." [28] He explained the rest of the experiment and then concluded: "There are very few people who are able to make experiments well, and often, by doing them poorly, they find just the opposite of what one ought to discover." [29]

Descartes' observations on the composition of the human eye and its mechanism were based directly upon his experiments with the dissection of animal parts which he received from his local butcher. In an extremely long letter to Mersenne in which he replied to the various objections to his *Dioptrique*, he describes in detail one of these experiments: "I took the eye of an old ox (this must be done, for that of young calves is not transparent), and having chosen half an eggshell, which was such that the eye could easily be placed inside without changing its shape, I cut out a circular piece with very sharp scissors which had the optic nerve at its center." [30] These natural organs, he believed, should be the models for artificial ones, and thus after having examined the process of vision, he turned in the next section to the question of how vision might be perfected. In the seventh discourse he described the cutting of lenses and evolved the ovals which still bear his name. He concluded that hyperbolic and elliptical lenses are preferable to all others, and of these the hyperbolic is preferable to the elliptical. In addition to his description of the lenses best suited for the microscope and telescope, he included a section on the magnifying glass. And in the final discourse he set up a refractive index for the different kinds of glass.

Although *La Dioptrique* was composed for a very practical aim, its ultimate importance turned out to be of a far more theoretical nature. Despite his efforts and those of Ferrier to perfect a machine for the grinding of hyperbolic lenses, Descartes encountered endless technical difficulties. Even if these could have been overcome, there would have remained the obstacle of chromatic aberration, or chromatism, which is due to the differences in refraction of the colored rays of the spectrum. This is much greater in hyperbolic than in spherical lenses. In the end, his research proved to be of very little immediate practical value, but it did pave the way for the later discoveries of Hooke, Grimaldi, and especially Newton. Descartes' achievements in optics were considerable, particularly if he is considered the originator of the law of refraction. Here as elsewhere, however, he was accused of plagiarism.[31] Both the German astronomer Johannes Kepler and the Dutch mathematician Willebrord Snellius were named as possible sources. In answer to such accusations, Descartes replied with his customary acidity:

> Whoever accuses me of having borrowed the ellipses and hyperbolas of my *Dioptrique* from Kepler must be either ignorant or malicious. As concerns the ellipse, I do not recall that Kepler speaks of it, or if he does, it is assuredly to say that it is not the anaclastic that he is seeking; and as for the hyperbola, I remember very well that he expressly tries to demonstrate that it too is insufficient. . . . Now I leave it to you to decide if I would have borrowed something from a man who tried to prove it false.[32]

Even Ferrier, whom Descartes had tried to persuade to join him and who eventually succeeded in constructing a very good hyperbolic convex lens, did not escape his sarcasm: "As for Ferrier, let him do as he pleases; it appears that he will accomplish nothing, and I believe that the most insignificant wheel turner or locksmith would be better able than he to demonstrate the effect of lenses." [33]

Despite the fact that Descartes' experiments in optics turned out to be of little practical value at the time and that he probably owed more to his predecessors than is generally acknowledged, his originality in the field cannot be questioned, for he found new applications of the ideas of others. *La Dioptrique* is the work of an extremely original thinker which led not only to the invention of an important class of curves but also to a clearer explanation of color and eventually to the undulatory theory of light. By combining mathematics, physics, and anatomy, *La Dioptrique* set a high standard of excellence for scientific treatises and helped to stimulate interest in the practical concern of how to perfect man's vision. Considered along with *Les Météores* and *La Géométrie*, *La Dioptrique* represents a decisive turn in the history of science. Descartes steadily increased the span of his mathematical method so as to encompass the entire world within his *mathesis universalis*. Even metaphysics was not exempt as he continued to expand his mechanistic concept of the universe. But although he arrived at a theory resembling, at least in its terminology, the French philosopher Offray de La Mettrie's definition of "man-machine" a century later, his mechanism was limited, for he ruled out neither the soul nor God. His scientific pursuits were thus restricted by his metaphysics and vice versa.

The three essays contain his principal concerns and achievements in science and, most specifically, in mathematics, but after 1637 Descartes was to pay more attention to the changes which his universal mathematics would require in the field of philosophy. After attempting an explanation of the physical universe, he turned to the question of the nature of man in all his complexity. Pure science would eventually wane in his interest to be replaced by metaphysics. Thus, as two modern critics have expressed it, when one considers Descartes' scientific pursuits, he appears "a philanthropist before humanity whose happiness he wants to assure and yet which refuses to accept it from his hands," and when he turns from science to metaphysics he seems "less concerned with giving humanity a mastery of the

world than with obtaining a clear idea of what man really is." [34]
At the time of the publication of the *Discourse* and during the
years which followed, however, it will be seen that his interests
could be neither exclusively scientific nor metaphysical.

CHAPTER 5
Sorrow and Persecution

THUS far in the life of the philosopher it appears that his activities were orientated almost exclusively toward matters intellectual. The thinker so outshines the man that one wonders if his concern for and with humanity ever went beyond dispassionate observation and became true involvement. Even his friendships up to this time, sincere though they were, had been largely founded on mutual scientific or philosophic interests, and his attachments had been limited to men of learning, people with whom he could correspond and converse in terms that only rarely left the realm of the abstract to express some small

135

measure of admiration or devotion. The real enthusiasm in his letters is directed more toward his own discoveries than to any desire to please or serve his friends. The bonds of blood or country had been broken early; his family counted for little with but few exceptions, and any nostalgia for his homeland was quickly dispelled. The formula expressed in the *Discourse*, "I think, therefore I am," seems well suited to characterize a man whose life would be directed by his head rather than his heart. He was, however, human, and just as during his youth he had momentarily found diversion in the more pleasurable pastimes of Parisian society without succumbing to debauchery, at the age of forty he entered into a relationship that reveals, if nothing else, that he was not entirely devoted to cerebration and that his private life was not always consistent with his public image.

Descartes' only romantic adventure began three years before and was to terminate three years after the publication of the *Discourse*. To call the episode a romance is perhaps too strongly suggestive of a deep and lasting love, for six years was the total duration of the affair. Most of it remains shrouded in mystery, undoubtedly because he preferred it so. Yet the few details which survive offer much the same allure as a melodramatic novel if one interprets the "facts" with any imagination. Some have been overly naïve and somewhat embarrassed in their evaluation of the affair, while others have sought to overemphasize the relative importance of what they consider either a tawdry or lurid liaison. When the facts themselves are so limited, it seems preferable to ignore the accounts that cannot be verified with a reasonable degree of historical accuracy and restrict what follows to a simple retelling of the events with as much objectivity as possible. Whereas many biographers prefer to dismiss the affair with but a passing reference, anyone interested in discovering the philosopher's feelings in all their complexity cannot overlook the only relationship in his life where by his own admission the sexual act played a significant role. His devotion to study and his dedication to reason and temperance in all things would seem to be belied by his behavior, which in this instance demonstrates that no matter how strong his desire to apply his principles of method to all realms of activity, his private life was at odds with his moral maxims and his otherwise methodical assurance. At the time his mind was occupied with the composition and publication of the *Discourse*, he met the woman to whom he gave at least momentarily his body and perhaps his heart.

Her name was Helen, a Dutch servinggirl whom he probably encountered while living at the house of Thomas Sergeant, a schoolmaster and bookseller in Amsterdam. She may even have worked in his host's employ. Her family name, usually given as Jans, is doubtful, for this was her father's first name, which has been misinterpreted as her family name from a certificate of baptism. Virtually nothing is known about her looks, her background, her morals, her intelligence, or what happened to her after she disappeared from Descartes' life. Some have suggested that she was what the French would usually imagine a Dutch girl to be: flaxen hair, blue eyes, rosy cheeks.[1] That she was of a lower social station than Descartes is evident from several references to her position as a household servant, and it can safely be assumed that she possessed the virtues and perhaps the foibles of others of her class. The fact that she was a Protestant has been cited as a possible reason for Descartes' failure to marry her, but certainly he could have found far more serious objections. It is known that they corresponded for a while, but since their letters have been lost, there is no way of telling anything about her character from her own words. She knew how to write, which in itself might classify her as above average for her station, but whether she expressed herself as an amorous adolescent (even her age is unknown) or in fairly literate terms will probably always remain a subject of supposition and a cause of frustration.

Descartes made no mention of his first meeting with Helen, but he did write down another date, Sunday, October 15, 1634, the date on which their illegitimate child was conceived. That he should record this date, rather than that of its birth or any other event connected with either the mother or the child, appears significant, especially since he chose to write it not in a letter (none of his friends was apprised of his affair) nor in one of his works (certainly the public had no right to be admitted into his private life) but scribbled on the flyleaf of a book in which he had jotted down random observations. The fact that he should retain this one date and that he should note it in the place where he did would seem to indicate that not only did he consider the event important but also that it was perhaps a unique occasion. To apply the word "mistress" to Helen or, as some have called her, "concubine" would seem to exaggerate the intimacy of their relationship, for later Descartes was to refer to the affair as if it had been but a momentary fall from his otherwise chaste life.

The winter following the conception of his child was a relatively quiet one—a lazy period, as it were, in a life which was usually inordinately active. Even his correspondence apparently lagged, for there is a lapse in his letters from September until the following April. In the early spring of 1635, when Helen's pregnancy began to show, he arranged for her to move to Deventer, where he had friends and where she would be cared for with discretion. He then set up his own residence at Utrecht, where he was attracted by the presence of his friend Reneri and where he began his correspondence with Constantijn Huygens, whom he had met just before leaving Amsterdam. Huygens had made a deep impression on his new friend, whose first letter upon his arrival at Utrecht was filled with eulogies: "Truly he is a man who is superior to all the praise that one might give him. . . . There are some qualities which elicit esteem for the possessors without making us love them, and others which produce love without in any way increasing our esteem; but I find that he possesses both to perfection." [2] Such was his initial reaction to Huygens. One can only wonder how much esteem or love was in his heart at this time for Helen. He is silent on the subject, and one searches in vain for passages in his correspondence that might permit a double reading in order to reveal his private thoughts.

On July 19, 1635, Helen gave birth to a daughter, who was baptized on August 7. The baptismal certificate lists the father as Reyner Jochems, or René, son of Joachim, but it is doubtful that he was present at the ceremony. Since he had lived previously in Devener, he could not return incognito. One might explain his absence by reasons of propriety, his desire to avoid any scandal for either the mother or himself. Scholars have pondered, for example, the question of why there was no entry in the registers which listed the names of all illegitimate children and have wondered if Descartes might have married Helen secretly. But the earliest extant copy of the *Kalverboek* which is now available dates from the eighteenth century, so there is no way of knowing if the child's name appeared there or not; and there is no mention of his name on any of the marriage records. The only official document which remains is the certificate of baptism, and even on that the name of Descartes is avoided. Given his allegiance to the Roman Catholic Church, such a marriage would have been highly improbable, and the fact that his daughter was christened in a Protestant church leads one to wonder if the father gave his tacit consent, for in the eyes of an orthodox Catholic, this was tantamount to damnation.

The child was called Francine, a name which, meaning little France, some have interpreted as a sign of nostalgia on the part of her father. Did he wish, as Gustave Cohen suggests, that his daughter had been born in his homeland? [3] The use of a diminutive was increased by both the mother and the father, who in turn called her Francintje and Francinette. Almost every account of Descartes' relationship with his daughter emphasizes his tenderness and love, stating that she brought a great joy into his life. And yet for two years after her birth, there is no evidence that he ever saw Francine. In fact, in his entire correspondence there is but one letter in which he refers to her explicitly, and even there he chooses to call her his niece. This was written on August 30, 1637, when he was living near Alkmaar, perhaps at Santpoort or even at Egmond. It is also the only letter in which he mentions Helen, who had by this time left Deventer and taken their child with her to the outskirts of Leiden where she was again employed as a domestic. The publication of the *Discourse* has been completed, and in a happy frame of mind, the philosopher writes to their usual intermediary in the hopes of having the mother and the child join him:

> Everything here is going as well as we could hope. I spoke yesterday to my landlady to find out if she would consent to have my niece here and how much she would want me to pay. Without any discussion she said that I could send for her whenever I liked and that we could easily agree upon the price, for it made no difference to her if she had one more child to look after.[4]

The philosopher's landlady obviously had several children, so that it was no extra burden to have another in the house. She was in need, however, of a new maid, and Descartes asked his correspondent to find one for her. It was just after this request that he spoke of Helen: "Indeed, Helen must come here as soon as possible. It would be best, provided things can be arranged satisfactorily, if she could come before St. Victor's Day, even if she has to find someone to take her place." [5] The feast of St. Victor occurred on September 30, and it was at this time that servants were customarily employed. Evidently Helen had agreed to work until that date, so that if she were to leave earlier, she would have to find a replacement. Descartes stated twice how very anxious his landlady was to find a servinggirl and then asked his intermediary to relay Helen's thoughts on the matter. Was he speaking merely of her proposed relocation, or was there the possibility that he planned to have both his child, masquerading as his niece, and his mistress, employed in the role of servant, under the same roof with him? At any event, he seemed decidedly anxious to keep her identity secret. Toward the end of the letter he wrote in the margin: "My letter to Helen is not pressing, and I prefer that you keep it until she comes to you, which she will do, I believe, toward the end of this week to give you letters for me, rather than send it to her via your servant." [6] It seems clear that even while living in different cities, the less attention drawn to Helen the better.

There is no proof that Helen ever brought Francine to live with her father, but one would assume so. This would seem to account for the period between 1637 and 1640 when he became something of a recluse. He received fewer and fewer visitors at his country house, excusing himself by saying that it was due to the humbleness of his home, but his reticence to see outsiders or even intimate friends at his own residence could well have been prompted by the presence of the little girl and her mother. These were, for the most part, happy years, when his principal concern was the study of nature, specifically in relation to medicine. The tone of his correspondence at this time reveals a concern for life, a certain enthusiasm and exuberance, and even a certain vanity: "It is true that I have never been less inclined to write than now," he confessed to Huygens. "The fact that my hair is turning gray warns me that I should spend all my time trying to set back the process. That is what I am working on now, and I hope my efforts will succeed even though I lack sufficient experimentation." [7]

Again to Huygens, a kindred soul whose understanding and praise Descartes considered an almost unimaginable happiness, he wrote about his plans for longevity:

> I have never taken such pains to protect my health as now, and whereas I used to think that death might rob me of thirty or forty years at most, it could not now surprise me unless it threatened my hope of living for more than a hundred years. It seems very clear to me that if we would simply avoid certain things in our daily routine, we would be able to achieve a much longer old age than we do at present. But since I need time and many experiments in order to examine everything concerning this subject, I am now at work composing a *Summary of Medicine*. Part comes from books, part from my own theories, which I hope to be able to use at least temporarily to gain a delay from nature and then afterward continue in my projects.[8]

His medical research gave him increasing assurance. Thirteen months after the letter quoted above, he wrote to Mersenne, who was concerned at not having heard from him:

> I should have to be very weary of living if I failed to take care of myself after having read your latest, where you say that you and others fear that I might be sick, for it has been more than two weeks since you have received a letter from me. But it has been more than thirty years, thank God, since I have had any sickness which deserved to be called such. Age has taken from me that impetuosity which once made me love a soldier's life. Since my profession now is largely one of timidity, and since I have gathered some knowledge of medicine, and since I feel alive and pamper myself with as much care as a rich man suffering from gout, it seems to me that I am at present farther from death than I was in my youth. If God does not grant me enough knowledge to avoid the ills which age brings, I hope that He will at least let me remain long enough in this life to have the time to bear them. . . . One

of the principles of my moral philosophy is to love life without fearing death.[9]

All the while that Descartes was experiencing such exuberance and advancing his theories of medicine, Francine, although she remained in the background, was growing up. Her father, who had busied himself with dissections and theories of the blood's circulation and the pineal gland, began to think of her education. She was now five, and he proposed sending her to France, where she would be under the supervision of Madame du Tronchet, a woman renowned for her virtue, the mother of an ecclesiastic, and also a distant relative. She seemed a perfect choice for rearing his daughter, and he entrusted her with the task of finding a suitable governess. Then, while Madame du Tronchet was making the necessary arrangements, Descartes was forced by an ironic turn of fate to suffer probably the greatest loss of his life. He who "never felt farther from death" learned that Francine had contracted scarlet fever. Doubly ironic, when viewed in retrospect, were his words written the previous year to Mersenne to whom he boasted of his accomplishments in anatomy. He had learned all about the various parts and functions of animal life, but, he concluded: "I still do not know enough for all that to be able even to cure a fever. For I believe I understand animal life in general, of which it is not a question here, but I still do not know about man in particular, which is the main concern." [10] Now that his daughter's life was at stake, would his medical studies be of any avail?

Descartes had left Santpoort in April, 1640 to return alone to Leiden. He was ready to publish his second work, one which he had begun ten years earlier as a short treatise on metaphysics and which he had now reworked during the past five months into its definitive form. Just as with the publication of the *Discourse*, he wanted to assure a favorable reception and supervise the printing personally. He would need at first a few sample copies so that he might send them to friends and scholars for correction and to sound out their reactions. While this was being done, he also needed to make certain that the printer did not allow any extra copies to circulate. Although the new work, written in Latin and entitled *Meditationes de prima philosophia*, was intended as an apology for his religious beliefs, a demonstration of God's existence and an examination of the real distinction between man's body and his immortal soul, he foresaw the likelihood of its being misinterpreted by the theologians, both in Holland and in France. One of his first steps, therefore, after sending it to the University of Utrecht for the approval of his friends Regius and Aemilius was to submit it to several Catholic priests in the neighborhood before forwarding it to Paris for the approbation of the Sorbonne.

It was during these preparations, which were to drag on for more than a year, that he received the news of his daughter's illness. Whether he arrived in time to try to save her is not known. What is certain is that Francine, her body completely covered with purple blotches, died on the third day of her malady, September 7, 1640. Baillet tells us that her father wept over her with a tenderness which made him realize that true philosophy does not stifle one's natural inclinations. He declared, again according to Baillet, that her death caused him the greatest sorrow that he had ever experienced in his life.[11] As is frequently the case with his first biographer, however, these statements can no longer be verified, and one wonders if he did in fact shed tears, and if so, just how profoundly the loss of his daughter affected him.

The week before Francine's death, he corresponded with Mersenne in an effort to dispel any objections on the part of the Jesuits. The week following her death, he again wrote to the Minim priest excusing himself for not writing sooner and giving the curious reason that he had been forced, because of unforeseen circumstances, to absent himself from the city.[12] There is no mention of where he went or why, but there is no doubt that his absence was caused by Francine. The rest of this letter is concerned with objections to his *Meditationes* and is couched in the most philosophical and scientific terms. It contains eighteen specific points which Descartes listed by number. Obviously there is no trace here of any grief.

Was it simply his desire to keep his private life to himself, or had he succeeded in adopting his philosophic principles to his actions so that he was above any outward display of emotion? Some three years earlier he had written to his good friend Huygens, who had just lost his wife, a letter of condolence which was far from the ordinary solace expected in such communications:

> If I were to measure you by the same standards as ordinary souls, I should fear that the sorrow which you experienced at the beginning of your late wife's sickness might have made her death insupportable; but, not doubting that you govern yourself entirely by reason, I am convinced that it is much easier for you to console yourself and to recover your customary peace of mind now that there is no remedy than it was when you still had occasion to vacillate between hope and fear. For it is certain that once hope is gone, the desire to save her disappears or at least diminishes; and once one no longer desires what one has lost, one's sorrow cannot be very great. . . . A strong and generous soul such as yours knows only too well on what terms God brought us into this world to want to resist the necessity of His law by useless hopes. Although one cannot submit to it without some difficulty, I hold friendship in such high esteem that I believe that everything one suffers for its sake is worthwhile, so that even those who die for the well-being of those they love seem happy to me up to the last moment of their lives.[13]

As a philosopher, he offered Huygens the solace, if such it can be called, of reason and stoicism; as his friend, he offered diversion now that mourning would be of no use either to the deceased, to Huygens, or to his friends. He pointed out, rather coldly and at the same time excusing himself for expressing his feelings in such "philosophic" terms, that it is a virtue to feel sorry for even the slightest afflictions which others suffer, but it is a kind of cowardice to feel sorry for ourselves. By his own lack of reaction to the death of his daughter, three years later, it would seem that Descartes had succeeded in subduing his emotions to his reason, in applying the same stoic attitude to his own life which he had recommended to Huygens. And six months after Francine's death he wrote to another friend, Alphonse Pollot, who had just lost his brother, in practically the same terms. "It would be barbarous," he said, "to feel no sorrow whatsoever when one has sufficient cause, but it would be cowardly to abandon oneself completely to one's grief." [14]

Descartes had every reason to grieve, for not only had he lost his daughter, but within the space of five weeks after her death he also lost his father and his sister Jeanne, who died at approximately the same time. Thus, in the same letter of condolence to Pollot, when he speaks of the recent loss of "two people who were very close to me," most critics have interpreted the allusion as referring to his daughter and his father. Even though he was not on particularly close terms with his parent, he had intended to return to France to visit the aging Joachim, then in his seventy-sixth year. When his father died on October 17, however, Descartes did not learn of his passing until well over a month later, a lapse occasioned by his elder brother's negligence or perhaps even by his ill will, for none of his family looked kindly upon René's profession. Not knowing that his father was already deceased, the philosopher continued to write to him until he finally received word from Pierre. His reaction is expressed in a letter to Mersenne:

> The last letter [from his brother] which you sent informs me of the death of my father. I am very sad and am sorry not

to have been able to go to France this summer so that I might have seen him before he died; but since God did not permit it, I do not intend to leave here before finishing my *Philosophy*.[15]

The "two people" whom he had lost recently could refer to his daughter and his father, but even though the exact date of his sister Jeanne's death is not known, it too could have produced this recollection of sorrow. And what of Helen? Although he made no direct mention of her at the time, immediately after Francine's death, she disappeared entirely from Descartes' life. Thus within the space of a few months, he had lost his daughter, his father, his sister, and his mistress. Helen, nonetheless, seemed to have left no sadness in the heart of the philosopher, and one can only speculate at what might have been his reaction to the whole affair which he so carefully kept as clandestine as possible. Was it his philosophic self-composure, his detachment, his desire for secrecy, or even a certain hardheartedness which prevented him from any outward show of emotion? At the moment when ordinary men might have sought increased solitude and withdrawn from society, Descartes made another one of his innumerable changes of residence and installed himself in an attractive country château at Endegeest. Well-staffed with servants and conveniently located so that it was within a short distance of university and court life, both of which come to play increasingly important roles in his life of "retirement," Endegeest was both a charming retreat and a place where he could entertain, a custom of which he had deprived himself during Francine's lifetime.

How was he to remember Helen, if remember her he did, now that she was no longer a part of his life? There is no evidence that he ever took any interest in her after the death of their daughter or that he was concerned either with her happiness or security. Their relationship had given rise to a certain amount of malicious gossip about the "irregularity" of the philosopher's mode of life; some went so far as to accuse him of being the father of countless illegitimate children, a common adventurer, to which others replied that "Frenchmen consider such actions as *galanterie*," and Descartes himself answered the accusation by saying that if he had any bastards, he would not deny it, but in truth he had none. He was careful, however, to use the term *fils naturels*, for he had in fact a *fille*. His feelings about Helen were kept hidden from even his closest friends, and the only remaining testimony concerning his affair is the account given by Clerselier. To him the philosopher confessed during a visit to Paris in 1644 that God had rescued him from a dangerous *engagement* which had occurred ten years earlier. The date coincides almost to the day with the conception of Francine. And he added that God, by a continuation of His grace, had preserved him up until now from falling back into temptation.[16] This account, however, comes to us at least thirdhand; *i.e.*, Descartes' conversation with Clerselier may have suffered some transformation when the latter recounted it to Baillet. And Baillet, as was his wont, could have added religious overtones in this instance in an effort to restore his subject to the purity of his earlier celibacy. If Descartes considered his brief liaison with Helen as sinful and therefore cause for remorse, he left no record of such a reaction.

Equally plausible, although equally impossible to verify, is the supposition that he looked upon his mistress as he might regard any other scientific experiment. Was it by accident, for example, that Francine was conceived in 1634, the very year when he had been at work on his treatises *De l'Homme* and *Traité de la formation du foetus*? At the time when he was especially engaged in physiological research, was it not possible, as one biographer suggested, "that he carried his theory of *bêtes-machines* a step higher than he confessed in public, and that this adventure was merely the result of a scientific curiosity?"[17]

To every question regarding his personal feelings toward Helen and Francine, Descartes remains silent. That his writings, especially his correspondence, contain almost no mention of them is not surprising when one remembers his conviction that the secret life was the good life. Nor is the omission necessarily a sign of indifference, for his stoicism did not go so far as to rule out any display of emotion. "I am not one of those," he wrote in January, 1641, "who believe that tears and sadness belong only to women and that to appear as a man of heart one must always force oneself to present a look of composure." [18] But rather than surrender himself to mourning, he seemed to accept the death of Francine, the loss of his father and sister, and the disappearance of Helen with a characteristically philosophical resignation. In his new residence at Endegeest he was ready to resume life, to savor and to study it, and to embark once again upon his quest. The five years spent with Helen and Francine were among the happiest of his life, but clouds had been forming which were soon to darken his relatively peaceful existence. What began as fairly restrained criticism of his work quickly developed into heated controversy and finally into persecution. There was virtually no time for sorrow, for his attention was soon to be diverted by attacks on both his work and his person. At the moment when he might have longed for peace and seclusion in his new country residence, he was challenged to defend his thought, his character, and eventually his life, for the charge of heresy, if he were convicted, brought with it the penalty of death.

The scene of the coming battle was the University of Utrecht. It was there that his philosophy had experienced its first success through the efforts of his friend Reneri. When the professor died in 1639, his defense of the philosopher's seemingly revolutionary theories was taken up by an even more enthusiastic disciple, Regius, also known as Henri de Roy. Whereas Reneri had been responsible for introducing Cartesian theories at the university, Regius was to become an almost fanatic propagandist for the new philosophy. He enjoyed great popularity with his students, who were enrolled not only in his courses in botany and theoretical medicine but also in such diverse disciplines as physics, theology, and law. They were anxious for their teacher, who because of his audacity appeared something of a hero in their eyes, to publish his theories, but Regius decided that it would be better to sound public opinion first by presenting them in the form of theses which would be debated in open hearings in much the same way that doctoral candidates today are often required to present an oral defense of their dissertations.

Prior to the public debate Regius, who had replaced his deceased predecessor in the friendship of Descartes and was now a frequent visitor at Endegeest, sent the proposed theses to the philosopher. Descartes' reply was a long letter in Latin in which he responded both to his disciple's earlier objections to his *Meditationes*, still to be published, and to the theses, which he examined point by point, correcting those which appeared either vague or misleading. One of the things which caused him some concern was the repeated mention of his name. This had already given rise to certain difficulties, for in his funeral oration for Reneri, another disciple, Anton Aemilius, had eulogized Descartes more than the deceased, calling him "the Atlas and Archimedes of our century." Such praise, especially when it was published, provoked envy among the other professors. Regius was even more lavish in his use of compliments, and, therefore, after reading the theses, his friend politely reprimanded him for being overly flattering: "I find my name again at the end of page eight. I might let it appear in a title, as might any gentleman, but only on the condition that you spare me the epithets which follow. And I should also prefer to be called by my true name, Descartes, than by the one invented here, Cartesius." [19] Regius complied with the philosopher's request, but to this day in the Netherlands he is still known as Cartesius.

Beginning on June 10, 1640 the theses proposed by Regius

were publicly disputed and immediately aroused a storm of controversy. Although the debate was largely limited to the subject of the circulation of the blood, a doctrine recently discovered by the English anatomist William Harvey and defended by Descartes, Regius was anxious to prove the superiority of the new philosophy over the old, and his rather immature enthusiasm caused him to offend several of his colleagues. Despite Descartes' counsel of moderation, he exposed himself, and indirectly his mentor, to severe attacks from the traditionalists. Among the first to react was a French doctor named Primerose, who published a pamphlet which declared that the position held by Regius concerning the circulation of the blood was completely erroneous. Regius, who was hotheaded and quick to call anyone who disagreed with his opinions a fool or a quack, immediately answered with another pamphlet entitled *A Sponge to Wash Away the Filth of the Remarks Published by Dr. Primerose Against the Theses in Favor of the Circulation of the Blood, Explained at the University of Utrecht*. Tempers flared on both sides. What had begun as a relatively technical, scientific dispute soon exploded into an argument involving medical, philosophical, and theological questions as well, for Regius, a scholar in many fields, was convinced that he had every right to explore the consequences of his theories in subjects that his colleagues considered their personal, unique, and virtually sacred property. They in turn banned together to attack less a specific theory than the general danger which they saw in novelty of any sort and the potential power of a system of thought which might subvert the principles of the university, of Protestantism, and even the state. Their criticism, therefore, would eventually be directed against Cartesian doctrine on religious rather than scientific grounds.

The leader of the opposition could not have been more ideally suited for his task, both by temperament and position. Gysbertus Voetius was one of the most influential men in

Utrecht. First professor of theology at the university and first clergyman of the city, he had the support of academicians and townspeople alike. Eager for power, he sought to appeal to both through his pious airs, his impassioned sermons, and his pedantic pretentions. Despite his great mediocrity in learning, he went about with pompous self-satisfaction in his own achievements, especially since the victory of the Gomarist party, and attained great success in the one field in which he possessed any real talent, polemics. His sermons, like his writings, were filled with the most virulent pleas for the castigation of his enemies. He attacked the rich and influential, which gave him the reputation of bravery and integrity. He came to be respected by most, feared by some, and actually beloved by others. It seems strange in retrospect that such a man could have given his support the previous year to the promotion of Regius, but this was probably due to flattery on the part of the latter. Voetius had been displeased by the increasing popularity of Descartes' philosophy, and in June, 1639, without mentioning the philosopher, he held his own series of debates in which he presented certain tenets culled from the *Discourse* and attempted to prove their atheistic tendencies. Undoubtedly the eulogy given to Descartes in the funeral oration for Reneri stuck in his craw.

Voetius, or Voet as he is sometimes called in French, was annoyed by Regius' success as a scholar and teacher, by the growing number of students who attended his lectures, in short by any threat to his own authority and power. He hated Catholics, philosophers, and foreigners. Thus Descartes was triply suspect. And his antipathy was such that he came to label them all as atheists, blinded as he was by his prejudice against those who did not share his views. He enjoyed nothing better than a good fight, and the theses proposed by Regius provided an excellent opportunity for the first skirmish. He would prove that Cartesianism was dangerous to Protestantism, that it was basically atheistic and therefore its inventor and adherents were deserving of banishment, if not death, and such teachings should be outlawed not only from the university but from the entire country. He did not begin, however, with such strong charges. Rather than attack Descartes directly, he chose to crush his disciple first, and to this end he used all of his influence with both the university and the Church, with his colleagues and his parishioners.

Unfortunately Regius did not follow Descartes' advice that he should proceed with caution and not appear as an iconoclast. Like his adversary, he also enjoyed a fight, and after answering the first objections to the theses in his characteristically heated manner, he decided to continue the discussions and prove his superiority, that is, the superiority of Cartesianism, over any and all dissenters. Thus, at the beginning, the dispute was conducted largely on academic ground between Regius and Voetius, with Descartes remaining in the background and directing his disciple with as much prudence as possible. It is not known whether he attended the June debates, but he had offered to do so if his friend, and in this case his spokesman, needed help:

> Should you want a fuller explanation about anything, you will find me always ready to serve you, either by letter or in person. And as concerns the defense of the theses, I shall even journey to Utrecht if you wish; but no one must know it, and I would remain hidden in the place usually occupied by Mademoiselle Schurmann when she comes to listen to your lessons.[20]

This passing reference to Anna Maria van Schurmann conjures up one of the most remarkable young ladies of the Netherlands, whose learning had earned for her a reputation throughout Europe. She was hailed as the Dutch Minerva, the Torch of Learning, the tenth Muse, and the fourth Grace. Well-versed in the classics, to the extent that her writing in both Latin and Greek was praised for its elegance and subtlety, she also knew Oriental languages and had studied Turkish, Syrian, and Arabic. She read the Bible in Hebrew and wrote French with such command that her style was often compared to Balzac's. In addition to her literary talents, she was a gifted painter and sculptor, and her works, which also included wood carving, engraving, and tapestry, commanded a high price. She was thirty-two when Descartes mentioned her in his letter to Regius, and they had been acquainted for some time. Most probably they met at one of the universities, either at Leiden or Utrecht, where she was in the habit of lecturing and disputing with professors and divines alike. Women, however, were not permitted because of academic protocol to enter into public debates, and it was for this reason that she was usually seated in a curtained pew or tribune, an *écoute* as it is termed in French, from which she could be heard but not seen. This was where Descartes wished to listen to the defense of the theses if he traveled to Utrecht.

Anna Maria van Schurmann was truly a prodigy of learning, one whose accomplishments dazzled all she met. Her own education was phenomenal by both its breadth and depth, and she undertook to champion the cause of women's being admitted into universities with much the same enthusiasm of a later-day suffragette. To this end she wrote a pamphlet entitled *The Learned Maid, or Whether a Maid May Be a Scholar? A Logical Exercise Written in Latin by That Incomparable Virgin Anna Maria van Schurmann of Utrecht.* Most modern readers would find the tract wearisome because of its repetition of certain formulas, but it does exemplify the type of logical disputation that was so popular in the public debates of the day and offers occasional turns of phrase which might be termed quaint. At one point, for example, she argues that all who have a "sublime countenance" are suited to study. Maids as often have a sublime countenance as men: Ergo, maids may study.[21] While not espousing the cause directly, Descartes, too, was interested in the education of women. Had he not written the *Discourse* in French so that it would be accessible even to them?

His acquaintance with Mademoiselle Schurmann never developed into a friendship; on the contrary, it was not long before they became antagonists. At one point they differed over the relative merits of two musical compositions, both based on the same line of verse. One was written by a Dutchman, and it was his work which she preferred. Descartes favored the work of a compatriot and expressed his reasons in a rather joking fashion. Their first real quarrel, however, occurred when he visited her one day and found her occupied in one of her favorite pastimes, reading the Bible in Hebrew. He was surprised that a person of her talent would give so much time to something he termed "of so little importance." Whether these were his exact words is not known, for the event, like so many of the most interesting anecdotes connected with his life, comes to us thirdhand.[22] The account continues that when she tried to show him the importance of such study, he replied that he, too, had once learned the language called holy and that he had even begun to read the first chapter of Genesis in the Hebrew text. But no matter how deep his meditations, he reflected in vain and could find nothing "clear and distinct." He realized that he could not understand what Moses meant, and instead of enlightening him, everything he read only served to confuse him more. Such a reply wounded Mademoiselle Schurmann so deeply that she disliked the philosopher from that day forward and never saw him again.

Whether Descartes was sincere in his denigration of Hebrew is open to question. He may have been merely teasing the young woman. And was she so overly sensitive as to make this the cause for their permanent rupture? Her reaction may have been due to her deep piety or may even have been the impulsive act of someone suffering from unrequited love.[23] There is no doubt, however, that she was deeply religious. She was said to have adopted certain Calvinistic principles when she was between three and four years old, and later her religious inclinations overcame her enthusiasm for learning. She burned her poems, renounced pedantry, and became a convert to mysticism under the direction of Jean de Labadie. Already at the time of the Utrecht controversies, she had begun to devote more and more of her energy to theological disputes, and for this she had chosen as her master Descartes' worst enemy, Gysbertus Voetius. It was he whom the philosopher blamed for diverting Anna's talents away from the more feminine arts. Under such a tutor it was no wonder that she had no taste for the new philosophy.

In the fall of 1640 Descartes wrote to Mersenne:

> This Voetius has spoiled the young Miss Schurmann; for although she used to have an excellent head for poetry, painting, and other such refinements, he has had her in his power so completely now for five or six years that she is concerned only with controversies over theology, which deprives her of the conversation of all respectable people.[24]

It was probably while under Voetius' spell that she came to regard Descartes with the horror of a virgin being attacked by the devil, for her tutor referred to him as an atheist and libertine, and when years later she recorded her opinion, she wrote in the margin under the heading of "Blessings from the Lord" the following: "God has separated my heart from that profane man and used him as a goad to revive piety in me so that I might give myself entirely to Him." [25]

Not long after her break with Descartes, Anna also turned away from her instructor and spiritual guide. Her enthusiasm for Voetius as a man of God was suddenly altered when he took it upon himself in one of his sermons to attack the frivolity of women's hairdos and even criticized those men who appeared in church looking too well groomed. Although deeply religious, Mademoiselle Schurmann was also a young woman not insensitive to current fashion. It appears that she took the minister's

"Descartes as a Young Man," anonymous, Musée des Augustins, Toulouse.

"Descartes,"
by Jan Lievens,
Groninger Museum,
Groningen.

"Descartes,"anonymous,
Institut Tessin, Paris.

"Anna Maria van Schurmann,"
self-portrait, Stadhuis, Franeker.

"Marin Mersenne,"
by Duflos,
Bibliothèque
Nationale, Paris.

"Descartes,"
by David Beck,
Royal Swedish Academy
of Sciences,
Stockholm.

"Gysbertus Voetius," by J. Suyderhoef,
Bibliothèque Nationale, Paris.

"Princess Elizabeth
of the Palatinate,"
by Guillaume van Houthorst,
Heidelberg Museum.

"Descartes,"
by Achille Jacquet,
Bibliothèque Nationale,
Paris.

"Queen Christina," by Sébastien Bourdon,
National Museum, Stockholm.

"Queen Christina of Sweden Surrounded by Scholars,"
by Dumesnil, Musée de Versailles.

"Descartes," by Frans Hals, Musée du Louvre, Paris.

remarks a bit too personally, for she would dress as she pleased, and it annoyed her to hear criticism, direct or indirect, especially from the pulpit. Her zeal for Voetius, however, had not yet begun to wane when Descartes described her in his letter to Mersenne, and in that same letter the philosopher was much more concerned with the master than with the pupil.

Voetius, who had written to the philosopher's Parisian correspondent, for some strange reason thought that he might enlist Mersenne's help in combating the increasing popularity of Cartesian doctrine. It must have delighted Descartes when the Minim priest sent him his replies to Voetius' objections in order that he might forward them to the irate professor. Rather than agree with the charges that his friend's philosophy contained heretical tendencies, Mersenne pointed out certain similarities with the teachings of St. Augustine; and in a subsequent letter, written in answer to Voetius' repeated inquiries, he stated that Descartes' doctrines, if rightly understood, were not inconsistent with those of Plato and Aristotle. It seemed almost inconceivable, as Descartes himself stated, that Voetius could have been blind to their friendship:

> Thank you for the news about Voetius. I find nothing unusual there except that he has ignored what I am to you, for everyone here, even those who know me but slightly, is aware of it. He is the most obvious pedant in the world, and he is bursting with resentment that there is a professor of medicine [Regius] at their Academy of Utrecht who openly acknowledges my philosophy, even gives special lessons in physics, and in just a few months enables his students to dispense entirely with the old philosophy. Voetius and other professors have done everything in their power to have him prevented from teaching by the town council, but on the contrary, it has allowed him to continue in spite of them.[26]

With a rather spiteful sense of humor, Descartes goes on to inform his friend that he has forwarded the enclosed letter to

Voetius by messenger, so that he would have to pay the postage, as if it had not been sent under cover, and thus Mersenne would have some small vengeance for the six livres he was forced to pay for the delivery of Voetius' theses.

Although he failed to draw Mersenne into his plot, Voetius continued to create as much hostility as possible. His position was made even stronger when in March, 1641 he was elected rector of the university. It was precisely at this time, as if in open defiance of his adversary's new status, that Regius proposed another series of debates. In April and again in May there arose new disputes, more animated than the first. Regius refused to limit his discussions to purely scientific or medical matters; instead, he undertook to defend the thesis that the union of body and soul consists only in the composition of the two substances and is not therefore an actual unity. Both his thesis and his language were considered in direct opposition to the official position of the university, which was based on the Aristotelian Scholastic theory of the substantial unity of form and matter, body and soul. Voetius immediately replied by countertheses and declared the new doctrine heretical. According to the rector, views such as those propounded by Regius could only promote skepticism and endanger faith.

Until this point in the controversy, most of the argumentation had been in the form of public debates; now it began to be carried on in writing. When Voetius published his countertheses, Regius became so angered that despite Descartes' counsel of temperance he in turn replied by publishing his views, although he did follow his friend's advice and tried to temper any expressions which the rector might find offensive. Voetius, however, insulted that Regius should have replied at all, discovered that his work had been printed without official permission and that the publisher was a Remonstrant. He succeeded in having the book confiscated, which made it all the more popular and hence Voetius all the more angry. He enlisted the help of his son Paul, who published additional theses under his father's direction. Had not Descartes, by his revisions of Regius' replies, employed another to be his spokesman? Why should he not use a mask as well? Descartes merely laughed at the work of the son, the "child" as he called him; yet Paul was then a professor at his father's university despite the fact that he was not yet twenty-two.

To Regius the philosopher suggested that he ignore such squabbles, for they did not merit the attention of intelligent people:

> I read and I laughed heartily at both the theses by young Voetius, the son of the other, who is only a child, and the judgment of your academy, which perhaps is equally deserving of being considered as still in its childhood. . . . I am rather annoyed at you. You seem to take such things to heart. You should be happy to see your adversaries fighting among themselves with their own weapons. Certainly no one of even average intelligence would read their writings without seeing that they obviously lack the reason necessary to refute you and that they also lack the wisdom to hide their stupidity. . . . Just laugh and, I beg you, calm yourself. Have no fear, your enemies will soon be punished. You will win eventually if only you keep still.[27]

Voetius had succeeded in getting the academic senate of his university to condemn the teaching of the new philosophy, and aside from Regius, all but two of the professors acquiesced to the rector's dictates. Regius was strictly forbidden to lecture on anything other than medicine and was forced to exclude from his courses any mention of Cartesian doctrine. Although Descartes laughed at the folly of Voetius, his son, and his fellow conspirators and counseled Regius to do likewise, he realized that he could no longer remain in the background. Rather than continue to rely on Regius to be his spokesman, he would henceforth write and sign his own rebuttals. He was being attacked by Catholics in France, by Protestants in Holland, and by Scholastics in both countries. "Actually," as he told Huygens, "I ask for nothing but peace from the two, but I realize that in order to get it I must wage war for a little while." [28]

The maneuver which he chose was one of extreme subtlety, almost Machiavellian in its strategy. It took the form of a letter, the *Épître au Père Dinet*, but was, in fact, a pamphlet designed to combat Protestant and Catholics alike in order to reconcile both toward acceptance of his work. Père Dinet was a Jesuit; yet in his letter Descartes attacked another Jesuit, Père Bourdin, who had previously condemned Cartesian philosophy at the College of Clermont at Paris. Although he sought the support of the Jesuits, he could cite this criticism as an answer to Voetius' charge that he was a Jesuit in disguise, if not a heretic or an atheist, for to the Dutch clergyman, they were all almost equally abhorrent. Certainly the Protestants in Holland would be pleased by his censure of a French Jesuit. At the same time, however, he appealed to Catholics and countrymen to judge his condition with compassion, for was he not being persecuted by Protestants and thus something of a martyr for the cause of his religion? To the Jesuits he would appear as a missionary and confessor in a land of heretics; to the Dutch Protestants he would play the role of censuring the Jesuits.

Not only did he attack Père Bourdin, with whom he was to become reconciled a few years later, but he also inserted in the account of his persecution a highly unflattering portrait of Voetius, although he was careful not to name him:

> He passes for a theologian and orator, a man of many disputes. He has drawn to him all sorts of little people by professing deep piety and an unconquerable zeal for religion, by attacking public officials, the Roman Church, and any opinion which is different from his own, by pricking the ears of the populace with buffooneries. Every day he edits pamphlets which no one reads, cites authors whom he knows probably only from tables

of contents and who more often than not speak against rather than for him. He speaks presumptuously and gauchely of all the sciences as if he knew them but appears learned only in the eyes of the ignorant.[29]

Voetius was not one to take such insults lightly and promptly demanded that an official censure be sent out on behalf of the university. The task of drafting the document fell to his son, but knowing that its publication would take time, and impatient for a quicker answer to his adversary, the father sought out a former student, Martin Schoockius, whom he enjoined to write a libelous pamphlet entitled *Admiranda methodus sive philosophia Cartesiana*. To the unsuspecting the work might at first have appeared as an exposition of Descartes' philosophy, whereas it was actually a refutation. Schoockius, then a professor at the University of Groningen in Friesland, was but a pawn, for the real author was Voetius. Alerted by his friends who sent him extracts of the work while it was being printed, Descartes undertook to refute its errors with the intention of publishing his version at the same time as the Voetius-Schoockius document appeared. The work was temporarily interrupted however, for Voetius put it aside to enter into another dispute, one which would involve Descartes as well.

At the small town of Bois-le-Duc there existed a certain Society of the Holy Virgin, which had lost its religious character and continued as a civil society after the victory of the Reformation and the expulsion of Spanish power. In order to insure the society's remaining nonsectarian and, more specifically, to prevent its becoming a secret center for Catholicism, the town authorities required it to admit members of the Reformed Church. When the burgomaster and thirteen of the most important Protestant citizens of Bois-le-Duc joined the society, Voetius accused them of idolatry and published his views in a pamphlet. After a moderate reply from the authorities, he gave a counterreply, an anonymous libel which was promptly forbidden in Bois-le-Duc. A tireless author, he wrote the book *De confraternitate Mariana*, and for more than four years he continued his denunciations in theses, lectures, sermons, and letters. To answer the charges that they had joined forces with the Catholics for political ends, the Protestant magistrates chose as their spokesman Samuel Desmarets, a French Protestant, who had come to Bois-le-Duc, often referred to as the Rome of the Low Countries, in 1636. By 1642, like Schoockius, he was a professor at the University of Groningen. He was also a minister. When Descartes sought to enlist his aid against their common enemy, Voetius' son referred to them as Herod and Pilate. Accusations and insults were exchanged by both sides, and finally Voetius procured an official condemnation of the society. He boasted of his triumph in a letter which Descartes felt he must answer publicly. He preferred to circumvent the religious aspects of the quarrel as much as possible, for he would write as a philosopher rather than as a Catholic: "I respect all theologians as servants of God, even those who are of a religion different from mine, because we all adore the same God." [30] The *Epistola ad Voetium*, published at the end of May, 1643, ran to some 282 pages and made it clear that its author had no respect for one theologian, namely Voetius, who obviously was not deserving of the name: "If someone passes himself off as a theologian but I know him to be a notorious liar and slanderer and if his vices are such that they constitute in my opinion a danger to public welfare, the title of theologian will not stop me from unmasking him." [31] What Descartes sought by his detailed description of all the wrongs done to him by Voetius and his conspirators was a public vindication. After examining point by point each of the accusations brought against him, he concludes with eloquence and no small measure of invective of his own:

> I do not need to invoke the religious liberty which is accorded to us [*i.e.*, French Catholics] in this republic. I confine myself to stating that your book contains such criminal lies, such

stupid insults, slander which is so abominable that no enemy would use the like against his enemy, no Christian against an infidel, without denouncing himself as a cheat and a scoundrel. . . . I understand the Dutch temperament well enough to know that their magistrates imitate God in that they are often slow to punish the guilty, but once the audacity of the evildoers has passed the limit where they deem repression necessary, they act without mercy and are not to be fooled by false words. By publishing your books, devoid of charity and proofs and filled only with calumnies, you have dishonored your profession and your religion. Take care that they do not judge punishment to be the only possible atonement. Adieu![32]

It was now Huygens' turn to suggest that his friend be more temperate in his rebuttals. Highly amused by the letter to Voetius, he realized that such attacks would only incite the philosopher's enemies the more, and he quoted the comparison of theologians to hogs: "When one is pulled by the tail, they all squeal."[33] In this case the squealing was to continue for another seven years. Voetius now assumed the role of martyr, one persecuted for his faith by this foreigner, this Jesuit spy, who had come to the Netherlands to stir up controversies. He so excited public sentiment in Utrecht that on June 16 the authorities issued a summons requiring Descartes to appear before the town council and prove his accusations, especially that Voetius and not Schoockius was the author of the pamphlet against him. With great politeness, Descartes answered by letter and in Dutch this time that it was after all up to the council to discover the author of the libel against him, and that he would appear later in person to give testimony if such were necessary. He contested their right, however, to summon him, for he was living at Egmond, which he considered to be out of their jurisdiction. The town council continued its deliberations and finally concluded in favor of Voetius. Descartes was cited a second time as being guilty of slandering the clergyman, but the citation never reached him. Thus in September he found himself threatened with expulsion and his books subject to a public burning. Feeling unsafe in the little town of Egmond, he went to The Hague, where he immediately sought assistance from the court. He had friends in high places and eventually obtained the intervention of the Prince of Orange, who wrote on his behalf to the magistrates of Utrecht. The town council was in an embarrassing situation, for it did not want to condemn its own rector and at the same time it wanted to do justice to the philosopher. It hesitated, therefore, to make any formal decision.

Descartes then decided to take the initiative upon himself and appealed first to the University of Groningen and then to the town officials for a judgment against Schoockius. The professor, who had previously declared that he was the sole author of the *Philosophia Cartesiana*, now admitted under oath that Voetius had urged him to write the work and, besides furnishing most of the material, had inserted the most virulent invectives. When Descartes sent the proceedings from the senate in Groningen back to Utrecht, he expected that he would at last be vindicated. But the town council did nothing except issue a proclamation which forbade the circulation of anything for or against Descartes. It had virtually no effect, however, for Paul Voetius continued to write slanderous pamphlets, and his father brought suit against Schoockius, a suit which he was soon forced to drop. Descartes sought to put an end to the whole affair, which had now dragged on for more than six years, by writing *An Apologetic Letter to the Magistrates of Utrecht Against the Two Voetiuses, Father and Son*. Once again he traced the quarrel step by step from its beginning and did not spare his adversaries the same type of sarcasm they had so lavishly heaped upon him. Schoockius was compared to Susanna among the Elders, and the *Philosophia Cartesiana* reminded him of the two mothers quarreling over the same child before Solomon. In a Protestant country such Biblical references were considered not only irreverent but virtually sacrilegious. And the magistrates of Utrecht, far from granting him the justice he claimed, remained deaf.

Utrecht was not the only scene of controversy unfortunately, and scarcely had the turmoil there subsided when new attacks began at the University of Leiden. Here, too, Descartes had disciples and adversaries. Adrian Heereboord defended his theories in much the same way, although with far more circumspection, as Regius had done. And Jacobus Revius, who had earlier tried to convert Descartes to Protestantism and been scandalized by the philosopher's adherence to Catholicism (the religion of his king and his nurse, as Descartes pointed out), played a role similar to that of Voetius. Once again Descartes was forced to appeal to the authorities of the university and to the magistrates of Leiden for support against the false accusations that were being hurled at him:

> I have written a long letter to the curators of the university to demand redress for the slanders of two theologians. I have not yet received their answer, but I do not expect much, for I know the temperament of the people here. They do not respect honesty and virtue, but instead they revere the beards, voices, and frowns of the theologians. . . . Those who are the most brazen and know how to scream the loudest, the more stupid they are, the more power they have. I expect that the wrong will be plastered over rather than remedied. . . . In case I cannot obtain justice, and I foresee that it will be extremely difficult, I believe I shall be forced to leave the country.[34]

He felt persecuted by men he had every reason to believe would never listen to the voice of reason. He complained that the reputation he had earned through his work had brought him nothing but trouble. It was like another Inquisition, worse than the Spanish, he said, and was it not ironic that he had earlier borne arms in order to help the Dutch in their fight for religious freedom? The orthodox Calvinists, however, were determined that his philosophy should be suppressed. A few years later they succeeded in forbidding theologians to make any mention of Cartesian doctrine in either their discourses or their writings. Not knowing exactly where to turn, Descartes thought seriously of moving once more. Certainly the years of a relatively peaceful existence in his country residence were at an end. His life, nonetheless, was not devoid of friends, and perhaps one of the strongest reasons for his reluctance to leave Holland during the attacks from the theologians was his attachment to a person who throughout this period of strife was his companion, his inspiration, one might well say his soul mate. One needs to go back several years in order to trace the development of a friendship that was to leave an indelible mark on both the philosopher's personal life and on his work.

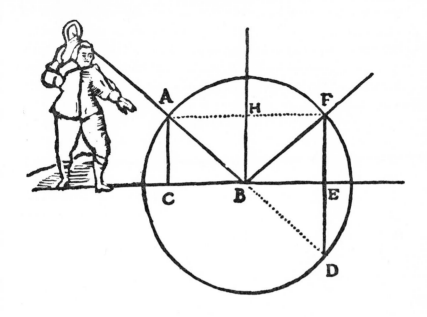

CHAPTER 6
A Royal Friendship

IN May, 1643, at the moment when Descartes was most embroiled in the attacks directed against him and his philosophy by Voetius, he received the first letter from the person who was to become his new disciple and his closest friend. The one to whom he could best open his heart as well as his mind, the one who understood his theories and yet was quick to point out their weaknesses, appeared not in the form of an aging philosopher or mathematician but as a young and extremely talented princess. When he was forty-seven and she but twenty-four, there began the correspondence which lasted until the philosopher's death, a testimony to the deepest and most enduring friendship he was ever to experience.

Elizabeth of Bohemia, Princess Palatine, could boast of one of the most illustrious lineages in Europe. Born December 26, 1618, she was the eldest daughter of Elizabeth Stuart and Frederick V. Her maternal grandfather was James I of England, and her mother possessed all the charm and beauty of her own ill-fated grandmother, Mary, Queen of Scots. Her father, the Palatine Elector, came from the distinguished strain of the House of Orange and was the son of Louise Juliana of Nassau, daughter of William the Silent and widow of Frederick IV. Elizabeth was thus to inherit many of the brilliant qualities of her parents' ancestry, as well as their misfortunes. At the time of Elizabeth's birth, Frederick V was still young and enthusiastic about his political aspirations. Swayed by his ambitious wife and by his own devotion to the Protestant cause to accept the crown offered by the revolting forces in Bohemia, he took the step which was to reduce his family to exile and poverty and the Palatinate to ruin. Frederick had expected support both from England and from the Lutheran princes of northern Germany, but his hopes were quickly deceived. In 1620 the Spanish and Bavarian troops, under the leadership of Count Tilly, won a decisive victory at the battle of the White Mountain. Some biographers believe that Descartes served in the forces which defeated the father of his future friend, but nowhere does he mention having witnessed or participated in the siege of Prague.[1] Frederick was now derisively called the *Winter König*. Driven from his original wealthy possession on the Rhine, he and his family were outcasts without land or money. The prosperity and power which had seemed so assured proved but an illusion. The Palatinate was turned over to Maximilian I of Bavaria, the Protestant religion was again forbidden in Bohemia, and the "Winter King" was forced to flee from Prague with his "Queen of Hearts," hoping to find safety and perhaps regain the crown that he had worn so briefly.

One of thirteen children, three of whom had died in early childhood, Elizabeth spent the years before she met Descartes first under the tutelage of her grandmother Juliana at the lonely castle of Krossen, and then in 1628 she rejoined her parents in Leiden, where they had been offered a residence and a subsidy by the States General of Holland. It was here amid rather frivolous surroundings that Elizabeth, the most serious child of the riotous lot that occupied the Children's Court, was instructed by Madame de Plessen, who had been Frederick's governess until he was seven. The young princess had very little contact with her mother who, it was said, preferred the antics of her monkeys and lapdogs to those of her babies; but under the strict direction of Madame de Plessen she attacked her studies with such seriousness that those about her often made fun of her old-maidish ways. She had always had a penchant for religion and excelled in the study of languages, both modern and ancient, which earned for her the nickname of *La Grecque*. Later university professors visited her to instruct her in philosophy and the sciences. While her brothers and sisters remained carefree and could jest that they frequently dined on diamonds and pearls, for such was their poverty that jewels had to be pledged for credit, Elizabeth seems to have been the only one to reflect soberly about her family's position.

The exact date of Descartes' first meeting with the princess is not known, but it most probably occurred during the winter of 1640, three years before the actual beginning of their correspondence. He was first introduced to her, one suspects, through the intermediary of his friend Pollot, at a reception given by Elizabeth's mother, the Queen of Bohemia. Retiring though she was, especially in the midst of the high-spirited badinage that usually surrounded the queen, Elizabeth did not fail to attract the philosopher's attention. In spite of her shyness, he preferred her to her more lively sisters. Even at their first encounter, Descartes was no stranger, for she had already read his writings and found in them a new appeal, a new explanation of the graver subjects that were to form the basis of their conversations and their letters.

She took almost no interest in current gossip or the social functions she was required to attend. One might say that her chief virtue, at times perhaps a hindrance, was her humility. She had no sense of her own importance or gifts, and yet she was not without a certain beauty. Quite tall, she had black hair, a bright complexion, sparkling brown eyes, thin dark eyebrows, a well-formed forehead, a pretty red mouth, admirable teeth, and an aquiline nose.[2] This last aspect, her nose, caused her some embarrassment, particularly in her youth. Often it would become exceedingly red, perhaps from indigestion. One anecdote relates that when her sister Louise reminded her that it was time to visit their mother's apartments, Elizabeth asked, "Would you have me go with this nose?" to which her rather impudent sister replied, "Well, you can't wait until you can get another one."[3] Extremely sensitive, Elizabeth would try to avoid society at such times. But it was not primarily her looks that so distinguished the princess; rather it was the charm of her mind, her utmost simplicity of character, which endeared her to those who knew her and was to win for her the admiration of Descartes. Her intelligence and forthrightness enabled him to see in her a reflection of his own ideas, only now graced by her femininity. He was not, however, unaware of Elizabeth's physical charm, for in his first letter to her (or is it only the language of the courtier?) he speaks of her body as "comparable to those which painters give to angels."[4]

Descartes' visits to Elizabeth were few. He appears to have been somewhat timid in her presence, so dazzled was he before this "beautiful object"—to use his own terms. Rather than pay his respects in person, he preferred to converse with her in written form. He had purchased property at Endegeest in 1637, and from there it was only a short trip to the residence of his royal friend. Endegeest lies slightly off the main road which leads from Leiden to the coast and the dunes at Katwijkaan Zee. He had only to pass through the woods of Wassenaar and of The Hague in order to arrive at her residence, but, on the contrary, it was the princess who sought out her newfound master in his country retreat. The little château is still intact, a house of simple design surrounded by a small park. His study was in one of the turrets on the upper floor, from which could be seen the windmills by the river and in the distance the towers of Leiden. Adjoining this was his laboratory where he carried on his chemical and biological experiments, and it may have been here that Elizabeth was first induced to attempt dissections.[5] He had chosen the house for its very seclusion. Although he often shunned society, he did not live as an ascetic. The house was well furnished, and his servants were devoted. He enjoyed tending his flowers, his cook was considered excellent by witnesses such as the young doctor and literary adventurer Samuel Sorbière, and his valet, who acted as both companion and secretary, was later to become a teacher of mathematics in Leiden. In short, his establishment at Endegeest, although rather rustic, was a perfect model of orderliness and comfort.

Perhaps he would not have minded if Elizabeth had come to see him alone, but apparently it had become fashionable for well-born young ladies of The Hague to organize little outings to visit the philosopher at his country house. For this, gossip had it, they disguised themselves as "*bourgeoises*," which probably meant that they simply traveled by barge without any ceremony. Not adverse to certain social functions, Descartes may well have resented these visits as intrusions upon his privacy. How many times Elizabeth and her companions journeyed to Endegeest is not known, but in May, 1643, when she and Descartes were in the closest physical proximity and their correspondence just beginning, he abruptly left the pleasures of Endegeest and moved to Egmond op de Hoef, where he leased a house for a year. He may have foresaken his beautiful country house because he found it too near the city and the university; the former furnished him with curious visitors, and the latter with disputes and attacks from the scholars. Elizabeth, however, may have had some bearing on this sudden change.

Close as they were geographically, it was always she, apparently, who had been coming to his house, and his choice of the remote Egmond, a small village situated in the marshes between the sand dunes along the coast and the pastureland of the interior, may have been a deliberate attempt to flee—not from the affection of a person he so obviously esteemed but from her physical presence. Some observers have seen in his move a thinly disguised effort to avoid a possible love affair, one which because of his age he felt would have been ill-requited. He was afraid, and the fact that he ran away from her at the very beginning could be interpreted as a sign of nascent love.[6] Even when he returned to The Hague, it was at a time when he did not expect to find her there. She was indeed absent, and her first letter, which shows no sign of annoyance at his change of residence, expresses her regret that she was not able to receive him.

From the outset their exchange of letters, of which fifty-nine remain (twenty-six from Elizabeth and thirty-three from Descartes), bears the mark of an animated conversation between two very exceptional people. There is virtually no mention of contemporary events or local gossip, for despite their intimacy these two were more interested in psychology and metaphysics than in details of the everyday affairs that surrounded them. They talked of science and philosophy, mathematics and literature. Frequently Elizabeth asked his advice both as a friend and as a doctor. He became in a sense the director of her thoughts and her moral conscience, a kind of *directeur spirituel*. Descartes' official published works reveal the philosopher and his intelligence. His correspondence with the Princess Palatine reveals much more of the man in often unguarded confessions of self-confidence and tribulation. One sees his consuming desire for independence bound with his basic goodness and generosity. Whatever might have appeared obscure or incomplete in his previous writings he sought to clarify and make utilitarian for his newly found friend.

In his replies to her questions he examined at length the question of the union of body and soul, which Elizabeth found the major stumbling block to her acceptance of his philosophy. He pointed out that man in essence is composed of this very union and that we often experience within ourselves an awareness of this union without being able to explain it. The evidence provided by living is thus much more important than that furnished by philosophizing:

> I can truthfully say that the principal rule which I have always observed in my studies and that which I believe has been the most useful for acquiring knowledge has been to devote only a few hours a day to thoughts which occupy the imagination exclusively and very few a year to those which occupy the understanding and to give all the rest of my time to the relaxation of the senses and the intellect. That is what made me retire to the country.[7]

Descartes was not denigrating completely the usefulness of metaphysical speculation, but he counseled that once certain basic principles had been comprehended, it was best to retain them in one's memory rather than spend one's time in perpetual meditation. This was particularly true for Elizabeth. He knew her temperament, her tendency to melancholy, and her difficulty in subduing her passions. She suffered both physically and mentally, and his advice to her was that of a family physician who was well aware of the psychological character of his patient. He gave her specific remedies for the blisters on her hands, the obstruction of her spleen, and the fits of depression to which she was subject; but he knew that if these cures were to be truly beneficial, she must try to attain as much peace of mind as possible and content herself with only happy thoughts. In addition to mineral waters and ointments he therefore prescribed that she look at the beauties of nature—the greenery of a forest, the color of a flower, the flight of a bird—and thus free herself from any exertion that might augment her sadness.

Elizabeth had many reasons to bemoan her fate and to think that destiny had marked her family for persecution. One form of exile and disappointment succeeded another. In January, 1629, the year after her return to her parents, her eldest brother, Henry, was drowned as he and his father were crossing the Zuider Zee to see the Spanish ships recently captured by the Dutch. As their vessel sank, the young prince became entangled in the wreckage, and before he could free himself, half-frozen in the chilly waters, he let out the cry "Save me father!" and then disappeared under the surface. It was a cry which Frederick could never forget, and his eldest daughter was just old enough to realize the extent of its sadness, the depth of the loss to her parents and to herself.

In 1632, when Elizabeth was fourteen, her father died. Some accounts attribute his death to the plague; others, perhaps more romantic and yet equally plausible, relate that the Winter King, having lost the will to live, died of a broken heart. He was suffering from a fever, by no means fatal by its nature, when he received the news of the death of Gustavus Adolphus. With the passing of the Swedish king, his hopes for the restoration of the Palatinate cause seemed futile. Utterly discouraged, he left his queen with a fatherless son, Elizabeth's new baby brother, and a lost cause to be fought by his family. The only reference to Elizabeth's sorrow at the death of her father occurs in a letter she wrote three years later to a cousin who had suffered a

similar bereavement. Although written years before her introduction to Descartes, the letter is interesting, for it gives much
the same stoic resignation that she was to seek from the philosopher when future troubles were to beset her. Speaking of
her cousin's affliction, she continues:

> I know its greatness by experience, which is still fresh in my
> memory. However, I will not trouble you by suggesting all
> the reasons which you already know, but will pray the Al-
> mighty to give you strength to bear it, which is the sole remedy
> which one can have, which I wish you, as I do all that could
> give you satisfaction, and should feel myself very happy if I
> could serve you in anything of which you would find me
> capable.[8]

During these years of political adversity one hope seemed the
most propitious for advancing the family's interests—that of
making advantageous marriages for the young princesses. Despite their varying talents and beauties, matches for Elizabeth
and her sisters were not easily arranged. Their pretentions were
high, but their finances were low. In this respect, Elizabeth's
fortune was as luckless as in other matters. In January, 1633, the
King of Poland, Ladislas IV, sent a deputy to Charles I of
England to negotiate for the hand of his niece. The reply seemed
favorable enough but was made with the stipulation that she be
allowed to retain her religion. Ladislas, who was then in his
forties and had been married before, might have been quite
agreeable to such a stipulation and undoubtedly a dispensation
could have been obtained from the Pope, but the difficulty of
the religion of their future offspring eventually deferred the
question to the Diet of Warsaw.

The Poles were adamant in their refusal to accept a Protestant.
Elizabeth was equally obdurate in her fidelity to the religion of
her family. For her to become a convert to Roman Catholicism
would have been a rejection of her entire spiritual education and
a treachery to the memory of her father, who had lost both his

crown and patrimony in the Protestant cause. Ladislas behaved alternately as a hotheaded boy and a middle-aged lover. Despite his tears and protestations, he dared not marry without the consent of the Polish Diet. The negotiations languished for three years and then were finally broken off. There were other suitors less highly placed, among them the Comte de Soissons, Bernhard of Saxe-Weimar, and the young Count Waldemar of Denmark, but Elizabeth appeared destined for spinsterhood. She never recorded her feelings about marriage, but her natural independence of mind and her inclination toward mysticism from a relatively early age did not engender romantic attachments. By the time she was eighteen, it would seem she had given up any thought of conjugal life. She was, nonetheless, capable of deep and lasting friendships with men and won the enthusiastic admiration of Descartes.

In addition to family misfortunes Elizabeth suffered from her own ill health. She complained in her letters to Descartes that the doctors who were visiting her every day were unable to find the cause of her malady and that their prescriptions were less efficacious than those which he had sent from a distance. Her body was frail, possessing, as she said, all the weaknesses of her sex, and she was frequently tormented by a low fever and a dry cough. Descartes, who had himself inherited from his mother a similar cough which he had overcome in his youth, was quick to diagnose the cause of her affliction as being largely psychological. Anyone surrounded by sadness, as was Elizabeth, needed to take special care not to brood over unhappy events, for this would have its inevitable effect upon the circulation of the blood, causing the heart to constrict and eventually alter the functioning of the lungs which would produce a cough. He told her to take the waters at the spa, if such was the advice of her doctors, but a surer cure would be found in ridding her mind from too many serious thoughts. Although a philosopher and scientist, Descartes the physician saw the dangers of overindulgence in matters intellectual. Good health, he told her, was the basis of all other benefits of this life. And he knew that his advice was much simpler in theory than in practice, particularly when one was beset daily with cares which were often inescapable. But he could offer her himself as an example of one who had overcome his own physical difficulty through sheer willpower.

The very receipt of a letter from him helped to dispel Elizabeth's melancholy, but only temporarily, for even though his correspondence assured her of the happiness to be found in their friendship, she could not view the annoyances and disappointments that surrounded her with the same objectivity as Descartes. She was sensitive and reacted to events emotionally. The kind of self-mastery her correspondent recommended took time, and she could usually become dispassionate only after having let passion play its role. Once having disciplined herself, she was subject to frequent relapses: "There is something surprising in misfortunes, even if foreseen, of which I am mistress only after a certain time. My body becomes so disordered that in order to cure it I need several months which hardly ever go by without some new subject of trouble." [9] Elizabeth knew as well as Descartes that the cause of her poor health was more mental than physical, and in describing her symptoms she often gave such an honest appraisal of herself as to have it sound less like a patient speaking to her doctor than like a sinner in the confessional.

Both Elizabeth and Descartes were simultaneously believers and doubters, but of a different order. The princess, reared as a Protestant, had a spiritual bent and was deeply attached to her faith; but she was accustomed to questioning all principles, even those of her religion, by subjecting them to a methodical doubt. She broached questions not as a confirmed skeptic but with a philosophical desire to gain rational assurance for her beliefs. This quest for certainty often caused her the deepest anguish, and she expressed her uneasiness to her friend: "I shall despair of finding certitude in anything in this world if it does not come

from you who alone have kept me from being skeptical. . . ." [10]
Descartes, a Catholic, once having accepted his faith, never questioned it. And once he had established the principle of the *cogito* and formulated his method, his doubting was but a procedure that he felt certain would soon be dissipated by the discovery of the truth.

Elizabeth's doubts were more all-encompassing and longer-lasting. She expressed them with such candor to the philosopher that she often feared lest someone without his understanding might misinterpret them. She was not satisfied, for example, with the explanations of God's relationship to actions resulting from man's free will. How could He be omnipotent and man still be free to act according to his own will? While stating her misgivings, she added, "I am afraid that you have not received my last letter because you make no mention of it. I should be annoyed if it fell into the hands of one of the critics who condemn as heresy the doubts which one raises about current opinions." [11] Because of her outspokenness, she often ignored one of Descartes' own maxims, which was never to put anything in writing which might be misinterpreted by unsympathetic readers. Her sincerity and frankness when writing to her friend were protected, however, for in her very first letter she had taken the precaution of asking that as her doctor, both physical and spiritual, he observe the oath of Hippocrates.

Elizabeth became increasingly skeptical, and her natural bent toward melancholy, combined with her ill health and increasing family problems, resulted in a pessimistic outlook which was diametrically opposed to Descartes' optimism. To his expressions of self-confidence she replied with doubts. In many of his letters he had spoken of the immortality of the soul in which he found but one more reason for overcoming the difficulties of life on earth. Elizabeth, on the contrary, saw it as possible justification for suicide and an escape from present misfortunes. Although two of her brothers were to die honorable deaths in battle, she was not seeking a Cornelian type of self-sacrifice to a higher ideal, but rather an answer to the predicament which she felt all too strongly of choosing between life filled with adversity and death with its release from suffering. Descartes responded in a detached tone, so characteristic of his philosophic generalizations, that only by false reasoning would one interpret the immortality of the soul as an invitation to suicide, for what assurance was there that the felicity which one so desired would be granted after death? He thus indirectly recalled to her one of the principal tenets of both her faith and his. But Elizabeth's religious beliefs were being severely tested by the unhappy circumstances of reality, and her friend's objective statements seemed insufficient consolation for events to which she could only react subjectively.

One such event was the death of her uncle, Charles I of England, who was beheaded by his rebellious subjects on February 9, 1649. When the news reached Elizabeth, she became disconsolate. Now that England had become a revolutionary Commonwealth every hope of restoring her family position appeared more futile than ever. She fell seriously ill and in her despondency could find no distraction from her sorrow except the writing of occasional verses. Descartes' effort to assuage her grief resulted in a letter couched in such terms as might aggravate her condition rather than bring comfort. He opens by referring to the fact that he too has recently had disturbing news, referring to the death of two of his friends, Monsieur de Touchelaye and Monsieur Hardy, although he does not name them. That Elizabeth has taken to writing poetry reminds him of Socrates, who did the same while he was in prison. The inference here is that great minds are often so inclined in moments of stress. "But," he continues, "I am certain that your Highness, being accustomed to fortune's adversities and having recently escaped the danger of death, will be less surprised and horrified at the news of a close relative's passing than if she had not suffered similar afflictions herself." [12]

What follows is an attempt to elevate her spirit by referring to the nobility of the king's death. Hoping to dispel her melancholic depression, he treats the decapitation with a philosophic objectivity that might have seemed cold:

> Although such a violent death may appear more frightful than that which comes to a man in bed, when one examines it carefully, it is actually far more glorious, far sweeter. This should console your Highness . . . It is certain that without his last trial the gentleness and other virtues of the dead king would never have been so noticed and so esteemed as they will be by all those who read his history . . . As to his physical suffering, I discount this completely, for it is so short that if assassins could use a fever or any of the other ills which nature employs to remove men from this world, they would be rightfully considered more cruel than when they kill with the swift blow of an ax. I dare not prolong my reflections on such a fatal subject, but I shall add only that it is much better to be entirely freed from a false hope than to be uselessly fostering a delusion.[13]

Is he referring to Charles or to Elizabeth in this last remark? More probably the latter, for he next proceeds to offer some political advice; namely, that her brother should accept the terms of the new electorate, even though it returned only a small portion of their hereditary claims. There is also a passing reference to his having received a letter from Christina. He is obviously flattered that the Swedish queen takes an interest in his work, but he is at odds to explain her silence in regard to Elizabeth: "I can only imagine that since the conditions of the peace treaty were not as advantageous to your family as they might have been, those who were responsible wonder if you bear them a grudge and for that reason are hesitant to express their friendship." [14]

Elizabeth's immediate reaction is not known, for the letters which she wrote during this period have been lost. Most probably it was the same as at the beginning of their friendship when, hearing that she had been seriously ill, Descartes proposed as a distraction and so that his letters would not be "entirely empty and useless" that they discuss Seneca. If the pessimistic princess would not accept his optimism, he would offer stoicism. He emphasized certain fundamental truths which would help to dispel her doubts. God's omnipotence and perfection should give us confidence so that we can accept with resignation the events of this life. The immortality of the soul he cited as proof that we should not become overly attached to worldly goods, since they are but momentary, and we need not fear death. A third point was that one should not consider the earth the center of creation, for this leads man to believe that it exists solely for him. Such presumption can result only in deception. And he concluded by accentuating the fact that each man is only a small part of the community in which he lives and should subordinate his personal interests to the good of humanity.[15] But the Roman philosopher's teachings accompanied by Descartes' commentary were unpalatable to Elizabeth, who was seeking a more practical, a more immediate remedy.

There emerges from their correspondence a pattern that becomes discernible fairly early. Whenever he moves to a plane that she considers too abstract or too philosophical, she becomes impatient. Despite her thirst for knowledge in every field, she doubts the possibility of ever arriving at a total comprehension of the mysteries of the universe. Her main concern is with herself and with her own problems. Their exchange of letters about Seneca forms a veritable treatise on morality, but her interest begins to wane as Descartes enters into metaphysical speculation. She thus continually forces him to return to the practical side, to how she can apply these principles to improving her own condition. She is far less concerned about scientific or even theological explanations than about the problem of morality. She continues, therefore, to pose questions that will examine the nature of good and evil and the role of one's feelings. In order to satisfy both her intellectual curiosity and her very real psychological needs, Descartes will elaborate the discussion begun in their letters on Seneca into his *Treatise on the Passions*. But this belongs to the later years of their friendship. What is most important in their relationship from the beginning is Elizabeth's perspicacity and refreshing candor. Whenever she did not understand something, she said so, and her often puzzling questions forced Descartes to be as explicit and as pragmatic as possible.

Although Elizabeth preferred to discuss questions of a moral nature, she was not indifferent to mathematics, and her superior intelligence showed itself at the outset when Descartes posed the problem of the three circles. "Given three circles, find the fourth which touches the other three" was the task which he set for her, a problem which had fascinated the ancients since Appolonius and which geometricians had passed on to future generations as a classic example of the application of algebraic principles to geometry in order to find an unknown quantity. Descartes had long ago solved it and used it in his *Géométrie*, *Météores*, and *Dioptrique*. He now proposed it to Elizabeth as proof that her mind was as capable of encompassing mathematical difficulties as it was of dealing with philosophical abstractions. This would be a rare talent indeed, but no sooner had he given her the problem than he began to regret having done so. "Experience has taught me that most of those who are adept at understanding the reasonings of metaphysics are incapable of grasping those of algebra." [16] Perhaps with her limited knowledge of mathematics, which was based upon the theories of Stampioen rather than upon his own, she would be unable to solve such a difficult problem. He could not resist this ironic reference to the young Dutch mathematician, Stampioen d'Jonghe, whose treatise on algebra, published in 1639, had provoked a prolonged quarrel and whom Descartes treated with disdain. In order to forestall any possible embarrassment he wrote to their customary intermediary, Pollot, in November, 1643:

> From what you have written me recently concerning Madame the Princess of Bohemia, I felt myself obliged to send her the solution which she thinks she has found and the reason why I do not think one can succeed by imagining only one root. This I should do with misgivings, however, for perhaps she would prefer to continue trying to find it herself than to see what I have written.[17]

He therefore enclosed his solution in a letter addressed to Elizabeth, which he had left undated, with instructions to Pollot to deliver it only if he thought it would be well received. Elizabeth did succeed in finding the solution by her own efforts and thereby did not disappoint her mentor. He was in fact delighted:

> The solution which it has pleased your Highness to give me the honor of sending is so correct that there is nothing lacking; and I was not only astounded at seeing it, but I cannot refrain from adding that I was also overcome with joy and have taken satisfaction in seeing that the calculations which your Highness used are exactly the same as those which I proposed in my *Géométrie*.[18]

His praise was not quite justified, for although Elizabeth had arrived at the correct answer, she did so by means different from his. This gave him the opportunity to expound his own system, thereby adding another convert. He stated his theories in such complicated equations that it is obvious Elizabeth was no novice at deciphering mathematical sign language. He reaffirmed, as he had in his *Géométrie*, the necessity of formulating equations and then reducing them to the second degree. The essential point for him, as for his pupil, was to arrive at the correct solution and reduce the amount of calculation to a minimum. With the problem of the three circles Elizabeth displayed the kind of intelligence he had hoped to find in his new friend. Descartes had known her scarcely six months before introducing her to the fundamental principles of his algebraic system, but other interests rapidly diverted their attention, and never again did their correspondence touch upon mathematics.

Following their discussion of the three circles, there occurs a hiatus in the letters which lasts for seven months, from November, 1643 until July of the next year. During this time Descartes was desperately trying to combat Voetius and his adversaries at Groningen. He was also making final arrangements for the publication of his *Principia philosophiae*, which he hoped to distribute to friends in France. His decision to revisit his homeland was prompted both by personal and professional reasons, the two often indistinguishable in his actions. His quarrels with the universities had left him tired and depressed; his lease on the property at Egmond op de Hoef was about to expire; he would have the opportunity of attending to some family business and of seeing old friends; and finally, a visit to France would prove propitious to his reputation both there and abroad. In short, the time seemed ripe for another temporary uprooting. The printers were slow, however, and to his annoyance he was forced to leave for Paris empty-handed toward the beginning of May, 1644.

He stopped at various small towns along the way, where he saw acquaintances, most of them clerics, to whom he promised copies of his new book as soon as it appeared. He visited his elder brother, Pierre, at Rennes and spent almost a month at Le Crévis, where he saw his brother-in-law. Most of this time was spent in settling the estate of his father, who had died on October 17, 1640. Descartes had thought of returning to France

three and a half years earlier, but by the time he wrote to an-
nounce his proposed trip his seventy-seven-year-old father had
been dead for ten days. News of his sister Jeanne's death, which
occurred at approximately the same time, had also been slow in
reaching him. Pierre may not have known his address or the
delay may have been caused by simple negligence. He seldom
received more than two letters a year from any of his family,
and these were always confined to matters of business. That
Descartes waited almost four years to visit his father's grave
would seem one more indication that he was not on friendly
terms with any of his relatives, and some accounts credit his
father as being responsible for their distance by disdaining his
son's profession and treating him as something of a black sheep.

Next he stayed with his half brother, Joachim, at Chavagne en
Sucé, where he attended the baptism of a nephew, also named
René, for whom he served as godfather. It was here that he
saw his younger sister Anne. Family affairs, nonetheless, seemed
to hold little interest for him, and soon he was back in Paris at
the house of the Abbé Picot, where he spent the month of
August.

For a man who had so recently been seeking solitude, his
activities in the French capital were remarkably animated. Before leaving Holland, for example, he was so annoyed by any
intrusion on his privacy that he avoided large gatherings. After
an interview with Elizabeth the appearance of several of his
countrymen at the palace filled him with such apprehension
that he fled without even bidding good night to Pollot. Instead,
he sent his excuses by mail:

> The sight of four or five French faces, who were leaving
> the queen's apartments at the very moment I was departing
> from the princess' was the reason I did not have the honor of
> seeing you recently. I left without saying adieu because, hav-
> ing heard them mention my name from a distance, I feared

they might detain me with their talk at a time when I felt like going to bed. I withdrew as fast as possible. . . .[19]

In Holland Descartes preferred to confront his enemies, and often his friends, by letters sent from his retreat. Now that he was in Paris, despite the relative calm and certainly the elite company of his host's residence, he was extremely energetic both in his social visits and in his continued protection by correspondence of his interests at home.

His *Principia philosophiae* finally appeared on July 10, 1644, and copies were sent to Paris, where his friends hurriedly distributed them. The Abbé Picot was so enthusiastic that he undertook to translate them, for the original was in Latin, the language used deliberately in this case in order to appeal to both the Church and the universities where Descartes hoped to have his book accepted and included in the curriculum.

The *Principia* is divided into four parts. The first, entitled "On the Principles of Human Knowledge," is a general statement of his philosophy. The second, "On the Principles of Material Things," treats the essential elements of universal science and studies the nature of matter, space, time, and movement. The third, "On the Visible World," studies the movement of the planets, the formation of the sun, and the nature and relationship of fixed stars, comets, and planets. The last part, "On the Earth," is concerned with the four elements—air, water, earth, and fire—and remarks on the earth's formation. It also includes a rather lengthy explanation of the properties of magnets. Much of the material in his new work, particularly the last three parts, had already been included, although in slightly different form, eleven years earlier in *Le Monde*.[20] But both the form and, to some extent, the content of the previous book had undergone certain changes. These were occasioned by his desire to avoid condemnation by the Church on the question of the earth's movement. In his attempt to assuage theologians who still considered the earth immobile, Descartes succeeded by rather devious reasoning and endless examples, obvious and often boring to the modern reader, in proving that the earth was indeed stationary if one considered the word "movement" in its ordinary sense. But when examined in its relative meaning, movement was everywhere, and nothing in the world was totally immobile. Thus:

> The pilot seated on the poop deck of a ship does not move in relation to the ship; he is moving only in respect to the shore passed by the vessel as it is carried along by the waves. And the pocket watch of the captain who walks on the bridge of this ship, how many different movements are to be discerned? The movement of the wheels while the watch is running; the movement of its owner; the movement of the ship, of the sea, of the earth itself.[21]

He ended by saying, in other words, that the earth moved without moving. He was thus able through a series of wily maneuvers prior to the book's official acceptance to reconcile his writings with the official doctrine of the Church, particularly with his former adversary the Jesuit Père Bourdin, whose earlier bombast was directed against his *Meditationes*. The public, however, was less interested in the scientific accuracy of his observations about the solar system than in the relative ease with which his method could be applied to areas of inquiry heretofore obscure. His theory of vortices provided a mechanistic explanation of the universe. The former Aristotelian distinctions between things terrestrial and celestial were abolished. Before Newton had formulated his law of gravitation, Descartes presented the world with a system whereby celestial phenomena could be explained by ordinary mechanical methods readily understandable to everyone.

Perhaps the easiest way for a modern reader to approach the complexity of the *Principia* is through the letter Descartes wrote to Abbé Picot, whose translation was carefully corrected and in some places amended by the author before the French version appeared three years later in 1647. It serves as a preface in which he sets forth his intent, gives a brief summary of the contents, and explains how the work is to be read and then put into practice. Like any author, Descartes wanted to reach as many readers as possible, and he feared lest they be intimidated by the very title of the work. Many would probably find the mere mention of philosophy distasteful because of the way it had been taught. So he begins by a definition of the word: "Philosophy signifies the study of wisdom, and by wisdom is meant not only prudence in one's affairs but a perfect knowledge of everything which man can know, as much for the way he conducts his life as for the preservation of his health and the invention of all the arts. . . ." 22 He accentuates the practical side of philosophy, something even more necessary for those whom fortune has smiled upon, for good health and riches are inferior to that greater happiness which derives from true wisdom:

> Living without philosophy is like keeping one's eyes shut without ever trying to open them; and the pleasure of seeing all the things which our vision discloses cannot be compared to the satisfaction found through the knowledge that philosophy gives. This study is more necessary for the conduct of our lives than is the use of our eyes in guiding our steps.23

Without attacking Aristotle directly, Descartes proceeds to criticize those who have misinterpreted him, namely the philosophers currently teaching in the schools. He next considers how one is to arrive at the highest degree of wisdom, granting of course that one can never equal God's perfect knowledge. His formula is relatively simple. It consists in making certain that one's first principles are absolutely clear and self-evident;

and from these all others can be logically deduced. His own first principle, the *cogito* from which he has deduced all that follows, led to his affirmation of the existence of God, who is the creator of everything in the world and, being the source of all truth, did not create our understanding in such a way that it could be mistaken in its judgment of things perceived clearly and distinctly. Descartes is trying to arrive at an absolute certitude of the kind found in mathematics. Herein lies one of his great innovations, however, for instead of beginning with the concrete and tangible, instead of moving from the visible to the invisible, his entire explanation of the universe rests upon his belief in God's existence. He has thus changed the traditional order, that taught in the colleges, of progressing from the physical sciences to the metaphysical. The first part of the *Principia* is a brief outline of his metaphysics, and the parts which follow contain the physics, which are based upon the first.

This revolutionary reversal was expressed in one of the most memorable images to be found in any of Descartes' writings. "All philosophy," he tells us, "is like a tree. The roots are metaphysics, the trunk is physics, and the branches are all the other sciences which can be reduced to three principal ones: medicine, mechanics, and morality." [24] Obviously it is not from the root or from the trunk of the tree of knowledge that one gathers the fruit, the most practical aspect of philosophy, but from those branches which are to be learned last. In his earlier works he had been preparing the way toward what would become an all-encompassing system, and now he lacked only the time and money necessary for further experimentation before completing his explanation of all phenomena—minerals, plants, animals, and most notably, man—in order to explain fully all aspects of the three sciences most useful to the conduct of our daily affairs. He asks posterity's forgiveness if lack of funds forces him to limit his investigations to studying for his own enlightenment.

The remaining sections of his letter to Picot discuss the manner in which the *Principia* is to be read. That knowledge should be pleasurable as well as practical is evidenced by his use of the word "novel," for that is how he wanted his book to be considered at first reading. He hoped that the public would not be puzzled by seeming obscurities but would skim the work in order to comprehend its broad outlines and the general nature of its subject matter. Then it should be read a second time with attention paid to the logical sequence of his reasoning, still without undue attention to difficult sections. These should simply be noted in the margin, and the book read without interruption to its conclusion. A third reading should dissipate any confusion; if not, he assures us, a fourth reading will surely result in making everything clear.

He also outlines how one with only a limited or uncertain knowledge is to proceed in arriving at a true comprehension and sensible application of his principles:

> First of all, a man . . . must try to construct for himself a moral code which will suffice to direct his actions, for that will suffer no delay, and we must try above all else to live well. After that, he must study logic, not as it is taught by the schools, for that is only a dialectic which enables us to communicate to others what they already know or to speak without true judgment about things one does not understand, and thus it corrupts common sense rather than increasing it; rather that logic which teaches us how to use our reason to discover truths which we previously ignored; and because it is largely dependent upon use, it is advisable to practice frequently those rules which concern easy questions, such as those in mathematics. Then, after one has acquired some facility, he should begin to apply himself in earnest to true philosophy, the first part of which is metaphysics, which contains the principles of knowledge, including the explanation of the principal attributes of God and of the immateriality of our souls.[25]

Thus one progresses from the roots of the tree until at last one is able to gather the fruit from the branches.

The publication of the *Principia* naturally occasioned much adverse criticism. The French philosopher and physicist Pierre Gassendi felt that it would be shorter-lived than its author, and Descartes' former disciple, Regius, now disavowed any connection with a philosophy he considered both obscure and uncertain. And in addition to quite virulent attacks by his opponents, even his publishers were complaining about the meager sales of his latest work. But the book did gain general acceptance among the Jesuit fathers whom Descartes sought to please, and it was not put on the Index, at least not during his lifetime.

It had, however, a second, more personal importance. During his stay in France, Elizabeth had received very few letters from him; but this lapse was more than compensated for by the dedication which he had left as a kind of farewell testimony of his devotion. The world at large knew little of their friendship, still less of their correspondence. Instead of the flattery or banality one might expect to find in the dedication of such a work to a person of high rank, the public was informed, in some of the most eloquent Latin that Descartes ever wrote, of his deep veneration for this extraordinary princess.

After discussing the distinction between genuine and false virtues, he finds that she possesses admirably all the requisites not only for virtue but also for true wisdom. She has not let the distractions of the court keep her from her education, not that of ordinary young ladies but one which has introduced her to both the sciences and the arts. These she has learned so well that she has been able to understand his writings better than anyone else. She is virtually unique in possessing that rare combination of talents which enables her to embrace mathematics and metaphysics with equal ease. And he concludes his eulogy by saying:

> What most augments my admiration is that such a perfect
> and diverse knowledge of all the sciences is not found in some

old doctor who has spent years instructing himself, but in a princess who is still young and whose face resembles that of the Graces more than that which poets ordinarily attribute to the Muses or the wise Minerva.[26]

In her he finds gentleness and magnanimity joined with the kind of temperament that will always enable her to rise above adversity. His zeal for philosophizing was no greater than his desire to remain her "very humble, very obedient, and very devoted servant."

The few letters which passed between Elizabeth and Descartes during his absence were largely concerned with matters of health. As her doctor he was pleased by her diet and daily exercise. These, he thought, would soon remedy her indigestion, for the body, especially in one so young, has remarkable powers of recovery if one does not abuse it by excesses. As her spiritual mentor, he reminded her of the mind's effect upon the body. A strong will, he counseled, could be far more efficacious than the advice of a doctor or an astrologer. By August 1, 1644, Elizabeth had received and read attentively the new work and was delighted by the dedication which informed the world of their friendship. On that date she wrote to thank him, saying that she would have been happy merely to share in the knowledge which the *Principia* gave to their century, but how could she ever repay his kindness in giving her not only knowledge but also a share in his glory by this public testimony of his admiration?

Interspersed with words of gratitude and protestations that she was unworthy of so high a compliment, she nonetheless managed to point out that all sections of the book were not absolutely clear. She had difficulty understanding some of his explanations concerning the formation of quicksilver, which to her appeared contrary to the definition he had given elsewhere of weight; she also found it difficult to comprehend the nature of fossils and why their shapes were not affected by heat. As usual she was quick to point out any inconsistencies, and this she did with page references, often with specific mention of a particular illustration which she analyzed with almost as much authority as her master. This short letter of thanks was both a genuine expression of her gratitude and a succinct critique of the obscurities that she had discovered. These were the words of an extremely intelligent young woman whose warm friendship Descartes rightly cherished and whose advice was well worth noting. She signed the letter with her usual formula, which in itself is revelatory of her character: "Your very affectionate friend to serve you, Elizabeth."

After nearly five months in France, Descartes was more than ready to return to Holland, where his friends were beginning to wonder how much longer he would be detained in Paris and feared lest he decide to settle there permanently. Although he was not totally adverse to the many charms of city life, particularly in the company of men like Picot and Clerselier, he disliked the crowds, the artificiality, and the countless opportunists that made serious conversation with the truly worthy people virtually impossible. He yearned for his former solitude, and with his family affairs settled and the remaining copies of the *Principia* left in the hands of Picot for future distribution, he reached Amsterdam on November 15, 1644 and went directly to Egmond-Binnen, a small town located close to the other Egmond (op de Hoef) he had left the previous May. He had still to attend to the problems at Groningen and Utrecht, but for the moment he desperately needed peace. He was tired, and the exertion caused by his travels had made him desire almost total isolation.

A few months later he told Pollot: "Since my trip to France, I have aged twenty years, so that now it is more effort for me to go to The Hague than it used to be to travel as far as Rome. It is not that I am sick, thank God, but I feel weak and need comfort and rest more than ever." [27] His life at Egmond-Binnen, however, was not that of a hermit. Aside from work in his study and in his laboratory, for now he was more devoted than ever to his experiments, he enjoyed visits from close friends, conversations with the neighboring peasants, and puttering in the garden.

More is known of the details of his daily life during this period than at any other, both from his own description and from the accounts of his friends. He retained his habit of rising late in order to pass the early hours in that state of semiconsciousness he had treasured since his youth as the most fruitful time for meditation. He enjoyed taking walks, probably accompanied by his little dog named Monsieur Grat, but as his life became increasingly sedentary he gave up riding, except for an occasional hunt, in favor of taking a carriage or preferably a canalboat. In the mornings he spent some time working and shortly after noon took his main meal, prepared by his cook, Louise. Both she and his valet, Maçon, were extremely faithful and hardworking. Descartes took an interest in their affairs as he did in those of the neighborhood rustics. Evidently he was pleased by their lack of prejudice, for he took the trouble to initiate many of them into the rudiments of his philosophy and found them enthusiastic disciples. They, in turn, must have been delighted to find that such a celebrated foreigner would converse with them so amicably and in their own language.

While Picot was visiting him, he found reason to complain about Louise's cooking. Descartes, on the other hand, had very simple tastes in food. He preferred fruits and vegetables, considering them more healthful than meat. Part of the garden was set aside for the kitchen, the rest for his botanical experiments. One peculiarity of his diet was his fondness for omelettes prepared with eggs that were ten days old. After the midday meal he devoted several hours to conversations with friends or to pastimes either in his garden or on short excursions. Then around four o'clock he began work in earnest, often in his laboratory, where he busied himself with dissecting various animals he had obtained from the slaughterhouse. He devoted himself with such attention to his experiments that he frequently worked late into the night.

Two anecdotes dating from this period serve to exemplify Descartes' relationships with the local townspeople. The first concerns a modest but rather bizarre young man named Dirk Rembrantsz,[28] a cobbler from the nearby village of Nieuw Niedrop. Hearing that the philosopher was kindly disposed toward the inhabitants of the region, he set off to see him. From his manner of dress Descartes' servants mistook him for a beggar and refused him admittance. Not easily discouraged, the young man tried again and was turned away a second time. On hearing the story, Descartes took pity and sent money with a note asking that he not disturb him any further. Rembrantsz returned the coins with a message that evidently the hour was not yet ripe for their meeting. Such an unusual response piqued Descartes' curiosity, so that when he appeared for the third time, he was received. Very quickly the master discovered his unusual talent for mathematics, introduced him to his own experiments, and soon the student made such remarkable progress that he was considered an authority in his own right. He eventually wrote several treatises on navigation and astronomy, and his village became a well-known center for Cartesian scholars. Descartes had earlier given similar instruction to one of his servants, Jean Gillot, who later became director of the school of engineering at Leiden.

The second anecdote illustrates that in addition to his willingness to encourage the natural talents in those of little education or social standing, Descartes took a genuine humanitarian interest in the well-being of his fellowman and in pursuing the cause of justice. A neighboring innkeeper had murdered a man, but the circumstances were so extenuating that Descartes sought for nearly two years to obtain clemency for the assassin. The peasant, named Meeus Jacobsz, had led a peaceful life up until this time and was well liked in the community. Meeus' mother had married a man who beat her, and after years of mistreatment, she left him. He in turn threatened to kill one of her children if she did not return. On the day of the murder, Meeus was with his son, who was on the verge of death from a fatal illness. He was suddenly summoned to his brother-in-law, who was being attacked by their mutual enemy. Was this not provocation enough? Even the relatives of the dead man pardoned him on the very day of the funeral. But the most that the courts were finally willing to concede was that Meeus should be exiled. And this would be more punishment to his wife and children than to the murderer. Descartes wrote to magistrates and friends and in 1647 sent an appeal to the High Council of The Hague to prevent the confiscation of Meeus' property so that his wife could continue to support their children. His taking the part of the innkeeper's practically destitute wife earned for him a high place in the eyes of the local peasants, who now referred to him as the *Franschman*, one to whom they could turn for help and advice.

Thus the years following his trip to Paris in 1644 were passed in only semiretirement. The philosopher's varied activities were such as to put most men's daily occupations to shame for their lack of diversity and depth of concentration. Besides his many other interests, he continued his correspondence, although this along with his official writings occupied less of his time than previously. For the next four years Elizabeth was the most important of his correspondents, and little by little their letters became more personal in nature. They touched on endless topics, but their main concern was with moral issues. Her ill health, added to her family problems, put her in constant search of some means of attaining greater immediate happiness. After their letters on Seneca, with passing references to Aristotle and Zeno, in which Descartes tried to reconcile the Stoics with the Epicureans, they turned to a more minute examination of the nature of the passions and their relationship to directing one's life toward the greatest possible enjoyment. These were ideas prompted by Elizabeth's constant questioning about how she could overcome her present misfortunes and which Descartes was later to codify in his *Treatise on the Passions*. Their discussion, however, was cut short by an event that occurred in November, 1645 that completely staggered Elizabeth. She fell into such a state of depression and disillusionment that it seemed as if all of Descartes' sound and patient advice had been for naught.

Her brother Edward, having taken up residence in France, had fallen in love with Anne de Gonzague, a sister of the Queen of Poland. To the landless prince, such a match seemed highly advantageous, but to his family it caused great grief. Anne, besides being clever and ambitious, was a fervent Catholic, and one condition of their marriage was Edward's conversion. That he should abjure his religion appeared as an act of treason to Elizabeth, who considered it an insult to their father's memory and their entire family tradition. Nothing could have wounded her more than to see her dearly loved brother renounce the religion to which she was so strongly attached. The marriage took place on November 5, and on November 30 Elizabeth, who was by now accustomed to confessing her troubles to Descartes, wrote him in bitter terms and seemed to forget that he himself was a Catholic:

> It [the folly of one of my brothers] has disturbed the health of my body and the tranquillity of my soul more than all the misfortunes I have suffered thus far. If you take the trouble to read the news, you must be aware that he has fallen into the hands of a certain sort of people who have more hatred for our family than love of their own religion, and he has allowed himself to be snared into changing his faith and becoming a Roman Catholic. . . . I must see one whom I loved with all my

heart abandoned to the scorn of the world and to the loss of his own soul (according to my belief). If you had not more charity than bigotry, it would be impertinent of me to speak to you of this matter, but I tell you all my faults as the one person in the world most capable of correcting them.[29]

Elizabeth bewailed the fact that, unlike her mentor, she could not reconcile free will with the decrees of Providence. No matter how she tried to steel herself against adversity, her will was powerless to overcome her emotions in the face of misfortune. How was Descartes, as a Catholic, as a philosopher, and most of all as a friend, to cope with the situation? His reply was couched in the most general terms, and in a rather dry, not to say cool, tone he gently reproached her for taking the affair so seriously. Most people, he said, would approve of this conversion, certainly those of his faith. He spoke, however, in a philosophic rather than a religious spirit. His faith was virtually absent from his arguments, which amounted to the impossibility of pleasing everyone in matters of religion. He wrote:

> All those who belong to my religion, who are probably the most numerous in Europe, are obliged to approve of this conversion, even if they see motives behind it which are suspect; for God uses different means to attract souls to Him, and one may enter a cloister with bad intentions and afterward live a very saintly life. . . . And if they [the Protestants] considered the fact that they would not be of their religion if their forefathers had not left the Roman Church, they would have no occasion to make fun of or criticize those who change their religion. . . . I cannot believe that those who counseled this conversion bore any ill will against your family. I do not presume, however, that my arguments will diminish your Highness' annoyance; I only hope that time will help to assuage it before this letter reaches you.[30]

If Elizabeth had shown a lack of tact in her letter, Descartes' reply was perhaps overly politic. He had even pointed out the advantages for her family's ambitions of having members in the opposing religious parties. It was obviously not the reply that Elizabeth had hoped for, and she did not write to him again for five months. Her silence during this period may have been caused by annoyance at the philosopher's seeming lack of concern for her agitation, or it may have been the result of her attention to her younger brother Philip, whose illness kept her at his bedside trying to persuade him to follow the doctor's orders. She was also involved in political affairs at this time, especially the treaty which this brother was concluding with the Republic of Venice. When next she wrote, it was to comment upon the rough draft which Descartes had sent her of his *Treatise on the Passions.*

Fresh troubles were brewing, however, ones in which Philip was to play a key role, and which were to have far more serious consequences for Elizabeth and her entire family than did Edward's conversion. A scandal of very ugly proportions was about to erupt which would bring shame to the Palatine house and cause such a rift between mother and daughter that the queen would exile Elizabeth, who never again was to take up permanent residence at The Hague. The affair reached its climax on June 20, 1646, when Philip stabbed a man in broad daylight in the public marketplace. The details of the assassination are complex and often contradictory, for different contemporary sources tended to accentuate the more lurid aspects of the case. One certainty is that Elizabeth suffered greatly, both from the immediate results within her family and from the harm done to her public image by scandalmongers.

Philip was barely twenty at the time, high-spirited and often impulsive. He became involved in the affair through his desire to play the protector both to his mother, who had a certain reputation for frivolity, and to his sister Louise-Hollandine, who, unlike Elizabeth, was often easily dazzled and sometimes indiscreet. The older brothers were away from court when a handsome young Frenchman named L'Espinay succeeded in ingratiating himself with both the widowed queen and Elizabeth's younger sister. L'Espinay boasted openly of his good fortune with women, and soon it was rumored that he had seduced both the mother and daughter. Some accounts went so far as to interpret Louise's short trip to Leiden as being necessitated by pregnancy.[31] Philip, infuriated by both the rumors and L'Espinay's conduct, challenged the French captain major to a duel. The two were separated before an actual fight could take place, but on the following day they met again. The French account of what happened reported that Philip had L'Espinay waylaid by eight or ten accomplices, and although the Frenchman defended himself as best he could, he was overcome. The Dutch version relates that Philip, instead of challenging his adversary to a continuation of the previous day's duel, rushed upon him and plunged his hunting knife into his neck. It is not known which story was told to Elizabeth's mother, but she refused to listen to her eldest daughter's defense of Philip, suspected her of complicity in the crime, and declared that she would never see her son again. Her other sons also took Philip's behalf, but even if the queen had relented, it would have been impossible for him to remain at The Hague. There were two public proclamations summoning the young prince to trial. He fled immediately and later joined the Spanish Army, where he became head of a regiment and was killed at the siege of Rethel in 1650.

Elizabeth may have approved of her brother's action, for she had always been extremely sensitive about matters concerning their family honor, but it is doubtful that she would have gone so far as to be his accomplice in such a bloody deed. She highly disapproved of Louise-Hollandine's conduct, probably for good reason, for several years later her younger sister ran off to Paris with another French officer named Laroque and, like their brother Edward, converted to Roman Catholicism. Elizabeth's pious ways and disapproving attitude throughout the whole affair undoubtedly served only to increase the friction between her and her mother, who had always been more partial toward the talents and frivolity of the Princess Louise. One will never know if the queen believed that Elizabeth was actually one of the instigators of the crime, but it is clear that her daughter was required to take a short "vacation" from the court, a trip expected to last only six months but from which she never returned. Some sources say that she left at the express command of her mother; others believe that her voyage was for political reasons and was intended to ameliorate her family's sorry financial state.

Descartes' reaction to the whole affair remains a mystery. It is known that rather than write to his friend, he went to the palace on the day after the murder to console her in person. Once the date for her departure had been set, she sent word to Descartes by special messenger to remind him of his promise that he would leave his "pleasant solitude" whenever she needed him. Time was short, and she needed him now, for she could not bear the thought of a six months' separation without one last interview:

> And it [my absence] would be even longer if I were not assured that you will continue to help me profit from your meditations in your letters, for without their help, the cold weather and the type of person I might find to converse with would strangle what little common sense I possess. . . . In Germany I have been promised enough leisure for study, and I shall take along no greater treasure than your writings. I hope you will allow me to bring those on the passions, although they have not succeeded in calming those which were aroused by our latest misfortune. Your presence is required to effect the cure which neither your maxims nor my reasonings can accomplish.[32]

Thus the only written testimony that exists from Elizabeth concerning the murder of L'Espinay is the rather pathetic reference to "our latest misfortune." Descartes' letters contain no mention of the affair. Perhaps he felt it was something he could broach only in private conversation. He complied with Elizabeth's request for a meeting before her departure, and when his friend and pupil left for Berlin on August 15, 1646, she was never to see Descartes again.

Although they remained separated the rest of their lives, absence did not diminish their friendship, and they continued to correspond. So that they might do so more freely, for as an exile Elizabeth's letters were more closely watched and she always feared their interception by spies, a code was devised. Their letters were forwarded via the intermediary of the Princess Sophia, an eager accomplice at the age of sixteen, whom Descartes compared to an angel acting as a messenger. His first letter to Berlin was concerned with Machiavelli's *The Prince*. During their last meeting, Elizabeth had suggested that they discuss the famous treatise just as earlier they had examined Seneca's *De vita beata*. With almost the same methodical logic that Descartes had displayed in his *Principia*, and as if by some prearranged program of study, they now turned their attention from private morality to public politics. Elizabeth had read the work six years earlier and possibly hoped to find in her tutor's commentary some solution to her present family troubles.

Although both French and Latin translations of Machiavelli's work were available, both Elizabeth and Descartes read it in the original. They both objected in theory to precepts that were so contrary to their standards of morality; but as two people who were well aware of the practical necessities of this life, they admitted that under certain conditions violence, duplicity, and even crime might be condoned. Descartes objected to the fact that not enough distinction was made between princes who had obtained their power legitimately and those who had usurped it. Most of the maxims were directed toward the latter. He pointed out, however, that justice between sovereigns often had limits different from that between private individuals. Such observations as "It seems that God gives the right to those He gives might" and "One has permission, as it were, to do anything as long as one obtains some advantage either for oneself or for one's subjects; and I do not disapprove in such circumstances that the fox should be combined with the lion, and that guile should be joined with force" [33] make it appear that Descartes shares many of Machiavelli's ideas. He certainly makes a strong case for the divine right of kings, but while using very similar arguments, he arrives at very different conclusions from those of the Italian diplomat.

Elizabeth was delighted by her friend's commentary, and although her copy of *The Prince* had been packed in a trunk which had not yet arrived, her memory of the text after six years served her well. Besides, she had specific references in Descartes' letter to serve as a basis for her own observations, which were in general less dogmatic, perhaps more human, be it only for a certain lightness of tone, than her mentor's. She agreed that these maxims were applicable to but a very small number of circumstances, but in this respect, she pointed out, Machiavelli erred in much the same way as the Holy Fathers and the ancient philosophers, probably because they all took pleasure in being paradoxical. Rather than find a guiding principle in *The Prince*, she preferred to adopt the one Descartes had used to close his letter:

> Each man is responsible for his own happiness and must try to remain outside of Fortune's empire; thus, even though one should lose no opportunity to accept the advantages which fortune offers, still one should not consider oneself unhappy if refused; and because there are reasons for and against in all worldly affairs, one should consider principally those which help us to approve of what happens.[34]

The change of climate seemed to agree with Elizabeth. At that time Berlin was far behind The Hague as an intellectual center, but she found there a warm welcome. It was, after all, the scene of her childhood, and although the grandmother who had raised her had died two years earlier, two of her aunts were still living there, the Princess Catherine and Charlotte, the Electress Dowager of Brandenburg, who was especially fond of her. Her health gradually improved, and the shame and depression which she had felt after the L'Espinay affair were rather quickly dispelled as is evidenced when she wrote to her friend saying: "Here I find little difficulty, being in a house where I have been cherished since infancy, where everyone conspires to caress me, although they sometimes distract me from more useful occupations. I easily bear this inconvenience for the pleasure of being loved by one's close relations." [35] She attended balls and various fetes, often against her will, but compared to her mother's court at The Hague, Berlin was as inferior in frivolity as it was in culture. There was no established bookseller in the town, and the name of Descartes was virtually unknown there until she introduced it.

Elizabeth was indeed a strange phenomenon, quite a sensation in fact, in Berlin society. It was a novel sight for the Germans to see a woman, much less a young and highly intelligent princess, taking part in philosophic discussions with doctors and divines. She in turn had difficulty finding those who could converse about scientific or serious works and was extremely critical of the pedantry and ignorance of the Berliners. When she tried to explain Descartes' theories, most of them either shrugged their shoulders, being incapable of understanding, or smiled condescendingly, thinking her slightly mad. The aging Duke of Brunswick did ask her to obtain a set of the philosopher's works so that he might have them bound for his famous library, but, as the princess wrote sarcastically, "Although I promised to get them for him to improve his library, I do not believe they will improve his stuffy brain which is already filled with pedantic ideas." [36] There was, however, a certain Dr. Weiss, who proved to be an exception. He had read the *Discourse*, had rejected Aristotle's philosophy in favor of Descartes', and shared the latter's theory about the circulation of the blood. To him she gave the *Principia* and promised to relay his reactions to her correspondent. There was also a Professor Knesebeck, who greatly admired her talents, and with her cousin Frederick William, Elector of Brandenburg, she had such influence that later, when a university was established at Duisburg, its strongly Cartesian scholarship can be traced to her suggestions.

Seven months, which was to have been the duration of Elizabeth's stay in Berlin, had passed, and still no definite date had been set for her return. In March Descartes was at The Hague and wrote to tell her that he planned to return to France in several months in order to manage some personal affairs. In response he received a nostalgic letter which nonetheless postponed the time of their next meeting to a rather indefinite future:

> I never regretted my absence from The Hague until you told me you had been there, and I felt deprived of the pleasure I should have had in your conversation while there. It seems to me that the peace I find here . . . surpasses all the good I might find elsewhere, so I can neither promise to return within a few months nor even predict how many, for my aunt is not in the mood to let me leave, and I would not press it before the return of her son, which . . . will not be before September. . . . I hope you may find all the success you look for in this journey, and if I did not know the constancy of your resolutions, I should fear your friends might induce you to stay there.[37]

Before leaving for France, Descartes wrote again and complained rather bitterly of the continued harassment from the universities. So great was his annoyance that he threatened to leave Holland altogether, to which Elizabeth replied that it would be unworthy of him to give in to his enemies. If he persisted in such a plan, she continued, with a certain amount of feminine guile, then she too would not return to The Hague. He left, however, for Paris on June 7, before her letter reached him. Again he stayed with the Abbé Picot and busied himself with a preface for the French edition of his *Principia* which had just been completed. Aside from a short trip to Brittany for his seemingly interminable family affairs, most of the time was spent in the capital with his usual small circle of friends. Clerselier was suffering from gout but had been busy with the *Meditationes*, which had appeared in French several months earlier. Mydorge, the mathematician, died rather suddenly while Descartes was in the country with Picot. Mersenne was recovering from a cut artery, the result of a surgeon's carelessness while bleeding him. It was probably during his stay in Paris that he was invited to dine at the Marquis of Newcastle's in the company of two of his adversaries, philosophers Thomas Hobbes and Pierre Gassendi. But the most important of his encounters took place on September 23 and 24, just before his return to Holland, when he went to see a young man, then only twenty-four, who was to become one of France's reigning geniuses: Blaise Pascal.

It is doubtful that Descartes had ever met any of the Pascal family, although Blaise's father had sided with Roberval against the principles of geometry contained in the essays published with the *Discourse* in 1637. Roberval was again present, much to Descartes' annoyance, when he arrived at ten thirty on a Monday morning to visit the young Blaise. Pascal had heard that the famous philosopher was in Paris and desired to see him, but he was unfortunately sick in bed at the time. It was, therefore, the elder who took the initiative. On this occasion the prodigious talent of whom he had heard so much was weak from fever and extremely sickly in appearance. They spoke of the adding machine which Pascal had invented and of his recent experiments with vacuums. The young man's natural timidity was heightened by his illness, so that he had difficulty expressing himself. Roberval, Descartes' old adversary, then took it upon himself to act as interpreter, and the discussion became quite heated. The two could not agree and, as had happened on other meetings, exchanged very sarcastic remarks. Descartes became particularly irritated whenever one questioned his theory that an absolute void was impossible. At noon, however, they took their leave in a fairly civil manner, and Roberval was allowed to ride in the philosopher's carriage, where they continued their bickering.[38]

The next morning at eight Descartes paid a second visit. This time he played the role of doctor as well as physicist and counseled Pascal to remain in bed all day, to stay there in fact until he became "sick" of it, and to drink as much liquid as possible. They continued their discussion on vacuums and the manner in which mercury descends from the top of a closed tube. The elder man put forth his theories of subtle matter, and it was probably during this second interview that he suggested the experiments that would later be completed by Pascal and his brother-in-law at Puy-de-Dôme to show the effect of atmospheric pressure on tubes filled with mercury. One would like to know the exact nature of their conversation during this second meeting, but such an account is lacking. The significance of their encounter, aside from successful experiments which would be derived from their talk and eventual letters, serves to emphasize not only their mutual interests but also their very different natures and opinions. In many respects they were diametrically opposed. As Pierre Frédérix has pointed out,[39] Pascal claimed that suffering is the only means of sanctification, whereas Descartes repeatedly talked of happiness. One was devout; the other, tolerant. According to Descartes, man is essentially good and can raise himself through reason to God. According to Pascal, man is essentially corrupt. Descartes proclaimed that the basis of all certainty in physics is metaphysics; Pascal thought that experiments are the only principles of physics. Yet, despite their differences, the two men pursued the same goal, that of adding both to man's knowledge and to his wisdom. Descartes returned to Holland in October, accompanied by the Abbé Picot, who spent several months with him at Egmond-Binnen. Elizabeth was still in Germany. She wrote to say how much she admired the French translation of his *Meditationes*, sympathized with him over the stupidity of his adversaries, which only proved how much the world needed a treatise on erudition, which she enjoined him to write. He declined rather emphatically, having had enough trouble with the academicians and having other work which he considered more important; namely, his *Treatise on Animals*. The winter was spent in relative quiet. By spring there was still no mention of Elizabeth's returning to The Hague. Descartes wrote to her only twice during these months. The next letter was not sent until the following summer when he was once again in Paris. The reason for this third trip to France was a royal pension of 3,000 livres which his friends had succeeded in obtaining for him the previous September, and he now returned, as it seemed to him, at the order of the king. The pension did not require that he take up residence in France, but doubtless there would be benefits to be gained from being close to the court. Then, too, there were the entreaties of his friends, not to mention, although Descartes did to Elizabeth, those matters of family business. He arrived in Paris toward the middle of May with high hopes that were soon to be crushed, for he could not have chosen a more inopportune time to collect his royal due.

Thinking that he would make his appearance in Paris in a manner more befitting his newly acquired rank, he decided against staying with Picot, as he had on previous occasions, and settled closer to the center of town, near la rue St. Honoré. The abbé found him a well-furnished house, adequately staffed so that he could receive his friends, dine in private, and study in peace if he desired. He had arrived unfortunately at the time of the Fronde. Cardinal Mazarin, always disliked by the middle class because of his foreign birth and accent as well as his avarice, was at odds with the *parlement*, which sought immunity from royal control. At first he had seemed to yield to popular feeling, but when he had Broussel, the leader of the agitation, arrested, barricades were raised in the streets, and there followed a period of complete disorder.

The Parisians were so engrossed in this political upheaval that it is little wonder they had no time for paying tribute to their visitor from Holland. Descartes was disillusioned almost from the moment of his arrival, and his first letter mentions an early return to "the innocence of the desert that I left where I was much happier." [40] Friends proved to be of little consolation. Mersenne was on his deathbed, and Roberval was more cantankerous than during their earlier meetings. It is doubtful that Descartes ever received the pension he had been promised, although he was forced to pay rather dearly for the useless parchment it was written on, and he keenly felt the uselessness of the entire trip. He did not want to reproach his friends for his unhappiness, but six months later he recalled his experience thus: "I considered them as friends who had invited me to dinner; and when I arrived, I found their kitchen in chaos and the kettle overturned; that is why I left without saying a word so as not to increase their grievance." [41]

Perhaps the only good result of his visit was the reconciliation which was effected between him and Gassendi by the young Abbé d'Estrées. As a patron of the arts he was anxious to dispel the dissension between the two philosophers and therefore invited them to an elaborate dinner. Unfortunately, Gassendi fell ill at the last moment and was unable to attend; but rather than let the opportunity pass, after the meal the abbé took his guests to the sick man's house where the former adversaries embraced each other openly. Soon afterward, Gassendi paid Descartes a visit, which was promptly returned, and the reconciliation was complete. Such happy encounters were rare, however, and Descartes would have left Paris much sooner had it not been for Picot's entreaties to prolong his stay. He moved back to the abbé's house for a time, but the city became increasingly difficult, and on August 27, the day after the barricades had been set up, he left Paris in all its confusion, never to return.

No sooner was he back at Egmond-Binnen than he wrote to Elizabeth. She had told him of a proposed trip to Sweden with the Dowager Queen of Sweden, Marie-Eleonora, then residing in Berlin. Such a voyage might have been very profitable for her family's interests, but unfortunately the present queen had changed her mind about having her mother accompanied by a princess who was of a different religion. Elizabeth was disappointed and could not but take such excuses as an indirect insult. He, on the other hand, had had enough of travels. She should not be upset, he told her, about not taking a trip which was bound to have its inconveniences, whereas its rewards remained very uncertain. His words were to prove only too ironic, for within the year this would be the very trip that he himself would take.

There remains but one more letter from Elizabeth. She wrote others, which unfortunately have been lost. It is known that she was seriously ill during the autumn of 1648 and almost died from smallpox. To her brother Charles she wrote words that might well have been addressed to her friend:

> You will have learned from the last post the reason that has hindered my paying my duty to you since I have been persecuted by this wretched illness, and though the fever has left me and with it the peril of my life, I am still quite covered with it and can use neither my hands nor my eyes. They feed me like a little child, but the doctors would persuade me I shall not be disfigured, which I leave to their faith, having none of my own on the subject; but at the worst I console myself that the illness will only have the effect of three or four years, at

the end of which age would have rendered me ugly enough without its aid.[42]

Elizabeth now disappeared temporarily from the philosopher's correspondence, although not from his thoughts. Her last letter was sent more than a year later to Sweden, where he had embarked on the final stage of his life. Another friendship, this time with a personage of even higher rank than a princess, had begun to eclipse the place which Elizabeth had so deservedly held in Descartes' mind and heart.

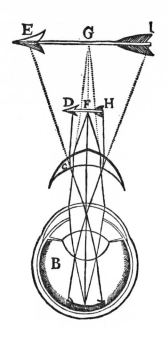

CHAPTER 7
The Snow Queen

CHRISTINA of Sweden was one of the most famous, some say infamous, queens in history. She was a legend in her own time, and her story continues to fascinate biographers and scandalmongers, scholars and the merely curious. She was neither beautiful nor saintly. Quite the contrary, she lacked virtually every feminine charm, and her morals were highly suspect. Physically Christina must have appeared rather repellent. She was indifferent to the way she looked. Her clothes were not only plain but neglected, and she rarely combed her hair more than once a week. She disliked women's dress. In place of the customary long skirts and elaborate coiffures she preferred short petticoats or a riding habit, and a ribbon sufficed for her hair. Slightly below medium height, she had one shoulder lower than the other—a fact which she tried to hide and, in so doing, changed her stance, so that when she walked her ungainly movements often provoked laughter. She paid no attention to her complexion or her figure. From childhood on she slept no more than five hours a night and was indifferent to heat and cold. Eating and drinking little, she hardly cared how her meals were prepared, which may account for the fact that later in life she suffered from indigestion. Some say she resembled a cavalry officer more than a woman. She wore low shoes like those of a man and had a deep masculine voice. Everything about her seemed to be at odds with her sex, even from the moment of her birth. Astrologers had predicted that her parents would have a male child, and when Christina was born, the nurses at first thought that she was indeed a boy. "She will be clever," her father observed much later. "She took us all in." [1]

Christina proved to be much more than clever. It was Gustavus Adolphus' wish that his daughter be given a man's education, and she proved more than equal to the challenge. As an infant she showed pleasure rather than fright at the sound of guns, and she was soon an excellent horsewoman. Her intense curiosity and incredible memory combined to produce what was reputed to be a truly encyclopedic mind. Her mother, Marie-Eleonora of Brandenburg, had been indifferent to her daughters from birth, so that when Christina's father died in battle in 1632 and she became queen at the age of six, her schooling was entrusted entirely to her ministers. She showed a natural bent for politics and learned early in life that one of a monarch's chief duties is to conceal his own personal feelings while getting others to reveal theirs. Certain critics have called this duplicity or deceit in Christina's conduct, while others have preferred to call it statesmanship. There is no doubt, however, that she took her duties as head of the state seriously, and throughout the struggle of the Thirty Years' War she strove by every means possible to obtain peace.

Christina also displayed a remarkable talent for the study of languages. She spoke Latin, French, German, Flemish, and Swedish all fluently. Reading Tacitus was like a game to her, and passages which even the erudite found difficult, she could translate and comprehend with ease. It is not surprising that such a virile personality found the company of most women at her court annoying if not intolerable. She had come to characterize them as either empty-headed or frivolous, incapable of conversing on her level, and therefore most of the time she ignored them.

Whatever Christina lacked in the way of feminine charm she more than made up for by her intellect. She had a vivacious, sometimes impetuous, manner. Intelligence seemed to sparkle from her bright, well-set eyes, and in conversation her observations were usually couched in such a reasoned way as to give them the definitive sound of formal pronouncements. Everything she undertook she did with enthusiasm, and her passion for riding and hunting was counterbalanced by her love for study. She was especially attracted to literature and philosophy. She loved discussions about both, but not for the sake of idle or abstract speculation. She was interested always in finding a practical application for her learning, a way of finding answers to the problems that were troubling her. She was particularly fond of examining the moral implications of what she read, for in the formative years of her life she was anxious to establish an ethical code that would answer her own needs and inner conflicts and at the same time be in harmony with ecclesiastical teachings. Although she did not overtly rebel against the strict Lutheran upbringing of her childhood until much later in life, she found certain tenets unacceptable or at least inexplicable. These she questioned at an early age, and after being reprimanded for her doubting nature, she preferred to keep silent rather than run the risk of scandalizing both her tutors and her subjects.

Soon books no longer sufficed, and Christina began to invite the most celebrated scholars of Europe to visit her court. Her reasons for doing so were various. She craved the company of men of learning so that she might converse with them personally and hear not only their explanations of their own works but also their interpretations of the knowledge and culture of the past which she had so assiduously studied. Christina was ambitious to become a patroness of the arts. Her motives may have been in part selfish ones, for she must at times have wearied of the isolation attendant upon her royal position. But she was also eager to increase her country's reputation abroad. Sweden was virtually unknown, at least culturally, in other European countries, and Christina was determined to make it the center of learning. To this end she had already spent large sums in collecting one of the finest libraries possible. It was not long before Stockholm was to represent a scholar's paradise and Christina was to earn for herself the distinction of being called the Minerva of the North. Descartes was among the first of Christina's important foreign visitors, but his decision to accept her invitation had been many years in the making and fraught with misgivings.

It was Descartes' good friend Pierre Chanut who served as the intermediary between the queen and the philosopher. It was he who first piqued Christina's curiosity so that she became anxious to learn more about the new philosophy that was rapidly gaining such controversial fame throughout Europe. The friendship between Chanut and Descartes appeared as deeply rooted as if they had known each other since childhood, but in fact they did not meet until 1644 in Paris, most probably at Clerselier's house. Clerselier, then a longtime friend of Descartes, was at work on a French translation of the *Meditationes*. Chanut, in addition to being a friend of Clerselier, was also his brother-in-law, having married his sister in 1626. He was, therefore, triply welcome as a friend, relative, and philosopher, for he had gained a reputation in his own right as a man of distinguished intelligence. Chanut rapidly became a sincere admirer of Descartes. He held a government post and introduced his friend to those he thought might be of use to him. He even tried to persuade Cardinal Mazarin to grant a pension to Descartes, but his negotiations proved, at least for the time being, unsuccessful.

In 1645 Chanut was sent as minister of the King of France to the Swedish court. That same year, he spent four days in October visiting Descartes in Amsterdam. From the very first, Chanut had been desirous of interesting Christina in his friend. He began by fairly guarded references to his works and to his genius and then by allusions to the personality of the man himself so that Christina would want to understand his philosophy and come to the conclusion that there would be no better way than to learn it from the author. Chanut undoubtedly thought he was acting in his friend's best interest; but as an accomplished statesman, he was anxious to please both the Swedish queen and the French king whom he served. In this case, his efforts to bring Descartes to Sweden fulfilled both personal and political aims. Naturally he wanted to have his friend near him and to further his career; at the same time he was contributing to Christina's project of transforming Stockholm into the new cultural center of Europe; and by strengthening his own position and that of Descartes in the Swedish court, he was indirectly and very diplomatically strengthening the prestige of France abroad.

The letters that passed between Chanut and Descartes are long and varied in their content, but they merit attention, for they reveal not only the gradual development of the latter's resolve to go to Sweden, despite many misgivings, but also they show Descartes playing the role of friend, philosopher, statesman, courtier, and sometimes even that of a rather aging recluse desirous of being wooed back into society. Chanut had been in Stockholm for more than a year when Descartes wrote to thank him for speaking to the queen in his behalf. The letter, dated November 1, 1646, begins by praising Chanut's intelligence and by excusing his own importunity in asking him to examine his writings. He has heard from Clerselier that Chanut is waiting for the arrival of the French version of his *Meditationes* in order to show them to Christina:

> I have heard so many estimable things about this queen that, even though I have often complained about those who wanted to introduce me to some high personage, I cannot refrain from thanking you for speaking to her about me. I saw Monsieur de la Thuillerie here since his return from Sweden, and he described her qualities in such a favorable way that being a queen appears one of her lesser talents. I should not have believed half of what he said if I had not seen through experience, in the princess to whom I dedicated my *Principia Philosophiae*, that persons of high birth, no matter what their sex, do not need to be advanced in years in order to surpass by far other men both in learning and in virtue. But I am very afraid that the writings which I have published do not merit her reading them and that she might not be grateful to you for having recommended them. Perhaps if I had discussed morality, it would have been more to her liking, but that is a subject which I must not write about.[2]

Behind the obvious flattery, both to Chanut and to the queen, for undoubtedly Chanut would either relate the contents of his letter or else show it directly to Christina, there can be seen far deeper motives than a simple desire to write a polite acknowledgment of thanks. Descartes knew his correspondent, and even though he had not yet met Christina, he could well imagine the kind of phraseology that would appeal to a twenty-year-old girl who was both powerful and popular. Although Chanut had not yet given him an opinion of his writings, Descartes wanted him to do so. He therefore told his friend that his works were not destined for the public but for an intellectual elite, *quelques personnes de bon esprit,* of which naturally Chanut was a member. But Descartes wanted to be read by as many persons as possible just so long as they did not misinterpret his thoughts. He was still being harassed at this time with accusations of heresy and atheism. That is why, so he said, he would not discuss morality, for his enemies would be certain to find his opinions counter to the state and the Church.

The wording of his remarks concerning Christina is equally well calculated to obtain his ends. He claims that he has never wanted to curry royal favor, and yet from his childhood he had remained fascinated by the ceremonials connected with those in high places. Certainly he was not unaware of the fact that he could already claim one member of a royal family as his friend and disciple. His mention of the Princess Elizabeth in this letter to Chanut also reveals his desire to bring her misfortunes to the young queen's attention and perhaps serve as intermediary in improving her condition. He flatters Christina by saying that neither age nor sex is responsible for one's depth of learning. Whether or not he was aware of her aversion to women, one can be sure that Christina would have been pleased by the remark, for she preferred to consider herself as having risen above the limitations of her sex and as being the equal of her male companions. And one final touch that should not be overlooked in the wording of his observations about the Swedish queen is the suggestion that a discussion of morality would have held more interest for her than his philosophical meditations. By this he means that a girl of her age, occupied whether she likes it or not by affairs of state, could not help but be interested in the question of right and wrong, and most particularly as it concerned love. Descartes confesses that this is a subject that he dares not treat, but his reticence will soon be broken in order to answer Christina's curiosity.

This first letter in the long correspondence concerning

Christina is a small masterpiece for its psychological insight into the nature of the recipients, for its less overt revelation of Descartes' own personality and motivation, and for the depth of its general observations. Two of these insights, given, as it were, in an offhand conversational tone, merit attention for the light they throw on Descartes' opinions when speaking in fairly abstract terms about universal emotions and for their relationship to his own feelings at the time. The first occurs toward the end of the letter, where he speaks about friendship:

> One can say a great many things in very little time, and I find that a long association is not necessary to establish close friendships when they are founded upon virtue. From the first moment I had the honor of seeing you, I was yours entirely; and because I have trusted ever since in your goodwill, I beg you to believe that I could not be more attached to you than I am if I had spent my entire life with you.[3]

Descartes is here dealing with a feeling that all mankind is capable of experiencing; he is also describing his own reactions since his recent meeting with Chanut; and finally, he is doing so in terms that his friend was certain to find flattering to his own *amour-propre*.

The second observation occurs in the final paragraph, in which Descartes discusses anger. He has been studying the passions and has found them all to be not only good and useful, but indeed essential to life:

> It is true that anger is one of [the passions] which I believe should be avoided, for it has an offense as its object, and because of that we should try to raise our minds high enough so that the injuries which others do to us do not succeed in affecting us. But I think that instead of being angry, it is fitting to be indignant, and I confess that I am often so against the ignorance of those who would be considered erudite, especially when I see their stupidity joined with malice.[4]

Here again Descartes is treating a universal human emotion, but he does so in terms of his own experience. He justifies indignation in general, but most especially his own indignation. He is still annoyed at the false accusations and misinterpretations of his works. He draws no fine line to differentiate between anger and indignation. Without any specific reference to past events or personal enemies, Descartes composes what might be taken for a maxim in defense of indignation. He has refused to enter upon the subject of morality, but by his seeming postscript on the passion of anger, has he not already touched upon that which he previously declared to be forbidden territory? The question of the passions and their relationship to morality will be at the center of his later preoccupations and discussions with Christina.

On December 1, 1646, exactly one month after Descartes had sent his thanks to Chanut for speaking of him to the queen, his friend replied by sending him three questions about love. Two of them were posed by Chanut; the third was from Christina. Descartes' answer covered eight pages and amounted in fact to a small treatise. He admitted that he would have written even more had he not feared that too many details might bore his reader. Chanut had asked first for a definition of love and then if our own understanding and inclination were sufficient to bring us to a love of God. Christina wanted to know which was worse, the excesses and misuse of love or hate? Descartes' reply traced the physiological sources of love and that which is truly a passion. In both he acknowledged the role played by the other passions, such as joy and sorrow, and most particularly desire, which by its relative importance had resulted in the classification of love into either *amour de bienveillance* or *amour de concupiscence*. The ideas which he expressed here are given fuller treatment in his *Treatise on the Passions*.

In his explanation of man's love for God, Descartes states that there are several reasons for doubting if human nature is capable of arriving at such a love by its own resources. He assiduously avoids the question of whether or not divine grace is necessary, an argument he prefers to leave to the theologians. Instead, he outlines what he considers the best way to arrive at this most perfect kind of love, always keeping in mind God's omnipotence and infinite greatness which does not negate man's free will but which accentuates his limited capacities. Love consists in our wanting to unite ourselves with an object, and as far as God is concerned, this would mean with the immensity of his creation of which we are but a small part: "One sees every day examples of this love, even in people of low station who willingly give their life for the good of their country or for the defense of some high-placed person whom they esteem. Consequently, it is evident that our love toward God must be without comparison the greatest and most perfect of all." [5]

This letter, like the previous one to Chanut, is not devoid of flattery addressed to the queen; it occurs in the middle of his discussion of the various kinds of love, of which the love of God is the highest. Descartes explains that ordinarily people use the term "respect" rather than "love" for their attachment to someone belonging to a much higher station in society. Love has an equalizing effect, and for that reason if a subordinate used its language while speaking to his superior, the latter might take offense. But true love disregards whether its object be of equal, greater, or less importance. By using the example of Chanut's relationship with the queen, Descartes is able to prove his point and also flatter them both:

> And if I asked you in all sincerity if you do not love this great queen whom you serve at present, you might say in vain that you have only respect, veneration, and wonder toward her, I should judge that you also have a very ardent affection. Because your style flows so well when you speak of her, and although I believe everything you say because you are very honest and I have also heard the same things said by others, I still do not believe that you could describe her as you do if

you did not have great zeal, nor that you could be near such a great light without receiving some of its warmth.[6]

The passage well demonstrates that while philosophizing, Descartes could simultaneously play the courtier.

Although love is the most useful passion that man can have, Descartes recognizes that it can be the most dangerous when misguided, far more so than hate. This is his reply to the third question contained in Chanut's letter, the one posed by Christina. He reasons that love carries one to greater excesses and is capable of causing more harm to others than hate could do because it is stronger. He traces its strength to its physiological origins, says that loving an unworthy object can make us worse than hating an object which we should love, for there is more danger in being associated with something which is bad than to be separated from something good, and concludes by citing the example of Paris, who for the love of Helen caused the burning of Troy and the ruin of his people.

As soon as Christina learned that Chanut had received a reply from Descartes, she gave him no peace until she had seen it. Chanut, it would appear, deliberately kept the letter from her for some time in order to pique her curiosity. When she finally obtained it, she was impressed enough by its contents to have a copy made and told Chanut: "I prefer the happiness of Monsieur Descartes to all the crowns of the world." [7] Chanut agreed that one day spent in rest and meditation is worth more than years passed in never-ending visits and boring official correspondence. Christina appears to have been generally satisfied by Descartes' reply to her question about the excesses of love and hate. Although she claimed to have no direct experience of these passions at the time, it was not long before her own attachment to the Italian nobleman Giovanni Monaldeschi was to end in his assassination, thus furnishing a dramatic example of Descartes' theory.

Only one point in this letter caused Christina considerable consternation. She found it impossible to reconcile the teachings she had received from her catechism, especially the dogma of the creation and the predicted end of the world, with Descartes' statement that the world is infinite both in the past and the future, in space as well as time. Chanut transmitted these objections to Descartes, who lost no time in replying.[8] He tried to resolve the queen's difficulties by pointing out that others before him had described the world as infinite without being censured by the church. He also took pains to differentiate between "infinite" and "indefinite," preferring to use the latter term to describe the world whose limits we cannot know and reserving the former to describe God. In all these explanations, he maintained a certain reserve and refused to come into direct conflict with orthodox opinion. Instead he turned the question back to the theologians to answer, and it is doubtful that Christina with her Lutheran background found any real satisfaction in his answer.

In September, 1647, Christina attended a lecture at the University of Uppsala given by the noted scholar and professor Freinshemius on the subject of the sovereign good, *De vero bono*. She was curious to know what Descartes' thoughts might be on this subject and asked Chanut to inquire. A letter was duly dispatched on September 21, but despite the irregularity and frequent delays in mail between Sweden and Holland at that time, the queen found Descartes' reply too long in coming and asked Chanut to renew his request on November 9. Descartes answered on November 20, but the letter did not reach Christina until January, 1648. This was the first time that Descartes dispensed with their intermediary and addressed himself directly to the queen.

After comparing the ancients' conception of the greatest good, which according to Zeno consisted in a virtuous life and to Epicurus in a life of sensual pleasure, with that of the Christian ideal found in God, he announced that man's greatest good lay in his will to do right: "I do not see how it would be possible to use our knowledge and our will better than to have always a strong and constant resolution to do exactly the things which we consider to be the best and to use all the strength of our intelligence in striving to understand them." [9] For Descartes, man's free will was his most noble possession, the quality which made him in some ways comparable to God and in some ways seemed to free him from subservience to God. Man's dignity and his greatest happiness, therefore, lay in the exercise of his free will.

In order to give a more complete explanation of his thoughts than was contained in this rather brief résumé to Christina, Descartes on the same day sent another letter to Chanut in which he enclosed his *Treatise on the Passions* and also six letters that he had written two years earlier to Elizabeth on the same subject. He would even have included her replies if he had not found it difficult to obtain her permission because of the distance which then separated them. His strategy in thus introducing the Palatine Princess into his correspondence with the queen was far from subtle. He knew that Christina might take offense at the fact that the letters had been originally written to someone else rather than addressed to her, and therefore he told Chanut that he should not show the letters but should mention them. Only if Christina then desired to see them should they be produced. The queen, as it turned out, never mentioned the letters to Elizabeth, probably because Chanut judged it wiser and certainly more politic to keep them to himself. Descartes' initial attempt at interesting his newfound royal admirer in his closest feminine friend proved futile.

Shortly after receiving the letters, Chanut wrote that the queen had read Descartes' definition of the greatest good and planned to take it along on a hunting party in order to study it further. Descartes was eager to know her reaction. Five months later he wrote Elizabeth that he still had heard nothing from either Chanut or the queen. Did this mean that she had not re-read his work as she had planned, or that she had done so and disliked it, or that she simply had not bothered to tell Chanut what her opinions were? Descartes was thus kept in suspense, and it was not until almost a full year later, on September 12, 1648, that Christina finally wrote to thank him. The letter was short, filled with polite phrases, but aside from saying that her esteem was confirmed, it contained no reference to the ideas which Descartes had set forth. By the same post he received a letter from Chanut telling him that he had read the preface of his *Principia Philosophiae* to Christina and that she was en-thusiastic to the point of wanting to undertake the study of the entire work. She willingly accepted Chanut's suggestion that in order to combat certain difficulties it would be wise to have the help of a scholar such as Freinshemius. The previous years he had been appointed historiographer to the queen and was also en-trusted with the supervision and collection of the royal library. Freinshemius in turn knew that he too would probably need help and suggested that Chanut serve as the third member of their studious endeavor. Chanut was vaguely amused at having to add lessons in philosophy to his other duties as a foreign minister, but he accepted the task with alacrity, assuring Des-cartes that once Christina had become versed in his thought, she would probably try to lure him to Sweden.[10]

The invitation was not long in coming. It might almost have been composed through mental telepathy. Descartes on February 26 was expressing his zealous admiration for Christina ("I hereby declare to your Majesty that there is nothing so difficult that she might command me to do that I should not always be ready to do my utmost to accomplish it, and that if I had been born a Swede I could not be more devoted."[11]), and on the following day Chanut sent word that the Queen of Sweden wanted to learn Descartes' philosophy from his own lips. His willingness to serve was now about to be tested.

Descartes wrote two letters of acceptance. Although both were addressed to Chanut, the first was obviously meant to be shown to the queen. He was ready to undertake the voyage, but since no date had been set, he preferred to postpone his departure until midsummer when the climate would be more temperate. This would give him time to put his affairs in order, for he planned to spend the winter in Stockholm. In the second letter, which was meant to be read by Chanut alone, he confessed that he had serious misgivings about the venture. Would the queen have sufficient time to devote to such studies, occupied as she was with affairs of state? Would she find his ideas less original and therefore less appealing once he had resolved their seeming difficulty? And what would be his own reception? His recent visit to Paris had left him disillusioned with society. It had proved costly, for he was even forced to pay postage for what turned out to be useless compliments, and the Parisians were so absorbed in the political struggles of Mazarin and the rising of the Fronde that they took little notice of Descartes: "But what disgusted me most was that no one wanted to know more of me than my face, so that I felt that they only wanted to have me in France as one would an elephant or a panther, because of its rarity and not in order to be useful." [12] Descartes did not want to run the risk of receiving similar treatment in the North.

But he had even more serious reservations about the voyage to Sweden which he did not state overtly in the letter to Chanut. He was a Catholic, and the strict Lutherans who composed the Swedish court might accuse him of trying to influence the queen in religious matters. It was already known that several of her court criticized Christina for spending too much time with her studies. Certainly his presence could only add to their aversion. Another reason for Descartes' prolonged hesitation was that his writings had created many enemies, and he feared that they might have written to Sweden. He knew that Christina would not be a prey to such libels, but some of her subjects might be less enlightened and try to prejudice the queen against him.[13] As if by premonition, Descartes continued to waver while trying to resolve all possible objections to the journey that was to prove his last.

Meanwhile Christina, acting in her frequently impetuous manner, dispatched Admiral Flemming for the purpose of escorting the philosopher back to Sweden. He arrived in Holland in early April, but for some reason Descartes did not realize that it was the queen who had sent him. In a letter to Chanut, he confessed ignorance not only of Flemming's mission but also of the fact that he was an admiral. He had not received Chanut's message until after Flemming's departure. The misunderstanding may have been due to language difficulties, or it may have been caused by Descartes' unwillingness to accept too readily an invitation that might have originated as a caprice. He wanted to be certain that Christina's desire to have him in Stockholm was genuine, and he saw no reason to travel with the Swedish admiral, thinking that his suggestion to return together was based merely on his friendship with Chanut. He claimed to be waiting for more specific instructions from the queen herself. He was, after all, comfortably established in his Dutch hermitage and was in no hurry to leave a land where, as he described it, "If there is not as much honey as in God's promised land, there is certainly more milk." [14] Flemming returned to Sweden empty-handed, and Descartes continued to write letters.

It was not until the end of July that he made his final decision, five months after the initial invitation. By then he had received a visit from Chanut, who on his way to France reiterated his praise of the queen. He also had the reassurance of Freinshemius that all would go well for him in Stockholm. Again there seems to have been a sense of foreboding shown by the care with which he set about putting his affairs in order. In addition to all the other difficulties he might encounter, there was always the possibility of being robbed, murdered, or shipwrecked en route.

On August 30, the day before he embarked, he wrote to the Abbé Picot: "Being about to leave for Stockholm and considering that I may die during the voyage. . . ." [15] About actually drawing up a formal will, he entrusted his business correspondence and the management of his affairs to Picot and included a list of all his debts. His heirs were to receive what little property he had, and he left a box of papers with one of his friends, the charitable Catholic physician Cornélis van Hogelande at Leiden which was to be opened only in the event of his death. He advised Hogelande that the letters should be burned except those written by Voetius to Mersenne. These he had inserted in the cover of the box and wanted them preserved as protection against any future slander.

Picot, besides being entrusted with Descartes' affairs, was the one responsible for his traveling companion, a young German named Henry Schluter. Descartes had met this talented manservant the previous year while visiting Picot in Paris and was so impressed that he asked the abbé if he might have the loan of his valet for six months. He felt that Schluter would be ideally suited to undertake such a trip. He possessed both the necessary qualities for a good servant and the kind of intelligence which would make him welcome company for his temporary master. In addition to speaking several languages, he was well versed in mathematics and had a good head for business. He also had some knowledge of Northern customs, for he was familiar with Holland and especially with Utrecht. His previous studies in college would enable him to assist Descartes in some of his experiments. The choice proved a felicitous one. Schluter became strongly attached to his new employer, and Descartes in turn had every confidence in him because of his industry and affection.

On August 31 Descartes left his retreat at Egmond-Binnen. Several friends came to bid him farewell, including a Catholic priest from Haarlem, named Bloemaert, whose defense he had taken earlier and who insisted on having a sketch made of the philosopher before his departure. Descartes, who usually took few pains with his appearance, preferring to dress in the plainest of fashion, had made rather elaborate additions to his wardrobe for the journey. If he were about to play the courtier, he would look the part. He is described by Brasset, secretary of the French embassy at The Hague, who was amused at the change in his friend's appearance, as wearing his hair in ringlets, long pointed shoes, and gloves trimmed with white fur.[16] At the age of forty-three Descartes' hair had begun to turn gray, and once installed at the Swedish court, he would order his wigs from Paris and be shaved in the French manner. If he were not vain, he was at least far from indifferent to his appearance.

The trip took slightly more than a month. The captain of the vessel was astounded at his knowledge of navigation. It is not surprising that he could keep him fascinated with his explanations of the constellations and the formation of storms, for earlier Descartes had done extensive research on the subject. He documented his own observations with the accounts of pilots and mariners in order to refute supernatural causes for what were purely natural phenomena and had published many of these findings earlier in his *Meteors* (1637). The work was definitive enough to have its principal tenets incorporated rather unscrupulously by the Jesuit father Georges Fournier in his *Theory and Practice of Navigation* (1643).[17] Thus, when the captain made his customary report to the queen upon their arrival, he told Christina that this was no ordinary man whom he had transported but a demigod. Descartes, he said, had taught him more in three weeks than he had learned in the sixty years he had spent at sea.[18]

Having reached Stockholm around October 1, Descartes went directly to Chanut's house where an apartment had been prepared for his lodging. Chanut, recently appointed ambassador, had not yet returned from France, but Madame Chanut was delighted at the idea of having one of both her husband's and her brother's closest and certainly most illustrious friends as a guest in her house. It was, therefore, a warm reception which awaited him, and he found himself in the midst of one of the most congenial families imaginable. Madame Chanut's agreeable nature and virtuous ways were reflected in her servants, who adored her, and especially in her two sons, Martial and Hector, who were well educated and models of good behavior. Although Chanut was not to return until the end of December, he had left letters for his friend most probably concerning the experiments with mercury which the two of them were conducting simultaneously with those being done by Pascal at Clermont. Here in the ambassador's house Descartes found both a charming refuge from the rigors of court life and the opportunity to work in peace while yet surrounded by a family whose principal concern was his happiness. In short, he seemed to have found the perfect atmosphere which neither his beloved Egmond-Binnen nor Paris had been able to afford him. It took only four or five days, however, for his initial enthusiasm to wane, and despite the efforts of those around him, he was no sooner installed than he began to talk of returning to his solitude.

The day after his arrival he went to pay his respects to the queen, who received him with such cordiality that it could only inspire jealousy among some of the other savants at her court. It was soon arranged that he would be dispensed from attending all official ceremonies at the palace and would come only at hours when he and the queen could converse freely in private. Christina with her usual enthusiasm suggested that they meet every morning at five o'clock in her library, heedless of the possible consequences of exposure to the freezing weather and so radical a change in the philosopher's way of living. The early hour was considered by her the best, for she rose habitually at four, and at this time she would not be harassed by affairs of state and her mind would be at its most rested and receptive. But before the lessons were to begin in earnest, she allowed him a month or so in which he was to familiarize himself with his new surroundings and become accustomed to Swedish ways. She wanted him to learn to love her country, for she had every intention of keeping him there.

During a long conversation in their second audience, which was granted two days later, the queen made no secret of the fact that she planned to have Descartes permanently installed at her court. She proposed that he become naturalized as the first step toward his being incorporated into the Swedish nobility. Titles held no personal appeal for him, and he had steeled himself, even before leaving Holland, against just this sort of ensnarement. While replying politely, he was nonetheless determined to return to Holland or even to France, so he said, if that country's internal problems were ever resolved peacefully.

Christina, in her second interview with the philosopher, also spoke of the Princess Elizabeth. In fact, according to Descartes,[19] she asked him many questions concerning his royal friend. He lost no time in reassuring Elizabeth that despite the change of climate and country he remained her faithful servant. On October 9, 1649, he described his first reactions to his new patroness, and although his tone is flattering, a close reading reveals the seeds of certain misgivings and future discontent. He begins by stating his certainty that there could be no cause for jealousy between two such superior people as the queen and herself, but perhaps he protests too much:

> One of the first things which she [Christina] asked me was whether I had any news of you, and I did not hesitate to tell her first of all what I thought of your Majesty; for, knowing the strength of her intellect, I did not fear that this would

occasion any jealousy on her part, just as I am certain that your Majesty could not feel any from my writing frankly my opinions of this queen.[20]

In addition to her generosity and majesty, her sweetness and goodness, he observed from his first two interviews with Christina that she was extremely interested in the study of literature and foreign languages. Recently she had invited a young Dutchman, Isaac Vossius, to tutor her in Greek. Vossius was then only thirty-two, and he was Descartes' chief rival for royal favor. Christina granted him more time than any of the other scholars who surrounded her. It is well known that from the time he left La Flèche Descartes held the study of the classics in little esteem. His opinion of them is clearly stated in the *Discourse.* He may have felt some jealousy toward Vossius, but it is doubtful that his disdain for the classics would have been expressed directly to the queen, as one contemporary states, by his telling her that he was astounded that she should amuse herself with such bagatelles; that he had had his fill when he was a little boy in school; but that fortunately he had forgotten everything about them when he reached the age of reason.[21] Such anecdotes are more likely the work of those at court who were anxious to discredit his reputation and augment rivalries between him and the jealous grammarians. However, it is evident from the terms of his own letter to Elizabeth that he was far from pleased with the queen's ardor for collecting "a lot of old books." He could not as yet judge what would be her liking for philosophy, but her taste for languages could only be a hindrance to their proposed plan of study.

After a few passing compliments to both the queen and his correspondent, Descartes concludes this first letter written after his arrival in Sweden by saying: "After all, nevertheless, even though I have a very great veneration for her Majesty, I do not think that anything would be able to keep me in this country longer than next summer; but I certainly cannot answer for the future." [22] On the same day that he wrote to Elizabeth he sent another letter to the Abbé Picot, for he was anxious that his countrymen should be informed of the warm welcome he had received from the queen. He told his friend that his establishment in the French ambassador's house was such that he believed himself in Paris rather than Stockholm but that despite his willingness to please the queen, he had not changed his resolution to return from Sweden and that he could easily leave the following January when the weather would be more suitable for traveling. [23]

For a period of from four to six weeks after his initial meetings with the queen, Descartes did not see Christina. She may have been devoting herself to her Greek studies, to affairs of state, or simply giving him, as she had promised, the opportunity to familiarize himself with his new surroundings. During this time, although not participating in the rigors of frivolities of court life, he must have missed his former solitude. And even before his lessons with his new royal pupil had begun, he undoubtedly felt some deception. He made several friendships, but he soon found that he had many enemies.

Among his new friends was the Comte de Brégy, the French ambassador to Poland. He had left Warsaw in order to further French diplomacy in Sweden and had arrived in Stockholm at the same time as Descartes. He, too, was lodged at Chanut's house. From their repeated meetings both at court and at home it was not long before the two became close friends. Brégy was a man of intelligence and breeding. Besides being already versed in Descartes' philosophy, he was also a friend of the Abbé Picot. The exact nature of his visit to Stockholm remains somewhat mysterious. Some said that he had come merely to pay his respects to the queen; others thought that he intended to help Christina in certain political maneuvers. The queen, with her usual prudent statecraft, sought to find out more about the ambassador before taking him into her confidence and questioned Descartes, who thus became indirectly involved for the first time in his life in affairs of state. In order to reassure her of Brégy's integrity he wrote several discreet letters to their mutual friend Picot, asking him to confirm his own opinion by inquiring into Brégy's general reputation in Paris.

By December Brégy, who had been called back to France because of the death of his father, returned to Paris having won Christina's affection. She presented him with a gift which included not only a large sum of money but also her portrait, in a box covered with diamonds, and a gold chain. Like Descartes, Brégy was envied his favor with the queen, and the two were linked both by their friendship and by the jealousy which they created in the Swedish courtiers who felt their nation had been invaded by foreigners. Proof of this enmity is to be found in a letter written to Brégy by the French classical scholar Claude de Saumaise *fils* on January 29, 1650:

> Everyone here is whispering in loud tones about your return, about your project, and about the Frenchmen who will compose the company of guards for her Majesty. They say that the country is overrun by foreigners, that this is insufferable, and that they would rather die. Among others, two officers have threatened to kill you.[24]

While awaiting Brégy's return to Sweden in early spring, Descartes kept him informed of various events, especially of Christina's concern, and revealed at the same time his own sense of isolation and homesickness:

> It seems to me that men's thoughts freeze here in winter just like the water. . . . I swear to you that the desire I have to return to my desert grows larger every day and that I do not know if I shall be able to stay here until you return. It is not that I do not have a perfect zeal for the service of the queen. . . . But I am not in my element here, and I desire only peace and tranquillity, rewards which the most powerful kings in the

world are unable to give to those who do not know how to
seize them for themselves.[25]

During Chanut's absence Descartes found companionship with
Freinshemius as well as with Brégy. His relationship with
Freinshemius had begun by correspondence long before he arrived in Stockholm. The professor from Uppsala was able to
provide stimulating conversation of the kind he needed and
often acted as intermediary between the philosopher and the
queen, particularly when it was a question of the granting of a
favor. It was he, for example, who had arranged that Descartes
be dispensed from attendance at court except for his interviews
with Christina. Since the time of their initial discussions concerning the greatest good, Freinshemius had been appointed royal
librarian. Christina had hopes of creating a library as well as an
academy that would rival the best in Europe. She was, therefore,
particularly delighted whenever books and manuscripts were
sent as presents from other monarchs, as they were from Louis
XIII at Chanut's request. Freinshemius was entrusted with the
duty of instructing Descartes in Swedish customs and culture.
Many of their conversations took place in the library, which
was also the meeting place for Christina's lessons in philosophy.
The librarian was frequently in attendance and undoubtedly
proud of his own achievements.

In connection with the royal library there occurs about this
time an extraordinary happening which is described in one of
Descartes' letters. It appears that at Dijon a learned man had
struggled all day with a key passage from a Greek poet without
being able to understand it. Tired and annoyed by the fruit-
lessness of his long effort, he went to bed. While deep in sleep,
his spirit was transported to Stockholm, where he was introduced
into the palace of the queen and led into her library. He looked
at all the books, and his eyes fell upon a small volume which
he opened. After having glanced through ten or twelve pages,

he ran across ten lines of Greek verse that completely resolved the difficulty which had troubled him for so long. The joy he felt at this discovery woke him up. He repeated the verses continually and then wrote them down on a scrap of paper so that he would not forget them. The next morning he thought about this nocturnal adventure, one of the most extraordinary of his life, and sent a letter to Descartes, via Chanut, to inquire if the queen's library, her palace, and the city of Stockholm were such as he had seen them in his dream. He asked him to look for the volume he had read to see if it did indeed exist and if it contained the ten lines of Greek quoted at the end of the letter.

Descartes was quick to answer the savant's inquiry, telling him that even the most talented engineer could not have described the plan of the city more correctly, that the library was exactly as he had depicted it, and that he had found the book in question and read the verses. Even though the book was extremely rare, one of his friends had promised to obtain a copy which he would send to Dijon as soon as possible as a token of his esteem. The story ends here, for there was no further correspondence between the two men. It was recounted in books published during both the seventeenth and eighteenth centuries, and while it remains one of those curious sidelights that literary historians employ to entertain their students, no attempt at a rational explanation has ever been given.[26]

Whereas Brégy and Freinshemius were to prove valuable friends, especially during Chanut's absence, Descartes soon discovered that he was surrounded by enemies. The grammarians were jealous of his favor with the queen and feared that he might supplant them. Naturally the Hellenists, and most particularly Vossius, were irritated by his derogatory remarks against Christina's learning Greek. The philosophers were unwilling to admit the superiority of his ideas to their own. The statesmen were suspicious of anyone who was of foreign extraction. And the Lutheran Swedes held a dim view of his avowed Catholicism. There was rivalry everywhere, and soon a veritable coterie of hostile voices was formed. One of his most vehement enemies, and one who was to play an important role in the near future, was Johan van Wullen, a doctor from Amsterdam. In the absence of Du Ryer, he had assumed the position of the queen's personal physician. Van Wullen, who had been antagonistic toward Descartes ever since the time of the quarrels over Cartesianism at Leiden, had gone to great lengths to try to prevent him from coming to Sweden. Among other reasons, he feared that Descartes' ideas on medicine might discredit his own. He lost no opportunity to condemn him, saying that no sensible person could possibly accept his philosophy, that his religious views were those of a heretic, and that his works were certain to be forgotten by posterity.

While waiting for Chanut to return and before beginning his lessons with Christina, Descartes found life increasingly difficult. Lodged as he was with Madame Chanut and her children, his former manner of living, especially the late rising hour and the time he used to spend in bed reflecting and writing, was completely disrupted. From the independence of a bachelor fairly set in his ways he was forced into a social atmosphere at odds with the kind of life he had so jealously prized up to this time. Both French and Swedes alike took little interest in his philosophic ideas, occupied as they were with their own personal affairs. Aside from a few experiments in physics and having his portrait painted on two separate occasions, once by the French historical painter Sébastien Bourdon and then by Van Dyck's pupil David Beck, he had little to occupy his time. He therefore withdrew more and more from the society which was for the most part either indifferent or hostile.

Rather ironically, instead of being able to devote himself wholeheartedly to his ordinary pursuits, he was obliged to honor the queen's first official request, the composing of verses for a ballet. Christina was an admirer of the dance and especially of spectacles involving pastoral or mythological settings which were then the vogue in France. To celebrate her birthday on December 8, she herself performed in the role of Diana victorious over love. By mid-December the court was organizing elaborate celebrations to commemorate the Peace of Münster, and the queen asked Descartes to contribute. She may even have asked him to dance. Such a request must have held some appeal for him, however, for it must be remembered that the philosopher was also a gentleman in the fullest sense of the word, one who was not adverse to distraction through fencing or riding and who had been greatly enthusiastic about poetry in his younger years. To be asked now to turn his talents to verse could well have proved a pleasant diversion.

The text of his work, which remained lost for more than two centuries, was discovered and published with a commentary in 1920.[27] Although Descartes was able to impress the Swedish court by his facile pen, the work appears virtually insignificant and certainly dull to the modern reader. He sought to depict the horrors of war, now that peace had finally been established, and did so by having the dancers dressed as crippled soldiers and impoverished peasants singing:

> *Qui voit comme nous sommes faits*
> *Et pense que la guerre est belle*
> *Ou qu'elle vaut mieux que la Paix*
> *Est estropié de cervelle.**

A few months later Christina again asked him to write for the court's entertainment, this time a comedy also in verse. This text has unfortunately never been recovered. All that is known

---

* Whoever sees the condition we are in
And thinks that war is beautiful
Or that it is preferable to peace
Is crippled in his mind.

is Baillet's remark that it was "rather mysterious but honest and in the style of the ancients." [28]

More important, however, than either of these literary efforts were two other projects, both prompted by Christina. Desirous of seeing his work set forth in a complete and systematic way, she made him promise to put his unpublished writings in order. He had arrived in Stockholm with a box of manuscripts, mostly unfinished fragments, all in great confusion. Amid this mass of material were two important treatises on *Man* and *The Formation of the Foetus*, which were later published together, mostly through the efforts of Clerselier. Besides these physiological writings, there were fragments on the nature of light and mechanics, mathematics and physics, and shorter works dating back to his youth. There were many notes of works to be undertaken and two fairly complete treatises, one in Latin, *Regulae ad directionem ingenii*, and the second in French, *La Recherche de la vérité par la lumière naturelle*. But by far the most important of these papers were the innumerable drafts of letters, many of which lacked dates and even the names of the persons addressed, which were later edited and published posthumously by Clerselier. It has only been in recent years that a correct and complete version of the correspondence has been given to the public.

The second project that Christina suggested to Descartes was a plan for the establishment of an academy of learned men. She intended to make him its director, an honor he declined by saying that foreigners had already caused too much trouble in similar institutions in other countries. He did, nonetheless, have many conversations with the queen on this subject and eventually drew up a set of rules governing the conduct of the debates. The queen was to preside over these meetings, whose aim it was to study and seek the truth. In general foreigners were not allowed, but one might be asked to attend at the queen's request and to speak—but only at the end, after all others had had their say. The academy was later inaugurated according to Descartes' statutes, but the weekly Sunday meetings did not begin until after his death.

Finally on December 20 Chanut returned from France. Three days later Christina received him with all due ceremony, an audience at which Descartes was present. This was the first time that Chanut had seen the queen since he had been promoted from resident to ambassador. One anecdote concerning their reunion related that Chanut, uncertain whether to appear bareheaded or covered before her Majesty, decided to follow the example of the Comte de la Thuillerie, who always remained hatless in her presence. The queen, seeing him thus, asked him to replace his hat. "I should do so, madame," he replied, "if it would make it more apparent that my master the king has an ambassador next to your Majesty; but, madame, he is such a polite prince and so well bred and your Majesty is so worthy of being served that he would not want to be in your presence other than bareheaded, and for that reason I should appear likewise." [29] Chanut, it would seem, knew how to phrase the language of diplomacy. However warm his reception, it was short-lived, for a few days later Christina left for the country, where she remained until January 14. It was only then that she decided to begin the study of philosophy in earnest. With her customary enthusiasm and energy she called Descartes to her and set up a schedule of lessons which were to begin at five in the morning three times a week. His period of relative calm was at an end.

Now he was forced to rise long before daybreak in the bitter cold. He could no longer enjoy the luxury of his bed until midmorning as had been his habit in order to savor the precious admixture of the previous evening's dreams with his waking meditations. In order to arrive at the palace at the appointed hour, he had to travel a considerable distance, and for this Chanut had the goodness to offer him the use of his carriage; but in freezing temperatures, in fact one of the most severe winters ever recorded, it was impossible to shield oneself completely against the cold. The queen at twenty-three had not only youth but incredibly good health. The early hour was no inconvenience to her. After dressing hastily, for it will be remembered she took virtually no pains with her toilette, she was ready to attack lessons with the same exuberance that characterized all her endeavors. What a strange contrast the philosopher and his pupil must have presented when they met in the queen's study.

In spite of her youth, Christina was not a novice in the realm of science and philosophy. From her vast reading she had acquired an encyclopedic knowledge that must have impressed her tutor. In fact, the extent of her knowledge was so varied that Descartes regarded it as a possible obstacle. It might impair some of the spontaneity required for her lessons with him. She was eager to learn anything new, and her agile mind flew from one subject to another with remarkable speed and seeming indifference. Although her studies up to this time had given her some insight into virtually every field of learning, she now needed a method of putting her knowledge into some sort of coherent system. Christina wanted Descartes to teach her moral philosophy. Her first questions, on the nature of the greatest good, remained the basis for all future inquiries. She hoped to learn from him an ethical code that would be as certain and as capable of demonstration as his writings on mathematics. But instead of furnishing his pupil with definitions of morality based upon his own method, he reverted to theology. He reaffirmed in religious terminology his own allegiance to orthodox Catholic doctrine.

Although Christina continued at this time to be instructed by the Lutheran clergy, many scholars are of the opinion that Chanut and Descartes were instrumental in initiating her to Catholicism and that they were indirectly responsible for her later conversion in 1652. The reasons for her adopting the Catholic faith are varied and complex and, if examined in detail, read like a romantic novel. There is no reason to believe, however, that in her relationship with Descartes he was trying to play the role of missionary. Her conversion is more properly attributed to psychological and historical reasons than to any deliberate effort on the part of Descartes, and her eventual abdication had nothing to do with her Catholicism. She did not accept Descartes' view that the universe was infinite, for she felt this to be in conflict with Christian doctrine. This was the first time she had met someone who taught that the new theories advanced by the natural sciences could agree with the teachings of the Church. According to him, any objections to his views came from theologians who were not sufficiently enlightened.

In all things Christina sought the practical side. She was not interested in research as an end in itself. She kept her own personal reality as the goal to be studied, explained, and hopefully mastered. In her *Reflections,* written toward the end of her life, she noted: "The greatest of all sciences is that of knowing how to live and to die well. All others are useless if they do not contribute to this end." [30] Descartes had chosen the contemplative life and usually preferred to be a spectator to the revolutions that were taking place about him. Christina, on the other hand, was a woman of action, possessed of a dominant will, in the process of forging history rather than watching it. Certainly the two discussed religious problems often, but Christina was more interested in his moral teaching, which tended to be humanistic rather than Christian.

It is impossible to reconstruct the exact nature of her lessons with Descartes, but the general intellectual climate of the time and certain historical events show that his teachings had at least an indirect effect upon her thinking and her own later actions. She was a highly complex personality, torn between conflicting duties and desires. Her ideal was to find some way to resolve the psychological struggle that was taking place within her and arrive at a means of governing her life so that she might be at peace in a world of contradiction. From the age of fifteen she had been thoroughly schooled in the doctrine of the Roman Stoics but found their theory of the passions unacceptable. In Descartes Christina found a new morality, for he explained the passions as natural phenomena, subject to the laws of mechanical necessity. They cannot, therefore, be suppressed, and absolute apathy, such as the Stoics recommended, was for him an impossible goal. Rather than try to obliterate our passions or escape from them, one should try to use and direct them according to one's reason. Descartes taught that the passions were neither good nor bad in themselves; they were simply necessary. It was only through the use that one made of them that they could be valued and judged.

Christina did not want to negate her passions. Her temperament was such that she could not have done so. In Descartes' theories she found a solution to her problem. She was not required to renounce her instincts, which were often at odds with her political and religious duties, but instead to aspire toward a self-mastery that would give her control over her passions. Thus she renounced the Stoic ideal for what might be termed a heroic one in her effort to find peace of mind and still enjoy the pleasures of her emotions. "The passions," she wrote, "are in themselves innocent and natural. They are the salt of life, which is insipid without them. That tranquillity so vaunted by philosophers is a dull and tasteless state. One is happy or unhappy only in proportion to the violence of one's passions." [31] Such thoughts are a faithful echo of Descartes' own explanation in his *Treatise on the Passions*, which she had read in manuscript form two years before his arrival in Stockholm.

Christina was so interested in her lessons that Descartes usually spent five hours with her every morning. The change in his routine and the bitter cold combined with the increased jealousy of the court after the success of his ballet to make him yearn more than ever to return to his Dutch retreat. The queen must have known this, for he was always extremely outspoken with her, and determined to keep him near her by promises of an estate and a handsome pension. Ironically, the property was to come from land recently acquired through the Peace of Westphalia, a monastery that the Lutheran queen had not hesitated to plunder after its secularization. How was Descartes, as a good Catholic, to accept such an offer? A rapid series of events made his refusal unnecessary.

On January 18, after returning from a walk with Descartes, Chanut fell ill. What first appeared merely as symptoms of a bad cold rapidly developed into pneumonia. Descartes, in addition to his early morning lessons, now attended his friend and helped Madame Chanut nurse him back to health. Apparently no demand, day or night, was too great while the ambassador's life was at stake. It was just at this time that Christina, heedless as she often was of the hardships of others, asked him to return to the palace in the afternoons so that they could discuss her plans for the academy. Chanut's malady lasted approximately ten days. Then, on February 1, after presenting his statutes for the academy to Christina, Descartes himself fell victim to the same disease from which his friend had just recovered. On that day, when he returned from the palace, he had seen Christina for the last time.

Descartes' symptoms, a high fever and inflammation of the lungs, were the same as those of Chanut, who was then convalescing. On February 2 he attended mass and received the sacrament but was too weak to remain on his feet the rest of the day.[32] He took to his bed, where his fever made him delirious. He refused to listen to the advice of friends and resisted any medical recommendations. The queen's doctor, Monsieur du Ryer, a defrocked priest turned physician who was also a friend of Descartes, was then away, and in his place she sent Dr. van Wullen, an avowed enemy of the patient. At first Descartes declined to see him or to be bled as was suggested. Christina sent messengers twice a day to inquire about his health. Many blamed her as being at least indirectly responsible, but she attributed his condition to the severity of the cold and to what everyone agreed was the worst winter in more than sixty years.

There were others who believed that he had been poisoned. Later there were rumors, ill-founded but numerous, that his rivals, especially the jealous grammarians, had done away with him. Equally erroneous but widespread was the theory that he had not had sufficient success with his royal pupil and that her disdain of his teachings had caused him so much chagrin that it hastened his end. From what is now known such hypotheses seem ludicrous. He was not the kind of man given to melancholy for lack of appreciation, and there is every reason to believe that his relationship with Christina was one of almost unqualified mutual admiration. The grammarians may have disliked Descartes' philosophy, but they wanted to rid their country of his ideas rather than his person. For that matter, poison was virtually nonexistent in the North as a method of disposing of one's enemies. There was even a more ridiculous supposition that his malady was caused from drinking too much brandy as a cure for gout, an ailment which he never had.

He finally consented to see Van Wullen but was obstinate in his refusal to be bled. "Gentlemen, spare French blood!" he shouted to the Dutch doctor and others who came to counsel him. Chanut was unable to convince his friend to take either medicine or food. Van Wullen's presence only aggravated him. "If I must die," he said, "I shall do so more peacefully if I don't see you." [33] He had his own ideas concerning what treatment was best for him and at first diagnosed his case as merely a severe attack of rheumatism. By the fourth day his mind was even more confused. Chanut, whose own health was still weak, made innumerable trips to his room trying to convince him to listen to the doctors' advice. The icy reception which Descartes had given Van Wullen soon made the others afraid to enter his room for fear of causing him even greater discomfort. Chanut and his wife, therefore, acted as mediators and kept the physicians informed as best they could of the patient's condition. By the fifth day his illness was considered incurable, and by the sixth, Van Wullen condemned him as lost.

During his delirium the Chanuts observed a curious thing. His rambling speech had nothing to do with mathematics or philosophy but rather was directed toward the greatness of God and the misery of man. Although he had lost the ability to reason logically about his own condition, he was still able to discourse quite coherently on the subject of piety.

Toward the end of the seventh day his fever left his head and spread to the rest of his body. He was once again in full possession of his intellect and able to realize the seriousness of his illness. He told the Chanuts that since it was God's will that had returned his reason, it must mean that he was to follow its dictates, which now told him that he should listen to the doctors. He allowed himself to be bled and an hour later requested a second bleeding. The treatment came too late, however, and did not diminish his fever. The inflammation in his lungs increased and caused him to cough and shudder. Convinced that the end was near and remedies useless, he returned to thoughts of death and religious reveries. "My soul," he said, "you have been a captive for a long time; now the hour has come when you must leave your prison, this body; you must bear this separation with joy and courage." [34] There was no need for those around him to warn or prepare him. He had already spent the night getting ready for what would be his final voyage.

The afternoon of the eighth day his breathing became heavy, and spasmodically he coughed phlegm which showed traces of blackish blood. Toward evening he asked that a mixture of wine flavored with tobacco be prepared to make him vomit. Dr. van Wullen, who knew that such a prescription would have been injurious in most cases, allowed the patient to have his way, for by this time he had abandoned all hope of his recovering. During the night Descartes continued to talk to Chanut about religion and his resolution to die in order to obey God's will. He was waiting for his confessor to arrive so that he might again receive the sacrament. He seemed at peace and said that he was suffering no pain. Around midnight his vision became blurred, his breathing was barely audible, and he seemed to lose consciousness.

The next morning, the ninth day of his illness, he asked his faithful valet Schluter to prepare some biscuits for him. He realized, even in his weakened condition, that for the good of his system he had to take something other than liquid nourishment. After eating, he felt and looked so much better that the Chanuts thought there might still be some hope. During the rest of the day, even he felt that his death sentence had been postponed and that he could live on for a considerable time. That evening, alone in his room with Schluter while the others were at dinner, he expressed the desire to sit by the fire, and his valet helped him to an armchair. Once there, however, he had a fainting spell, and when his senses returned a few moments later, his looks had changed completely. "Oh, my dear Schluter," he said, "this is the fatal stroke. I must leave now." [35] The valet, frightened by these words, immediately helped his master back to bed and sent for Chanut and the priest.

The ambassador and his family entered the dying man's room with Père Viogué, who had heard Descartes' confession on the first day of his sickness. The priest, perceiving that he was unable to speak, asked him to make some sign if he could still hear him and if he wanted to receive the final blessing. Descartes turned his eyes to heaven in such a moving way that those present saw therein a complete resignation to the will of God. Père Viogué pronounced the usual exhortations, and Chanut, reading the language of his friend's eyes, said that he was leaving this world satisfied with his fellowman, full of confidence in God's mercy, and eager to discover a truth for which he had been searching all his life. After the benediction, everyone knelt in prayer, and it was then, at four o'clock in the morning of February 11, 1650, that René Descartes died in a state of utmost tranquillity. He had lived for fifty-three years, ten months, and eleven days. "Our lives," he had told Chanut, "should be measured not by their length but by their virtue, and I should have lived a useless one if I had not at some moment learned how to die." [36]

Epilogue

Of all those who knew Descartes, no one was more sadly affected by his death than Chanut. The task of informing relatives and friends of the great man's passing fell to him, as did the making of an inventory and arranging for the funeral. Still not completely recovered from his own illness, Chanut first sent word to the queen, who then appeared deeply moved at the news of the premature death of her illustrious tutor. Later she was to remark that his oracles had misled him, referring to Descartes' experiments in later years to prolong human life. Even more sarcastic was the account given by the *Anvers Gazette* which printed: "In Sweden a fool has just died who used to say that he could live as long as he wanted." [1] However momentary her grief, Christina wanted to honor his memory by erecting a magnificent tomb in Stockholm's largest church where Swedish royalty was buried. She also offered to pay the expenses for an elaborate funeral procession.

Chanut objected that such ceremonies were not in keeping with either the dead man's simplicity or dignity. Many arguments followed about a suitable place for his remains. There was no Catholic cemetery in the city; and if he were buried according to Christina's wishes, the Lutherans, who had always been antagonistic toward him, might well have claimed that he had been converted to the Protestant Church. As it turned out, they could point with pleasure to his final resting place, for he was interred in nonconsecrated ground, like an atheist as far as they were concerned. Actually, Chanut, preferring unholy ground to that blessed by Lutherans, had chosen a cemetery ordinarily reserved for children who died before baptism.

The funeral took place on February 13. It was conducted without pomp, almost in secret, and was attended only by Roman Catholics. Special permission had been obtained from the queen for a single priest to deliver the final prayers according to Catholic ritual, and Chanut's elder son, who had taken such pleasure in the philosophical and religious discussions held with his mother and Descartes, was one of the pallbearers. The younger son, then only twelve years old, was judged not strong enough for such a burden. The expenses were paid from the estate of the deceased, and the tomb, like the ceremony, was of the utmost simplicity. For the four sides of the monument, which was of stone rather than the marble proposed by Christina, Chanut wrote lengthy Latin inscriptions to summarize his friend's life and work. Eulogistic verses were soon composed by other admirers, and a few months later a commemorative medal, carrying the philosopher's portrait and words of elaborate praise, appeared in Holland.

The day after the funeral an inventory was taken of the deceased's effects. Chanut saw to it that the faithful Schluter was rewarded, and Descartes himself, a few hours before he died, had dictated a letter to his brothers in Brittany asking them to look after his childhood nurse, whom he had cared for throughout his life. Strange that she, like the little cross-eyed girl he remembered from his youth, should be mentioned only once in his entire correspondence. Descartes' papers were given by his heirs to Chanut, who in turn entrusted them to Clerselier for publication. Among them, however, were the letters from the Princess Elizabeth which Chanut withheld from the inventory. When he wrote to inform her of the philosopher's death, he explained that he had set her letters aside:

I do not doubt, madame, that it would be advantageous to your reputation if one knew that you had serious and learned correspondence with the most talented man in many centuries; and I knew from Monsieur Descartes himself that your letters were so full of knowledge and intelligence that it could only be to your glory if they were seen. And yet I thought that out of respect toward your Royal Highness and faithfulness toward my dead friend I should not read them or permit them to fall into the hands of anyone without your permission. . . .[2]

Since Descartes had failed to make any mention of Elizabeth on his deathbed, Chanut attempted to compensate for this omission by becoming the spokesman for the deceased and ended his next letter in terms of flowery respect and admiration:

I believe, madame, that if he had known on the preceding day that he was so close to his end, still having the power of speech, he would have told me of his last wishes, particularly to make it known to your Royal Highness that he would die with the same respect for you that he had during life, a respect which he often told me about in words full of reverence and admiration.[3]

Elizabeth undoubtedly felt the loss even more deeply than Christina; yet she stubbornly refused to permit her letters to be published with those of Descartes. Chanut was particularly anxious to have the ones that pertained to the greatest good, which were necessary for a complete understanding of what Descartes had written on the subject. Perhaps the ambassador pressed his point too far by assuring her that even a copy would suffice and that it would be useful if not to the public at least to the Queen of Sweden. Despite his arguments and entreaties, Chanut was not compelled to return Elizabeth's letters which remained unpublished for more than 200 years.[4]

Descartes' other papers were entrusted to Clerselier. The inventory was made an easy task, for at the queen's request Descartes had put all of his unpublished works into order shortly before his death. His efforts were almost completely nullified, however, when in 1653 his papers were sent to France. The ship which was carrying them sank on the outskirts of Paris, and the box containing his manuscripts lay in the waters of the Seine for three days. When the papers were finally recovered, they were hung up to dry by servants. The resulting confusion made Clerselier's task of rearranging them an extremely arduous one.

The philosopher's own physical remains suffered somewhat the same series of misadventures as his writings only with more macabre overtones. Although he had doggedly asserted his orthodoxy to the end and those who described his passing emphasized his piety, the Church placed his writings on the Index in 1663. This did not detract from his growing popularity, however. If anything, his writings took on some of the allure of forbidden fruit and became increasingly *à la mode* as a topic of conversation in Parisian salons. The controversy which his writings had stirred up during his life became even more vehement in the years following his death, and the battle between his admirers and his adversaries became embittered. The pedagogues joined the ecclesiastics in proclaiming his system heretical. Even the Sorbonne became alarmed at the rapid spread of a doctrine which they considered revolutionary and therefore condemned his system in 1685. His followers both in Holland and France were no less ardent. As his works became increasingly popular, his countrymen began to clamor for the return of his body.

What followed was indeed a "burlesque necrology." [5] After innumerable difficulties the Swedish government finally gave its consent in 1666 to have his remains shipped back to France under the surveillance of the Chevalier de Terlon, who had ordered a brass coffin only two and a half feet long. He imagined that the skeleton of the dead man would not be intact and that one could place the bones on top of one another without any impropriety. As it turned out, the skull was kept in Sweden until 1822, and the casket, opened many times, was robbed by converts to Descartes' philosophy seeking souvenirs with much the same fervor as religious fanatics stealing sacred relics. For the voyage from Stockholm to Copenhagen the chevalier was forced to have the casket sealed and marked with his coat of arms, not only to insure the safety of its contents, but to assuage the superstitious seamen who thought that transporting the dead was an evil omen. After three months in Copenhagen, Terlon decided it would be more prudent to transport the body by land and thus avoid possible dangers at sea, particularly piracy by the English, who, it was felt, would be sure to erect a magnificent mausoleum in their country, so great was their admiration for the philosopher. The cortege proceeded slowly and uneventfully to France where, ironically, it was stopped in Descartes' own native province by custom officials who suspected the bearers of smuggling contraband. Once again the casket was opened, and it is not surprising that when the remains finally reached Paris in January, 1667, the chevalier ended by demanding that there be added to the inscription on the tomb the words "This transferral was accomplished under Louis XIV by the Chevalier de Terlon, His Ambassador." [6]

Even after the arrival of his remains in Paris, Descartes was denied the quiet resting place he had sought in life. While waiting for the arrangements to be made for this second burial, the body remained for six months in a chapel of the Église de Saint Paul. It was finally decided that the most suitable place would be the Église de Sainte-Geneviève-du-Mont, where elaborate ceremonies were finally held on June 24, 1667, but not without some strong opposition on the part of the clerics, who demanded endless testimonies as to the catholicism of the dead man's thinking and the piety of his actions. This, however, was not to be his final resting place. During the French Revolution the church was closed, and in 1793 it was decreed that the body should be transferred to the Pantheon, an honor which he never received. His remains were placed in the garden of the Musée des Monuments Français until 1819 when they were taken to Saint Germain des Prés. Today a small commemorative stone in the south wall can still be seen as his final tribute, and above the engraved marble is a bust not of Descartes but of Jean Mabillon, the Benedictine historian, whose body along with that of the scholar Bernard de Montfaucon flanks that of France's most illustrious philosopher. His skull, if it really is his skull, was placed upon its return from Sweden in the Musée de l'Homme, where the curious can view it in a glass case along with those of the Duc de Saint-Simon, the author of historical memoirs, on one side and on the other, the notorious bandit Cartouche.

Descartes' final years have been compared to the fable of the poor musician whose song could make whoever listened to it happy. People were too busy with their own affairs, however, to listen to his song attentively, and the musician became disillusioned. Finally from afar the snow queen summoned him, and having heard that she loved music more than anything else, he went and played his beautiful song. But his fingers became colder and colder, and when the music stopped, the queen looked up to see the musician stretched out, pale and motionless, frozen to death.[7]

On those whom he left behind, Descartes' passing had little lasting effect. They were too busy with their own affairs. Chanut left Sweden to become ambassador to Holland in 1653 and then returned to France, where he relinquished his post as treasurer to his son. He died in 1662. Elizabeth's situation went from bad to worse. Any hope of assistance from the Swedish court vanished on the death of her friend. She accepted the post of abbess at Herford, a Lutheran monastary in Westphalia. Religious leaders George Fox and William Penn found refuge at her retreat, which was open to all regardless of sex or religion. Her great physical suffering gradually increased and had its effect upon her intelligence. She continued to receive her friends but often without recognizing them, and she sometimes listened without answering. In 1680, the woman who had inspired the *Treatise on the Passions* and had contributed such memorable pages to Descartes' correspondence died at the age of sixty-two, as her sister Sophie said, "like a candle guttering out." [8]

And what of Christina? Hers was certainly the most eventful career of those who had been close to Descartes during his later years. Four years after his passing she abdicated and left Sweden for Holland. After her conversion to Catholicism and when the French clerics were demanding proof of Descartes' orthodoxy before granting his remains an official burial, Christina sent her written testimony that it was he and Chanut who had been God's instruments for her enlightenment. Her words arrived too late, however, to be of any use. Her main regret was that Stockholm had been robbed of its "treasure," and she declared that had she still been queen, she would never have allowed the removal of his body. She scandalized the French court by her treatment of Monaldeschi, for which Horace Walpole called her the "heroic murderess." After a short time in Paris, she spent most of the rest of her life in Rome, where she died in 1689, considered alternately sinner and saint.

Like the poet Racine, Descartes has no statue in the French capital. His style lacks the dramatic and poetic achievements of the great seventeenth-century playwrights; yet his music (for his writings can be compared to compositions ranging from occasional songs to operas), even if it did not affect the snow queen, resounded throughout the world and still appeals to modern ears. Truth had always been the final goal of all his studies, just as virtue had been the ruling principle of his actions. The search for one and the practice of the other had brought him at least inner peace and happiness. Clerselier was thus able to remark that Descartes often viewed the events of this world with the eyes of one watching a theatrical performance. Although he participated as a man of action, he remained fairly dispassionate. He tried always to perform what he considered to be his duty as best he could by practicing good and refusing to allow outward events, so often tempered by the vanity or jealousy of others, to affect his inner tranquillity.[9]

From his earliest writings and throughout the rest of his work Descartes gives the impression of an original thinker. It was in order to free himself from the prejudices of the past that he constructed his method. Many modern scholars have demonstrated his debt to previous theologians and philosophers, notably Saint Augustine, Saint Thomas Aquinas, and Aristotle.[10] Descartes may not have freed himself entirely from the influence of his predecessors, but this does not negate the originality of his application of the ideas already expressed by others. He transformed the thought of previous ages and gave it a new direction, a new interpretation, a new and more practical application and significance. In almost every realm of thought Descartes can be considered a pioneer, one who at times took current ideas but elaborated them to different conclusions. Not only did he free himself and his age from many misconceptions and erroneous explanations of natural phenomena, but he also foreshadowed the development of modern scientific and philosophic thought, so that he can in turn be heralded as the forerunner of Darwin's theory of evolution and even Einstein's theory of relativity. All three worked in the same spirit of geometrization, seeking invariant laws of nature. Descartes' research in cosmology and genetics produced an evolutionary though mechanistic view of the physical world that links him with Darwin. And Einstein's theory of relativity can be traced back to Descartes' description of shape, rest, and motion and his formulation of the theory of inertia.

Descartes' writings touch upon virtually every branch of the sciences with the exception of chemistry, which was then in its infancy. He made important contributions to mathematics, physics, astronomy, mechanics, geography, botany, anatomy, zoology, psychology, and even medicine. Although he wrote on the subject of music and composed verses for a ballet, his contribution to the fine arts is relatively small; yet much of his correspondence could be read and appreciated for its purely literary merit. Equal in importance to his scientific discoveries are his philosophical works, especially those concerned with metaphysics and ethics. It was his consuming desire to understand clearly both his thoughts and his actions that made a philosopher of Descartes; it was his desire to benefit mankind that made him an author. Thought was not sufficient in itself but needed to be transformed into action: "Every man is obliged to procure, as far as possible, the good of others, for one is worth nothing unless one is useful to someone else." [11] He was, therefore, not only a savant in the realm of science and technology but also a philosopher whose meditations had both a practical and a humanitarian goal.

In the history of science the twentieth century is indebted to him for his innovations in mathematics, particularly algebra. He was the first to introduce exponents and thereby laid the groundwork for calculating with powers. He advanced the treatment of negative quantities and stressed the equal importance of negative roots. He established as a means for limiting their number the theorem which still bears his name. He gave a new and ingenious solution for equations of the fourth degree. By this application of algebra to geometry, the algebraic treatment of curves, he is the forerunner of the greatest discovery in modern mathematics, that of differential calculus, by Newton and Leibniz. He showed how to draw tangents and normals at every point of a geometrical curve and how to express properties of curves by an equation between two variable coordinates, thus originating analytical geometry.

As a physicist Descartes' experiments in optics led to the discovery of the law of refraction, which he was the first to state in its present trigonometrical form. His research with lenses causing light rays to converge to a point resulted in the classification of curves now known as Cartesian ovals. His general method in physics, because of its *a priori* character, has been severely censured, but if he ignored the necessity of prolonged experiment and observation for the formulation of leading principles, he had a far greater appreciation than Bacon of the role mathematics was to play in deductions from these principles. His doctrine of space, although diametrically opposed to the Kantian, may well have helped because of its very clarity to prepare the way for later theories.[12] Among his other scientific contributions, he was the first to give a complete description of the causes of a rainbow.

It is not primarily as a scientist, however, that Descartes continues to dominate modern thought. Many of his contemporaries surpassed him: Galileo's theories are considered more advanced, Fermat's geometry more exact, and Harvey's explanation of the circulation of the blood more acceptable. What Descartes could not foresee was that, by the time physics, chemistry, and biology had been defined as distinct sciences, the impossibility of reducing them to a single law would be far more evident than it was in his own time. And yet as a philosopher, he had no equal in the seventeenth century, and his influence upon the centuries to follow ranks with that of Plato and Aristotle, Bacon and Newton. Even those philosophers who disagreed with his theories acknowledged their debt to his method. Thus, in the eighteenth century, Montesquieu observed: "Descartes taught those who came after him how to discover his own errors," and Voltaire expressed much the same thought when he wrote that Descartes was admirable even in his mistakes: "He was wrong, but at least it was with method. The men of his time learned from him how to use his weapons against him. If he did not pay off in acceptable currency, he nonetheless decried the counterfeit." [13]

The Encyclopedists, while not sharing his explanation of man and the universe, were enthusiastic about his accomplishments, for they saw in him a precursor of their own revolutionary doctrines. The image that French mathematician Jean Le Rond d'Alembert and his friends constructed of Descartes misinterprets his intentions but reflects to what extent reason, under the guise of Cartesianism, had become virtually the unique criterion, the rallying point, for the abolition of the *ancien régime:* "One can consider [Descartes] as the leader of a band of conspirators who first had the courage to rise up against a despotic and arbitrary power and who, by preparing a glorious revolution, laid the foundations for a more just and happier government which he was not able to see fulfilled." [14] Even Rousseau, the champion of feeling, for whom one would think the philosophy of clear ideas would hold little appeal, conserves something of the Cartesian spirit: "I was then in that state of uncertainty and doubt which Descartes requires." And farther on he writes: "My rule of abandoning myself to feeling rather than to reason is confirmed by reason itself." [15]

Each succeeding century seems to have found its own image in Descartes and interpreted his doctrines according to its own needs. Whereas it was his scientific writings that most appealed to the seventeenth century and his method that impressed the eighteenth, the nineteenth took particular interest in his metaphysics. The romantics were pleased by his psychological observations, by his separation of the material from the spiritual, the external from the internal, and his insistence upon the knowledge of the self. The philosopher Auguste Comte found in him a positivist, and Karl Marx claimed him as a forefather of dialectical materialism.

In the twentieth century scholarly research in Cartesian studies has multiplied to such an extent that it now offers a many-sided perspective that continues to enrich our understanding and appreciation of his work while it provokes still further reflection. Descartes' faith in human reason gave him a non-Christian, in fact nonreligious conception of man. His belief in human dignity and the possibility of progress and happiness gave a unity to his philosophy. There was for him no place for the contradictions and conflicts which so troubled the religious thinking of Pascal or Kierkegaard. In essence his view of the human condition is diametrically opposed to modern existentialism, and yet its most illustrious contemporary exponent, Jean-Paul Sartre, can quote Descartes with impunity. He too finds in Descartes that which is in accord with his own philosophy; namely, his emphasis upon freedom:

> We shall not reproach Descartes for having given to God what properly belongs to us; instead, we shall admire him for having established the basis for democracy in an authoritarian age and for having followed to their logical conclusion the exigencies of the idea of autonomy, and for having understood . . . that the unique basis for existence was freedom.

And again, Sartre unites his own conception of liberty with that of Descartes: "After the Stoics, Descartes made a capital distinction between freedom and power. Freedom is not being able to do what one wants, but wanting what one can do." [16]

When asked what remains of Descartes' work in the twentieth century, one modern critic replied: "Everything or nothing, as you like. Nothing of his work. Everything of the Cartesian spirit." [17] Of all his writings virtually none are read today except by specialists and scholars aside from an occasional student who skims the *Discourse on Method* in order to write a term paper. The Cartesian spirit, however, is everywhere and so ingrained in our way of thinking that we are oblivious to it. The plaque in the Bibliothèque Nationale which states about Voltaire, "Here lies his heart but his spirit is everywhere," is even more applicable to Descartes. We know not where his heart is, but his spirit is that of every thinking man. Its timelessness remains completely independent of his philosophy. His greatness, in fact, lies not in his having established certain well-defined truths but rather, as Charles Péguy observed,[18] in his having introduced a spirit of restlessness and anxiety, a spirit essentially radical and fearless in its questioning of all established principles and in its submission of everything to the test of human reason. Every age, it can be said, is in a state of revolt against the past. What Descartes sought was not so much a complete break with his heritage as a reevaluation by means of his method that would bring tradition into a more modern perspective and make it practical for the temperament of his time. Today man continues to question his values in the light of reason. Whenever contemporary philosophy falls into a state of pessimism or dogmatism, then the fundamental principles and method of Descartes are again invoked in order to restore faith in the human condition and in the possibility of man's being able to govern, at least to a limited degree, his own destiny.

Notes

Chapter 1

1. *Cf.* Adam, *Vie de Descartes,* in *Oeuvres,* XII:3.

2. "Car, étant né d'une mère qui mourut, peu de jours après ma naissance, d'un mal de poumon, causé par quelque déplaisirs. . . ." Lettre à Elisabeth, 1645, *Correspondance,* IV:220–221. Many biographers have erroneously accepted Descartes' word for the date of his mother's death, and Adam and Milhaud are among the few to cite the birth of her last child as its cause. See *Corr.,* I:430–431. Descartes does make another reference to his mother, but only to list her name as "J. Brochard, ma mère," in a letter concerning his inheritance. Lettre à son frère aîné, 3 avril 1622, *ibid.,* p. 24.

3. "Celui-là n'était bon qu'à se faire relier en veau." Sacy, *Descartes par lui-même,* p. 104.

4. "J'ai plus de soin et crois qu'il est plus important que j'apprenne ce qui m'est nécessaire pour la conduite de ma vie, que non pas que je m'amuse à publier le peu que j'ai appris." Lettre à Mersenne, 15 avril 1630, *Corr.,* I:130.

5. "Je ne suis pas de ceux qui estiment que les larmes et la tristesse n'appartiennent qu'aux femmes, et que, pour paraître homme de coeur, on se doive contraindre à montrer toujours un visage tranquille. J'ai senti depuis peu la perte de deux personnes qui m'étaient très proches. . . ." Lettre à Pollot, mi-janvier 1641, *Corr.,* IV:247.

6. "Aussi serait-ce être trop lâche de s'abandonner entièrement au déplaisir; et ce serait faire fort mal son compte, que de ne tâcher pas, de tout son pouvoir, à se délivrer d'une passion si incommode. La profession des armes, en laquelle vous êtes nourri, accoutume les hommes à voir mourir inopinément leurs meilleurs amis; et il n'y a rien au monde de si fâcheux, que l'accoutumance ne le rende supportable." *Ibid.*

7. ". . . pays des ours, entre des rochers et des glaces." Lettre à Brasset, 23 avril 1649, *Corr.,* VIII:218.

8. ". . . lorsque j'étais enfant, j'aimais une fille de mon âge, qui était un peu louche; au moyen de quoi, l'impression qui se faisait par la vue

en mon cerveau, quand je regardais ses yeux égarés, se joignait tellement à celle qui s'y faisait aussi pour émouvoir en moi la passion de l'amour, que longtemps après, en voyant des personnes louches, je me sentais plus enclin à les aimer qu'à en aimer d'autres, pour cela seul qu'elles avaient de défaut; et je ne savais pas néanmoins que ce fût pour cela." Lettre à Chanut, 6 juin 1647, *Corr.*, VII:345.

9. The quotation comes from Ovid, Tristia, III:25. Consult Lettre à Mersenne, avril 1634, *Corr.*, I:253, and Sacy, *Descartes par lui-même*, p. 37.

10. These conditions are quoted in their entirety by Rochemonteix, *Un Collège de Jésuites*, pp. 52–57.

11. "Parce que Sa Majesté désire remédier . . . aux abus qui se commettent en son royaume, le plus qu'elle pourra, ayant recogneu que le désordre s'est aussy bien glissé parmi les lettres que aultres arts, les docteurs recoyvant indifféramant aux degrés de *licenciés, bacheliers* et *docteurs* tous ceux qui se présentent pourvu qu'ils ayent de l'argent, Sa Majesté ordonne qu'il y aura au collège huit docteurs, à chacun desquels sera payé par ledit collège cinq cents escus par an, quatre qui seront en médecine et quatre en jurisprudence, lesquels ayant recogneu les escoliers et aultres qui se présenteront devant eux, capables desdits degrés, les passeront sans prendre aulcune chose d'eulx; et afin qu'il ne s'y puisse commettre aulcune fraude, ne pourront lesdits docteurs admettre personne à nul desdits degrés, qu'il n'ai subi examen public, auquel assisteront quatre des Pères, qui signeront avec les docteurs les lettres de degrés que l'escolier aura pris." *Ibid.*, p. 56.

12. Baillet gives 1604 as the date of Descartes' entry at La Flèche. More recent works tend to favor 1606 as more probable. *Cf.* Gouhier, *Les Premières Pensées de Descartes*, pp. 158–159.

13. There were 500 *gentilshommes* the following year (1607). The increase was probably the result of Henry IV's high recommendation to his nobles. *Cf.* Haldane, *Descartes*, p. 13.

14. Details concerning the occult are taken from Gadoffre's edition of the *Discours*, pp. 77, 116.

15. The author was Henri-Corneille Agrippa. The incident is related by Louis Batifol, "Un Magicien brûlé vif." *Revue de Paris* (15 mars 1902), pp. 369–393.

16. ". . . que la lecture des bons livres est comme une conversation avec les plus honnêtes gens des siècles passés, qui en ont été les auteurs, et même une conversation étudiée en laquelle ils ne nous découvrent que les meilleures de leurs pensées." *Discours, Oeuvres*, VI:5.

17. *Opuscules de 1619–1621, Oeuvres*, X:183.

18. Lettre à Chanut, 1 novembre 1646, *Corr.*, VII:199.

19. Details of the ceremony and bibliographical references are given by Rochemonteix, *Un Collège de Jésuites*, pp. 138–143.

20. Dimier *La Vie raisonnable de Descartes*, p. 6.

21. The details of the *Henriade* of 1611 come from an eyewitness account by Jacob Rezé, *Lacrymae Collegii Flexiensis regii Societatis Jesu*. See Rochemonteix, *Un Collège de Jésuites*, pp. 144 *et seq*.

22. "Sur la mort du Roy Henry le Grand et sur la descouverte de quelques nouvelles planettes ou estoiles errantes autour de Jupiter, faicte l'année d'icelle par Galilée, célèbre mathématicien du grand-duc de Florence." *Ibid.*, pp. 147–148.

23. *Ibid.*

24. "Au reste, n'espérez pas, avec toutes ces machines, de faire des merveilles du premier coup; je vous en avertis, afin que vous ne vous fondiez pas sur de fausses espérances, et que vous ne vous engagiez point à travailler que vous ne soyez résolu d'y employer beaucoup de temps; mais si vous aviez un an ou deux à vous ajuster de tout ce qui est nécessaire, j'oserais espérer que nous verrions, par votre moyen, s'il y a des animaux dans la Lune." Lettre à Ferrier, 13 novembre 1629, *Corr.*, I:82.

25. "J'ai été nourri aux lettres dès mon enfance, et, pour ce qu'on me persuadait que par leur moyen on pouvait acquérir une connaissance claire et assurée de tout ce qui est utile à la vie, j'avais un extrême désir de les apprendre." *Discours, Oeuvres* VI:4.

26. "Car je me trouvais embarrassé de tant de doutes et d'erreurs, qu'il me semblait n'avoir fait autre profit, en tâchant de m'instruire, sinon que j'avais découvert de plus en plus mon ignorance." *Ibid.*, p. 4.

27. "Car je ne me sentais point, grâces à Dieu, de condition qui m'obligeât à faire un métier de la science pour le soulagement de ma fortune." *Ibid.*, p. 9.

28. "Et je dois rendre cet honneur à mes maîtres, que de dire qu'il n'y a lieu au monde où je juge qu'elle s'enseigne mieux qu'à la Flèche." Lettre à Debeaune, 12 septembre 1638, *Corr.*, III:75.

29. ". . . pourvu seulement qu'on s'abstienne d'en recevoir aucune pour vraie qui ne le soit, et qu'on garde toujours l'ordre qu'il faut pour les déduire les unes des autres, il n'y en peut avoir de si éloignées auxquelles enfin on ne parvienne, ni de si cachées qu'on ne découvre." *Discours, Oeuvres*, VI:19.

Chapter 2

1. Charles Adam prefers 1622 for the date of their meeting and is skeptical about most of Baillet's information concerning this first Paris visit. See *Oeuvres*, XII:36–39.

2. The amount of time Descartes spent in the army varies. Some accounts say three years, while others limit it to less than two.

3. Charles Adam has reproduced large extracts from the journal in the *Oeuvres*, X:17 *et seq.*

4. "Pourquoi le sabot ou toupie des enfants reste debout en tournant . . . René, le Poitevin, me fit songer qu'un homme pouvait se maintenir dans les airs." Cohen, *Ecrivains français en Hollande*, p. 377.

5. ". . . à cette condition toutefois qu'éternellement caché dans l'ombre de vos coffres ou de votre cabinet, il n'ait pas à affronter le jugement des hommes. Ceux-ci ne détourneraient pas les yeux, comme je m'assure que vous le ferez, de ses imperfections, pour les fixer sur les pages où je ne nie pas que soient tracés, pris sur le vif, quelques linéaments de mon esprit. Ils ne sauraient pas surtout que tout ceci a été composé à la hâte, pour vous seul, parmi l'ignorance des soldats, par un homme oisif, soumis à un genre de vie entièrement différent de ses pensées." *Oeuvres*, X:140–141.

6. "À vrai dire, en effet, vous seul m'avez retiré de mon désoeuvrement et fait ressouvenir de ce que j'avais appris et qui m'était maintenant presque échappé de la mémoire; quand mon esprit s'égarait si loin des occupations sérieuses, vous l'avez ramené dans la bonne voie. Si donc il sort de ma tête quelque chose qui ne soit peut-être pas à mépriser, vous aurez le droit de le réclamer entièrement pour vous." 23 avril 1619, *Corr.*, I:14.

7. "Lorsque vous vous vantez de pareille chose devant des personnes qui me connaissent, cela nuit beaucoup à votre réputation. . . . Et vous avez beau montrer des lettres de moi qui en témoignent, on sait bien que j'ai coutume de m'instruire même avec des fourmis et des vermisseaux, et on pensera que c'est de cette façon que je me serai instruit avec vous." Septembre ou octobre 1630, *ibid.*, p. 145.

8. "J'ai reçu votre lettre; je l'attendais, et j'ai eu le plaisir d'y reconnaître, au premier coup d'oeil, des notes de musique; vous ne pourriez faire voir plus clairement que vous ne m'oubliez pas. Mais j'attendais autre chose encore, et c'est le plus important: Dites-moi ce que vous avez fait? Ce que vous faites? Et comment allez-vous? Car je ne m'intéresse pas seulement à vos études, mais aussi à vous-même, croyez-moi, et non pas à votre esprit seulement, bien que ce soit le principal, mais à toute votre personne." 24 janvier 1619, *ibid.*, p. 1.

9. Cohen, *Ecrivains français en Hollande*, p. 382.

10. Descartes is referring to the Scholastic philosopher Raymond Lully's *Ars brevis quae est imago artis generalis* or his *Ars brevis ad absolvendam omnium artium* (1481). See *Corr.*, I:453–454.

11. "Et certes, pour ne vous rien cacher de ce qui fait l'objet de mon travail, je voudrais donner au public, non pas un *Ars brevis* comme

Lulle, mais une science toute nouvelle, qui permette de résoudre en général toutes les questions qu'on peut se proposer en n'importe quel genre de quantité, continue ou discontinue, chacune suivant sa nature." 26 mars 1619, *ibid.*, p. 7.

12. Virgil, *Aeneid*, III:7.

13. "Je n'ai pas voulu partir d'ici, sans vous renouveler une fois encore par écrit l'assurance d'une amitié qui doit durer entre nous. N'attendez plus rien cependant de ma Muse: je fais mes préparatifs pour me mettre en route demain, et mon esprit est déjà parti en voyage. Je suis encore dans l'incertitude: 'Où le destin va-t-il m'emporter? Où me sera-t-il donné de faire halte?' Car les bruits de guerre ne sont pas encore assez sûrs pour que je me rende en Allemagne, et je soupçonne qu'il y aura des rassemblements de troupes, mais point de bataille." 23 avril 1619, *Corr.*, I:13.

14. Henri Gouhier disagrees with both Baillet's and Adam's account of the relationship between Descartes and Faulhaber. See *Les Premières Pensées de Descartes*, pp. 129 *et seq.*

15. "Ces longues chaînes de raisons, toutes simples et faciles, dont les géomètres ont coutume de se servir pour parvenir à leurs plus difficiles démonstrations, m'avaient donné occasion de m'imaginer que toutes les choses qui peuvent tomber sous la connaissance des hommes s'entresuivent en même façon, et que, pourvu seulement qu'on s'abstienne d'en recevoir aucune pour vraie qui ne le soit, et qu'on garde toujours l'ordre qu'il faut pour les déduire les unes des autres, il n'y en peut avoir de si éloignées auxquelles enfin on ne parvienne, ni de si cachées qu'on ne découvre." *Discours, Oeuvres*, VI:19.

16. The following summary of the dreams is taken largely from Baillet's *Vie*, II:81–86.

17. Here ends the account as it is given in Baillet's *Vie*, II:81–86.

18. *Cf. Corr.*, I:7.

19. Chevalier, *Descartes*, p. 46.

20. Georges Poulet discusses the symbolism of the melon in his *Études sur le temps humain*, pp. 31–32.

21. Two such interpretations are found in Galston's "Descartes and Modern Psychiatric Thought," pp. 118–128, and in Schönberger's "A Dream of Descartes: Reflections on the Unconscious Determinants of the Sciences," pp. 43–57.

22. Freud's letter is given in full in Maxime Leroy's *Descartes, le philosophe au masque*, pp. 89–90.

23. Poulet, *Études sur le temps humain*, p. 38.

24. *Ibid.*, p. 40.

25. *Ibid.*, p. 47.

26. *Ibid.*, pp. 46–47.

27. Maritain, *The Dream of Descartes*, p. 23.

28. *Oeuvres*, X:213. Henri Gouhier gives an interesting account of the various French interpretations of the Latin original in *Les Premières Pensées de Descartes*, pp. 67–68.

29. There is some confusion over this date, which is more often given as November 11, 1620. Compare *Oeuvres*, X:175 to XII:61, and also Gouhier, *Les Premières de Descartes*, pp. 74–75.

Chapter 3

1. "Je ne fis autre chose que rouler ça et là dans le monde. . . . Je déracinais cependant de mon esprit toutes les erreurs qui s'y étaient pu glisser." *Discours, Oeuvres,* VI:28–29.

2. "Toutefois, ces neuf ans s'écoulèrent avant que j'eusse encore pris aucun parti, touchant les difficultés qui ont coutume d'être disputées entre les doctes, ni commencé à chercher les fondements d'aucune philosophie plus certaine que la vulgaire." *Ibid.,* p. 30.

3. *Cf. Oeuvres,* XII:337, and Cohen, *Ecrivains français en Hollande,* p. 415.

4. *Cf.* Cohen, *Écrivains français en Hollande,* p. 414.

5. Baillet, *Vie,* II:501.

6. *Ibid.,* p. 460.

7. *Ibid.,* p. 131.

8. *Cf. Oeuvres,* XII:85–86.

9. "Ce fut là que je fis confesser à toute la troupe ce que l'art de bien raisonner peut sur l'esprit de ceux qui sont médiocrement savants, et combien mes principes sont mieux établis, plus véritables et plus naturels qu'aucun des autres qui sont déjà reçus parmi les gens d'étude." Lettre à Villebressieu, eté de 1631 (?), *Corr.,* I:198.

10. Most of this account of the meeting with Chandoux comes from Baillet's *Vie,* II:160–166. There is a conflict, however, between the date given by Baillet and that given by Cohen for Descartes' departure for Holland. If Cohen is correct, Descartes visited Beeckman again on October 8, 1628. The meeting with Chandoux took place in November, 1628, and Cohen makes no reference to it.

11. For this suggestion I am indebted to Gilbert Gadoffre, professor of French at the University of Manchester. Although it remains in the realm of supposition, no one, to my knowledge, has suggested this in print.

12. "Je dors ici dix heures toutes les nuits et sans que jamais aucun soin me réveille; après que le sommeil a longtemps promené mon esprit dans des bois, des jardins et des palais enchantés, où j'éprouve tous les

plaisirs qui sont imaginés dans les Fables, je mêle insensiblement mes rêveries du jour avec celles de la nuit." 15 avril 1631, *Corr.*, I:186.

13. "Au lieu qu'en cette grand ville où je suis, n'y ayant aucun homme, excepté moi, qui n'exerce la marchandise, chacun y est tellement attentif à son profit, que j'y pourrais demeurer toute ma vie sans être jamais vu de personne. Je vais me promener tous les jours parmi la confusion d'un grand peuple, avec autant de liberté et de repos que vous sauriez faire dans vos allées, et je n'y considère pas autrement les hommes que j'y vois, que je ferais les arbres qui se rencontrent en vos forêts, ou les animaux qui y passent. Le bruit même de leur tracas n'interrompt pas plus mes rêveries que celui de quelque ruisseau. . . . Quel autre lieu pourrait-on choisir au reste du monde, où toutes les commodités de la vie et toutes les curiosités que peuvent être souhaitées, soient si faciles à trouver qu'en celui-ci? Quel autre pays, où l'on puisse jouir d'une liberté si entière, où l'on puisse dormir avec moins d'inquiétude, où les empoisonnements, les trahisons, les calomnies soient moins connus, et où il soit demeuré plus de reste de l'innocence de nos aïeux?" 5 mai 1631, *ibid.*, p. 190.

14. Extracts from Beeckman's *Journal* in the original Latin are given in *Oeuvres*, X:331 *et seq.*

15. 18 juillet 1629, *Corr.*, I:44.

16. "Or j'estime que tous ceux à qui Dieu a donné l'usage de cette raison, sont obligés de l'employer principalement pour tâcher à le connaître et à se connaître eux-mêmes. C'est par là que j'ai tâché de commencer mes études; et je vous dirai que je n'eusse su trouver les fondements de la Physique, si je ne les eusse cherchés par cette voie." 15 avril 1630, *ibid.*, p. 135.

17. "Ne craignez point, je vous prie, d'assurer et de publier partout, que c'est Dieu qui a établi ces lois en la nature, ainsi qu'un roi établit des lois en son royaume. Au contraire, nous ne pouvons comprendre la grandeur de Dieu, encore que nous la connaissions. Mais cela même que nous la jugeons incompréhensible, nous la fait estimer davantage; ainsi qu'un roi a plus de majesté, lorsqu'il est moins familièrement connu de ses sujets, pourvu toutefois qu'ils ne pensent pas pour cela être sans roi, et qu'ils le connaissent assez pour n'en point douter. On vous dira que, si Dieu avait établi ces vérités, il les pourrait changer comme un roi fait ses lois; à quoi il faut répondre que oui, si sa volonté peut changer. Mais je les comprends comme éternelles et immuables. Et moi je juge le même de Dieu. Mais sa volonté est libre. Oui, mais sa puissance est incompréhensible, et généralement nous pouvons bien assurer que Dieu peut faire tout ce que nous pouvons comprendre, mais non pas qu'il ne peut faire ce que nous ne pouvons pas comprendre; car ce serait témérité de penser que notre imagination a autant d'étendue que sa

puissance. J'espère écrire ceci, même avant qu'il soit quinze jours, dans ma *Physique;* mais je ne vous prie point pour cela de le tenir secret; au contraire, je vous convie de le dire aussi souvent que l'occasion s'en présentera, pourvu que ce soit sans me nommer. . . ." *Ibid.,* pp. 135–136.

18. "Mais je ne veux pas me mêler de la Théologie, j'ai peur même que vous ne jugiez que ma Philosophie s'émancipe trop, d'oser dire son avis touchant des matières si relevées." 6 mai 1630, *ibid.,* p. 140.

19. "J'ai mille choses diverses, à considérer toutes ensemble, pour trouver un biais par le moyen duquel je puisse dire la vérité, sans étonner l'imagination de personne, ni choquer les opinions qui sont communément reçues." 23 décembre 1630, *ibid.,* p. 183.

20. ". . . et s'il fut venu, je voulais acheter des meubles, et prendre une partie du logis, pour faire notre ménage à part. J'avais déjà fait provision d'un garçon qui sut faire la cuisine à la mode de France." 18 mars 1630, *ibid.,* pp. 124–125.

21. "Si vous avez quelques meubles qu'il vous fallut laisser à Paris, il vaudrait mieux les apporter, au moins les plus utiles; car si vous venez, je prendrai un logis entier pour vous et pour moi, où nous pourrons vivre à notre mode et à notre aise. N'était que je ne saurais vous faire donner d'argent à Paris, sans mander où je suis (ce que je ne désire pas), je vous prierais aussi de m'apporter un petit lit de camp; car les lits d'ici sont fort incommodes, et il n'y a point de mâtelas." 18 juin 1629, *ibid.,* p. 42.

22. "J'étudie maintenant en Chimie et en Anatomie tout ensemble, et apprends tous les jours quelque chose que je ne trouve pas dedans les livres. . . . Au reste, je passe si doucement le temps en m'instruisant moi-même, que je ne me mets jamais à écrire en mon Traité que par contrainte, et pour m'acquitter de la résolution que j'ai prise, qui est, si je ne meurs, de le mettre en état de vous l'envoyer au commencement de l'année 1633. Je vous détermine le temps pour m'y obliger davantage, et afin que vous m'en puissiez faire reproche si j'y manque. Au reste, vous vous étonnerez que je prenne un si long terme pour écrire un Discours qui sera si court, que je m'imagine qu'on le pourra lire en une après-dînée; mais c'est que j'ai plus de soin et crois qu'il est plus important que j'apprenne ce qui m'est nécessaire pour la conduite de ma vie, que non pas que je m'amuse à publier le peu que j'ai appris." 15 avril 1630, *ibid.,* p. 130.

23. "Et si ou vous demande où je suis, je vous prie de dire que vous n'en êtes pas certain, parce que j'étais en résolution de passer en Angleterre. . . . Si on vous demande ce que je fais, vous direz, s'il vous plaît, que je prends plaisir à étudier pour m'instruire moi-même, mais que, de l'humeur que je suis, vous ne pensez pas que je mette

jamais rien au jour, et que je vous en ai tout à fait ôté la créance." 2 décembre 1630, *ibid.*, p. 181.

24. "Ne me demandez point, s'il vous plaît, quelle peut être cette occupation que j'estime si importante, car j'aurais honte de vous la dire; je suis devenu si philosophe, que je méprise la plupart des choses qui sont ordinairement estimées, et en estime quelques autres, dont on n'a point accoutumé de faire cas." 15 avril 1631, *ibid.*, p. 186.

25. ". . . ce qui m'a si fort étonné, que je me suis quasi résolu de brûler tous mes papiers ou du moins de ne les laisser voir à personne. Car je ne me suis pu imaginer que lui, qui est Italien et même bien voulu du Pape, ainsi que j'entends, ait pu être criminalisé pour autre chose, sinon qu'il aura sans doute voulu établir le mouvement de la Terre; lequel je sais bien avoir été autrefois censuré par quelques Cardinaux, mais je pensais avoir ouï dire que depuis on ne laissait pas de l'enseigner publiquement, même dans Rome; et je confesse que, s'il est faux, tous les fondements de ma Philosophie le sont aussi. . . . Mais comme je ne voudrais pour rien du monde qu'il sortît de moi un discours, où il se trouvât le moindre mot qui fût désapprouvé de l'Église, aussi aimé-je mieux le supprimer, que de le faire paraître estropié." Fin novembre 1633, *ibid.*, pp. 241–242.

26. ". . . vous n'aurez que meilleure opinion de moi, de voir que j'ai voulu entièrement supprimer le traité que j'en avais fait et perdre presque tout mon travail de quatre ans, pour rendre une entière obéissance à l'Église. . . . Pour moi, je ne recherche que le repos et la tranquillité d'esprit, qui sont des biens qui ne peuvent être possédés par ceux qui ont de l'animosité ou de l'ambition; et je ne demeure pas cependant sans rien faire, mais je ne pense pour maintenant qu'à m'instruire moi-même, et me juge fort peu capable de servir à instruire les autres." Février 1634, *ibid.*, pp. 250–251.

27. "Toutefois, parce que j'aurais mauvaise grâce, si après vous avoir tant promis et si longtemps, je pensais vous payer ainsi d'une boutade, je ne laisserai pas de vous faire voir ce que j'ai fait, le plus tôt que je pourrais; mais je vous demande encore, s'il vous plaît, un an de délai, pour le revoir et le polir." Fin novembre 1633, *ibid.*, p. 242.

28. Lettre à Mersenne, mars 1636, *ibid.*, pp. 300–301.

29. ". . . mais je vois aussi qu'elles sont telles, et en si grand nombre, que ni mes mains ni mon revenu, bien que j'en eusse mille fois plus que je n'en ai, ne sauraient suffire pour toutes." *Discours*, in *Oeuvres*, VI:65.

30. "Mais sitôt que j'ai eu acquis quelques notions générales touchant la physique, et que, commençant à les éprouver en diverses difficultés particulières, j'ai remarqué jusques où elles peuvent conduire et combien elles diffèrent des principes dont on s'est servi jusqu'à présent, j'ai cru que je ne pouvais les tenir cachées sans pécher grandement contre la

loi qui nous oblige à procurer autant qu'il est en nous le bien général de tous les hommes." *Ibid.*, p. 61.

31. Lettre à Mersenne, mars 1636, *Corr.*, I: 301.

32. "Car je ne mets pas *Traité de la méthode*, mais *Discours de la méthode*, ce qui est le même que *Préface* ou *Avis touchant la méthode*, pour montrer que je n'ai pas dessein de l'enseigner, mais seulement d'en parler. Car, comme on peut voir de ce que j'en dis, elle consiste plus en pratique qu'en théorie; et je nomme les Traités suivants des *Essais de cette méthode*, parce que je prétends que les choses qu'ils contiennent n'ont pu être trouvées sans elle. . . . Comme aussi j'ai inséré quelque chose de Métaphysique, de Physique et de Médecine dans le premier *Discours*, pour montrer qu'elle s'étend à toutes sortes de matières." 27 février 1637, *ibid.*, p. 329.

33. "Ainsi mon dessein n'est pas d'enseigner ici la méthode que chacun doit suivre pour bien conduire sa raison, mais seulement de faire voir en quelle sorte j'ai tâché de conduire la mienne. Ceux qui se mêlent de donner des préceptes se doivent estimer plus habiles que ceux auxquels ils les donnent; et s'ils manquent en la moindre chose, ils sont blâmables. Mais ne proposant cet écrit que comme une histoire, ou, si vous l'aimez mieux, que comme une fable, en laquelle parmi quelques exemples qu'on peut imiter, on en trouvera peut-être aussi plusieurs autres qu'on aura raison de ne pas suivre, j'espère qu'il sera utile à quelques-uns, sans être nuisible à personne, et que tous me sauront gré de ma franchise." *Discours*, in *Oeuvres*, VI: 4.

34. "Et si j'écris en français, qui est la langue de mon pays, plutôt qu'en latin, qui est celle de mes précepteurs, c'est à cause que j'espère que ceux qui ne se servent que de leur raison naturelle toute pure jugeront mieux de mes opinions que ceux qui ne croient qu'aux livres anciens; et pour ceux qui joignent le bon sens avec l'étude, lesquels seuls je souhaite pour mes juges, ils ne seront point, je m'assure, si partiaux pour le latin, qu'ils refusent d'entendre mes raisons pour ce que je les explique en langue vulgaire." *Ibid.*, pp. 77–78.

35. *Cf. Oeuvres*, I: 342, where Adam speaks of 66 pages.

36. "Au reste je n'y veux point mettre mon nom, suivant mon ancienne résolution, et je vous prie de n'en rien dire à personne." Mars 1636, *Corr.*, I: 301.

37. Reneri's role may have been less important than usually supposed. *Cf.* the work of Sassen in refuting Baillet's account. Serrurier, *Descartes*, p. 86.

38. "On trouvera aussy en plusieurs endroits des distinctions fort mal mises et quantité d'autres fautes de peu d'importance, lesquelles on excusera facilement, quand on sçaura que l'Autheur ne fait pas profession d'estre Grammairien et que le Compositeur, dont le Libraire s'est

servi, n'entend pas un mot de François." Quoted by Cohen, *Écrivains français en Hollande*, p. 506.

39. *Ibid.*, p. 507.

40. *Cf.* Lettre à Mersenne, 27 février 1637, *Corr.*, I:329–330.

41. A. Boyce Gibson discusses the relative importance of science and metaphysics in *The Philosophy of Descartes*, pp. 60 *et seq.*

42. Janet, Espinas, Cantecor, and Gilson have all discussed the question of Descartes' exactness in recording his feelings while at La Flèche.

43. "Le premier était de ne recevoir jamais aucune chose pour vraie que je ne la connusse évidemment être telle: c'est-à-dire d'éviter soigneusement la précipitation et la prévention, et de ne comprendre rien de plus en mes jugements, que ce qui se présenterait si clairement et si distinctement à mon esprit, que je n'eusse aucune occasion de le mettre en doute. Le second, de diviser chacune des difficultés que j'examinerais, en autant de parcelles qu'il se pourrait, et qu'il serait requis pour les mieux résoudre. Le troisième, de conduire par ordre mes pensées, en commençant par les objets les plus simples et les plus aisés à connaître, pour monter peu à peu, comme par degrés, jusques à la connaissance des plus composés; et supposant même de l'ordre entre ceux qui ne se précèdent point naturellement les uns les autres. Et le dernier, de faire partout des dénombrements si entiers, et des revues si générales, que je fusse assuré de ne rien omettre." *Discours*, in *Oeuvres*, VI:18–19.

44. "La première était d'obéir aux lois et aux coutumes de mon pays, retenant constamment la religion en laquelle Dieu m'a fait la grâce d'être instruit dès mon enfance, et me gouvernant, en toute autre chose, suivant les opinions les plus modérées, et les plus éloignées de l'excès, qui fussent communément reçues en pratique par les mieux sensés de ceux avec lesquels j'aurais à vivre. . . . Ma seconde maxime était d'être le plus ferme et le plus résolu en mes actions que je pourrais, et de ne suivre pas moins constamment les opinions les plus douteuses, lorsque je m'y serais une fois déterminé, que si elles eussent été très assurées. Imitant en ceci les voyageurs qui, se trouvant égarés en quelque forêt, ne doivent pas errer en tournoyant, tantôt d'un côté, tantôt d'un autre, ni encore moins s'arrêter en une place, mais marcher toujours le plus droit qu'ils peuvent vers un même côté, et ne le changer point pour de faibles raisons, encore que ce n'ait peut-être été au commencement que le hasard seul qui les ait déterminés à le choisir: car, par ce moyen, s'ils ne vont justement où ils désirent, ils arriveront au moins à la fin quelque part, où vraisemblablement ils seront mieux que dans le milieu d'une forêt. Et ainsi, les actions de la vie ne souffrant souvent aucun délai, c'est une vérité très certaine que, lorsqu'il n'est pas en notre pouvoir de discerner les plus vraies opinions, nous devons suivre les plus probables.

. . . Ma troisième maxime était de tâcher toujours plutôt à me vaincre que la fortune, et à changer mes désirs que l'ordre du monde, et généralement, de m'accoutumer à croire qu'il n'y a rien qui soit entièrement en notre pouvoir que nos pensées, en sorte qu'après que nous avons fait notre mieux, touchant les choses qui nous sont extérieures, tout ce qui manque de nous réussir est, au regard de nous, absolument impossible. Et ceci seul me semblait être suffisant pour m'empêcher de rien désirer à l'avenir que je n'acquisse, et ainsi pour me rendre content. . . . Enfin, pour conclusion de cette morale, je m'avisai de faire une revue sur les diverses occupations qu'ont les hommes en cette vie, pour tâcher à faire choix de la meilleure; et sans que je veuille rien dire de celles des autres, je pensai que je ne pouvais mieux que de continuer en celle-là même où je me trouvais, c'est-à-dire que d'employer toute ma vie à cultiver ma raison, et m'avancer, autant que je pourrais, en la connaissance de la vérité, suivant la méthode que je m'étais préscrite. J'avais éprouvé de si extrêmes contentements, depuis que j'avais commencé à me servir de cette méthode, que je ne croyais pas qu'on en pût recevoir de plus doux, ni de plus innocents, en cette vie." *Ibid.*, pp. 22–27.

45. "Ses syllogismes et la plupart de ses autres instructions servent plutôt à expliquer à autrui les choses qu'on sait, ou même, comme l'art de Lulle, à parler sans jugement de celles qu'on ignore, qu'à les apprendre; et bien qu'elle contienne, en effet, beaucoup de préceptes très vrais et très bons, il y en a toutefois tant d'autres mêlés parmi qui sont ou nuisibles ou superflus, qu'il est presque aussi malaisé de les en séparer que de tirer une Diane ou une Minerve hors d'un bloc de marbre qui n'est point encore ébauché." *Oeuvres*, VI:17.

46. "Ceux qui cherchent le droit chemin de la vérité ne doivent s'occuper d'aucun objet à propos duquel ils ne puissent obtenir une certitude égale aux démonstrations de l'arithmétique et de la géométrie." *Ibid.*, X:366.

47. "Tout ce que nous concevons clairement peut être fait par Dieu en la manière que nous le concevons. . . . Mais nous concevons clairement l'esprit, c'est-à-dire une substance qui pense, sans le corps, c'est-à-dire, sans une substance étendue . . . et d'autre part nous concevons aussi clairement le corps sans l'esprit (ainsi que chacun accorde facilement). Donc, au moins par la toute-puissance de Dieu, l'esprit peut être sans le corps, et le corps sans l'esprit. Maintenant les substances qui peuvent être l'une sans l'autre sont réellement distinctes. . . . Or est-il que l'esprit et le corps sont des substances qui peuvent être l'une sans l'autre (comme je le viens de prouver). Donc l'esprit et le corps sont réellement distincts." "Réponses de l'auteur aux secondes objections." *Ibid.*, VII:169–170 (French translation in Pléiade edition, p. 398).

48. "Touchant les objets que nous proposons à notre étude, il faut rechercher, non point ce que d'autres ont pensé, ou ce que nous-mêmes nous entrevoyons, mais ce dont nous pouvons avoir une intuition claire et évidente, ou ce que nous pouvons déduire avec certitude; car ce n'est pas autrement qu'on en acquiert la science." *Ibid.*, X:366 (French translation by Jacques Brunschwig in Garnier Frères edition of the *Oeuvres philosophiques*, p. 85).

49. "Par *intuition* j'entends, non point le témoignage instable des sens, ni le jugement trompeur de l'imagination qui opère des compositions sans valeur, mais une représentation qui est le fait de l'intelligence pure et attentive, représentation si facile et si distincte qu'il ne subsiste aucun doute sur ce que l'on y comprend; ou bien, ce qui revient au même, une représentation inaccessible au doute, représentation qui est le fait de l'intelligence pure et attentive, qui naît de la seule lumière de la raison, et qui, parce qu'elle est plus simple, est plus certaine encore que la déduction; celle-ci pourtant, nous l'avons noté plus haut, ne saurait, elle non plus, être faite de travers par un esprit humain. Ainsi, chacun peut voir par intuition qu'il existe, qu'il pense, que le triangle est délimité par trois lignes seulement, la sphère par une seule surface, et autres choses semblables, qui sont bien plus nombreuses que ne le remarquent la plupart des gens, parce qu'ils dédaignent de tourner leur esprit vers des choses si faciles." *Ibid.*, p. 368 (French translation by Jacques Brunschwig in Garnier Frères edition of the *Oeuvres philosophiques*, p. 87).

50. "On peut dès lors se demander pourquoi, en sus de l'intuition, nous avons ajouté ici un autre mode de connaissance, celui qui se fait par *déduction;* nous entendons par là tout ce qui se conclut nécessairement de certaines autres choses connues avec certitude. Il a fallu procéder ainsi, parce que la plupart des choses sont l'objet d'une connaissance certaine, tout en n'étant pas par elles-mêmes évidentes; il suffit qu'elles soient déduites à partir de principes vrais et déjà connus, par un mouvement continu et ininterrompu de la pensée, qui prend de chaque terme une intuition claire: Ce n'est pas autrement que nous savons que le dernier anneau de quelque longue chaîne est rattaché au premier, même si nous ne voyons pas d'un seul et même coup d'oeil l'ensemble des anneaux intermédiaires dont dépend ce rattachement; il suffit que nous les ayons examinés l'un après l'autre, et que nous nous souvenions que du premier au dernier, chacun d'eux est attaché à ses voisins immédiats. Nous distinguons donc ici l'intuition intellectuelle et la déduction certaine, en ce que l'on conçoit dans l'une sorte de mouvement ou de succession, et non pas dans l'autre; et parce qu'en outre, pour la déduction, il n'est pas besoin comme pour l'intuition d'une évidence actuelle, mais

que c'est à la mémoire qu'elle emprunte, d'une certaine manière, sa certitude. De là suit qu'on peut dire de ces propositions qui se concluent immédiatement à partir des premiers principes, qu'on les connaît, selon le point de vue auquel on se place, tantôt par l'intuition, tantôt par la déduction; mais que les premiers principes eux-mêmes ne sont connus que par l'intuition, tandis que les conclusions éloignées ne sauraient l'être que par la déduction." *Ibid.*, pp. 369–370 (French translation by Jacques Brunschwig in Garnier Frères edition of the *Oeuvres philosophiques*, pp. 88–90).

51. "Telles sont les deux voies les plus certaines pour parvenir à la science; du côté de l'esprit on ne doit pas en admettre davantage, et toutes les autres sont à rejeter comme suspectes et exposées à l'erreur; ce qui ne nous empêche pas pour autant de croire revêtues d'une certitude supérieure à toute connaissance les choses qui nous ont été révélées par une voie divine, puisque la foi que nous leur accordons, et qui porte toujours sur des choses obscures, n'est pas un acte de l'intelligence, mais un acte de la volonté; ce qui n'empêche pas non plus, si cette foi possède des fondements dans l'entendement, que ceux-ci ne puissent et ne doivent, plus que tout le reste, être découverts par l'une ou l'autre des voies déjà mentionnées. . . ." *Ibid.*, p. 370 (French translation by Jacques Brunschwig in Garnier Frères edition of the *Oeuvres philosophiques*, p. 90).

52. "Et le secret de toute la méthode est là: en toutes choses, repérer soigneusement ce qui est le plus absolu." *Ibid.*, p. 383 (French translation by Jacques Brunschwig in Garnier Frères edition of the *Oeuvres philosophiques*, p. 103).

53. "J'appelle absolu tout ce qui contient en soi, à l'état pur et simple, la nature sur laquelle porte la question: par exemple, tout ce qui est considéré comme indépendant, comme cause, comme simple, universel, un, égal, semblable, droit, ou autres choses de ce genre; et je l'appelle en même temps le plus simple et le plus facile, en vue de l'usage que nous en ferons dans la résolution des questions. Quant au relatif, c'est ce qui participe de cette même nature, ou du moins de quelqu'un de ses aspects; en vertu de quoi l'on peut le rapporter à l'absolu, et l'en déduire en parcourant une série; mais en outre il enferme en son concept d'autres choses que j'appelle relations: de cette nature est tout ce qu'on nomme dépendant, effet, composé, particulier, multiple, inégal, dissemblable, oblique, etc. Ces termes relatifs s'éloignent d'autant plus des absolus qu'ils contiennent plus de relations de cette sorte, subordonnées les unes aux autres; et la présente règle nous avertit qu'il faut distinguer tous ces rapports, et respecter leur connexion mutuelle comme leur ordre naturel, en sorte que nous puissions parvenir du

dernier terme jusqu'à celui qui est le plus absolu, en passant par tous les autres." *Ibid.*, p. 382 (French translation by Jacques Brunschwig in Garnier Frères edition of the *Oeuvres philosophiques*, pp. 102–103).

54. "Pour parfaire la science, il faut passer en revue dans leur totalité et une par une, d'un mouvement continu et absolument ininterrompu de la pensée, toutes les choses qui concernent notre propos, et les embrasser en une énumération suffisante et ordonnée." *Ibid.*, p. 387 (French translation by Jacques Brunschwig in Garnier Frères edition of the *Oeuvres philosophiques*, p. 108).

55. "Cette énumération ou induction est donc le recensement de tout ce qui se rapporte à une question proposée, recensement si attentif et si exact que nous puissions en conclure avec certitude et évidence que nous n'y avons laissé par mégarde aucune omission; en conséquence, chaque fois que nous en aurons fait usage, à supposer que la chose cherchée nous échappe, nous serons au moins plus savants en ce que nous verrons avec certitude qu'on n'aurait pu la découvrir par aucun des moyens que nous connaissons; et si, comme il arrive souvent, nous avons pu passer en revue tous les moyens qui s'offrent aux hommes pour y parvenir, nous pourrons déclarer hardiment que sa connaissance échappe entièrement aux prises de l'esprit humain. Il faut remarquer en outre que par énumération suffisante ou induction, nous entendons seulement celle d'où l'on conclut à une vérité avec plus de certitude que par tout autre genre de preuve, à l'exception de l'intuition simple; chaque fois qu'une connaissance ne peut se réduire à cette dernière, il ne nous reste, puisque nous avons rejeté tous les enchaînements syllogistiques, que cette seule voie à laquelle nous devions porter une confiance effectuées d'une chose à une autre, pour peu que l'inférence ait été totale. En effet toutes les déductions immédiates que nous avons effectuées d'une chose à une autre, pour peu que l'inférence ait été évidente, ont déjà été réduites à une véritable intuition. Mais si nous effectuons une inférence à partir de propositions nombreuses et dispersées, il arrive souvent que la capacité de notre esprit ne soit pas assez grande pour qu'il puisse embrasser tous ces termes en une intuition unique; en ce cas, la certitude de l'opération dont nous parlons doit lui suffire." *Ibid.*, p. 389 (French translation by Jacques Brunschwig in Garnier Frères edition of the *Oeuvres philosophiques*, pp. 110–111).

56. "Ainsi, en résumé, la méthode cartésienne consiste à décomposer les choses en leurs éléments simples, dont la vérité est reconnue intuitivement, puis, à l'aide de ces éléments, à recomposer les choses par une déduction qui va de propositions évidentes en propositions évidentes, et à combler les lacunes de cette décomposition et de cette composition alternantes, s'il s'en présente, par des inductions analogiques." Liard, *Discours*, pp. 8–9. In addition to Liard's introduction, the notes to the

Bordas edition by J.-M. Fataud and Ferdinand Alquié's edition of the *Oeuvres philosophiques*, Tome I, which contains Jacques Brunschwig's excellent translation, have all been of immeasurable assistance for the preceding discussion of Descartes' method.

57. "La première est, qu'il tâche toujours de se servir, le mieux qu'il lui est possible, de son esprit, pour connaître ce qu'il doit faire ou ne pas faire en toutes les occurrences de la vie." Lettre à la Princesse Elisabeth, 4 août 1645, *Corr.*, VI:280.

58. 24 mars 1637, *Corr.*, I:336.

59. "Descartes, dans l'histoire de la pensée, ce sera toujours ce cavalier français qui partit d'un si bon pas." Péguy, *Note.*

60. "C'est un héros; il a repris les choses par les commencements, et il a retrouvé de nouveau le vrai sol de la philosophie, auquel elle est revenue après un égarement de mille ans." Hegel, *Histoire de la philosophie*, cité pare Rabier, édition Delagrave du *Discours*, quoted in Classiques Larousse edition of the *Discours*, p. 75.

Chapter 4

1. *Cf. Regulae, Oeuvres*, X:377–378.

2. "Mais il me semble qu'il manque beaucoup en ce qu'il fait continuellement des digressions et ne s'arrête point à expliquer tout à fait une matière; ce qui montre qu'il ne les a point examinées par ordre, et que, sans avoir considéré les premières causes de la nature, il a seulement cherché les raisons de quelques effets particulier, et ainsi qu'il a bâti sans fondement." 11 octobre 1638, *Corr.*, III:77.

3. "Je prétends qu'on ne doit pas seulement croire que j'ai fait quelque chose de plus que ceux qui m'ont précédé, mais aussi qu'on se doit persuader que nos neveux ne trouveront jamais rien en cette matière que je ne pusse avoir trouvé aussi bien qu'eux, si j'eusse voulu prendre la peine de le chercher." Fin décembre 1637, *Corr.*, II:66–67.

4. Daniel Lipstortius, who in 1653 published memoires concerning Descartes which he had received from Jean de Raey, was one of Baillet's sources. *Cf.* Baillet, *Vie*, pp. xix–xv, and Haldane, *Descartes*, pp. 26–27.

5. Lettre à Mersenne, 29 juin 1638, *Corr.*, II:293.

6. Milhaud, *Descartes savant*, Chap. 3. See also Gibson, *The Philosophy of Descartes*, pp. 188–189.

7. The examples used in this paragraph are taken from Adam's *Vie*, pp. 52–53. The author points out that Descartes still used "*caractères cossiques*" in 1619 and that his reform was accomplished in steps. See also pp. 211 *et seq.*

8. Gérard Milhaud believes that the obscurities were not intentional

but the result of a defense mechanism. See "Sur les obscurités de la géométrie de Descartes," pp. 21–26.

9. "Toutefois je puis assurer que je n'ai rien omis de tout cela qu'à dessein. . . . Mais j'avais prévu que certains gens, qui se vantent de savoir tout, n'eussent pas manqué de dire que je n'avais rien écrit qu'ils n'aient su auparavant, si je me fusse rendu assez intelligible pour eux; et je n'aurais pas eu le plaisir, que j'ai eu depuis, de voir l'impertinence de leurs objections." 20 février 1639, *Corr.*, III:185.

10. "Pour des problèmes, je vous en enverrai un million pour proposer aux autres, si vous le désirez; mais je suis si las des Mathématiques, et en fais maintenant si peu d'état, que je ne saurais plus prendre la peine de les soudre moi-même." 15 avril 1630, *Corr.*, I:131.

11. "Mais je n'ai résolu de quitter que la Géométrie abstraite, c'est-à-dire la recherche des questions qui ne servent qu'à exercer l'esprit; et ce afin d'avoir d'autant plus de loisir de cultiver une autre sorte de Géométrie, qui se propose pour questions l'explication des phéno-mènes de la nature. Car s'il lui plaît de considérer ce que j'ai écrit du sel, de la neige, de l'arc-en-ciel, etc., il connaîtra bien que toute ma Physique n'est autre chose que Géométrie." 27 juillet 1638, *Corr.*, II:362–363. Desargues (1593–1662) was a geometrician and architect whom Descartes admired and who defended him against Père Bourdin.

12. "Et je ne suis nullement pressé d'entendre votre jugement; car j'ose me promettre qu'il me sera d'autant plus favorable qu'il viendra plus tard. Surtout je voudrais qu'il vous plût prendre la peine d'examiner ma *Géométrie*; c'est une chose qui ne se peut faire que la plume à la main et suivant tous les calculs qui y sont, lesquels peuvent sembler d'abord difficiles, à cause qu'on n'y est pas accoutumé, mais il ne faut que peu de jours pour cela; et si vous passez du premier livre au troisième, avant que de lire le second, vous y trouverez plus de facilité que peut-être vous ne croyez. Si j'avais des ailes pour voler, comme Dédale, je voudrais m'aller rendre pour huit jours auprès de vous, afin de vous en faciliter l'entrée; mais vous la pourrez assez ouvrir de vous-même, et je me promets que vous ne plaindrez point, par après, le temps que vous y aurez employé. 22 février 1638, *ibid.*, pp. 139–140.

13. Lettre à Mersenne, 17 mai 1638, *ibid.*, p. 271.

14. "Je n'ai jamais rien vu de sa façon qui ne puisse servir à prouver son insuffisance." À Mersenne, 20 avril 1646, *Corr.*, VII:42.

15. The question of Descartes' knowledge of Viète and his indebted-ness is discussed in detail by Charles Adam in his *Vie*, XII:215–219.

16. J. F. Scott, *The Scientific Work of René Descartes*, p. 92.

17. *Ibid.*, pp. 94–95.

18. *Ibid.*, p. 199.

19. Jules Vuillemin, *Mathématiques*, pp. 56, 72–73.

20. "Nous avons naturellement plus d'admiration pour les choses qui sont au-dessus de nous, que pour celles qui sont à pareille hauteur ou au-dessous. Et quoique les nues n'excèdent guère les sommets de quelques montagnes, et qu'on en voie même souvent de plus basses que les pointes de nos clochers, toutefois, à cause qu'il faut tourner les yeux vers le ciel pour les regarder, nous les imaginons si relevées, que même les poètes et les peintres en composent le trône de Dieu, et font que là il emploie ses propres mains à ouvrir et fermer les portes des vents, à verser la rosée sur les fleurs et à lancer la foudre sur les rochers. Ce qui me fait espérer que si j'explique ici leur nature, en telle sorte qu'on n'ait plus occasion d'admirer rien de ce qui s'y voit ou qui en descend, on croira facilement qu'il est possible en même façon de trouver les causes de tout ce qu'il y a de plus admirable dessus la terre." *Les Météores*, in *Oeuvres*, VI:231.

21. *Le Mercure français*, X:285–286, année 1624, quoted by Adam, *Oeuvres*, XII:201.

22. "Car je n'ai point l'esprit assez fort, pour l'employer en même temps à plusieurs choses différentes; et comme je ne trouve jamais rien que par une longue traînée de diverses considérations, il faut que je me donne tout à une matière, lorsque j'en veux examiner quelque partie. Ce que j'ai éprouvé depuis peu, en cherchant la cause de ce Phénomène, duquel vous m'écrivez; car il y a plus de deux mois qu'un de mes amis m'en a fait voir ici une description assez ample, et m'en ayant demandé mon avis, il m'a fallu interrompre ce que j'avais en main pour examiner par ordre tous les Météores, auparavant que je m'y sois pu satisfaire. Mais je pense maintenant en pouvoir rendre quelque raison, et je suis résolu d'en faire un petit Traité, qui contiendra la raison des couleurs de l'arc-en-ciel, lesquelles m'ont donné plus de peine que tout le reste, et généralement de tous les phénomènes sublunaires." Lettre à Mersenne, 8 octobre 1629, *Corr.*, I:48–49.

23. "Car, encore qu'elle paraissent fort irrégulièrement éparses çà et là dans le Ciel, je ne doute point toutefois qu'il n'y ait un ordre naturel entre elles, lequel est régulier et déterminé. Et la connaissance de cet ordre est la clef et le fondement de la plus haut et la plus parfaite Science, que les hommes puissent avoir touchant les choses matérielles; d'autant que par son moyen on pourrait connaître *a priori* toutes les diverses formes et essences des corps terrestres, au lieu que, sans elle, il nous faut contenter de les deviner *a posteriori*, et par leurs effets. . . . Je crois que c'est une Science qui passe la portée de l'esprit humain; et toutefois je suis si peu sage, que je ne saurais m'empêcher d'y rêver." 10 mai 1632, *ibid.*, 225–227.

24. *Ibid.*, p. 47.

25. "Toute la conduite de notre vie dépend de nos sens, entre lesquels

celui de la vue étant le plus universel et le plus noble, il n'y a point de doute que les inventions qui servent à augmenter sa puissance ne soient des plus utiles qui puissent être." *Oeuvres,* VI:81.

26. "Et il est malaisé d'en trouver aucune qui l'augmente davantage que celle de ces merveilleuses lunettes qui, n'étant en usage que depuis peu, nous ont déjà découvert de nouveaux astres dans le ciel, et d'autres nouveaux objets dessus la terre, en plus grand nombre que ne sont ceux que nous y avions vus auparavant: En sorte que, portant notre vue beaucoup plus loin que n'avait coutume d'aller l'imagination de nos pères, elles semblent nous avoir ouvert le chemin, pour parvenir à une connaissance de la Nature beaucoup plus grande et plus parfaite qu'ils ne l'ont eue." *Ibid.*

27. "Je ne doute point que vous n'entendiez plusieurs jugements de mes écrits, et plus à mon désavantage que d'autres: Car les esprits qui sont d'inclination à en médire, le pourront aisément faire d'abord, et en auront d'autant plus d'occasion, qu'ils auront été moins connus par les autres." 25 janvier 1638, *Corr.,* II:83.

28. "Car j'ose assurer qu'il en a aucune de fausse, parce que je les ai faites moi-même et nommément celle que vous remarquez de l'eau *chaude* qui gèle plus tôt que la *froide;* où j'ai dit non pas *chaude* et *froide,* mais que *l'eau qu'on a tenue longtemps sur le feu* se gèle plus tôt que l'autre." 1 mars 1638, *ibid.,* p. 163.

29. "Mais il y a peu de gens qui soient capables de bien faire des expériences, et souvent, en les faisant mal, on y trouve tout le contraire de ce qu'on y doit trouver." *Ibid.,* p. 164.

30. "Je pris l'oeil d'un vieux boeuf (ce qu'il faut observer, car celui des jeunes veaux n'est pas transparent), et ayant choisi la moitié d'une coquille d'oeuf, qui était telle que cet oeil pouvait aisément être mis et ajusté dedans sans changer sa figure, je coupai en rond avec des ciseaux fort tranchants. . . . Et la pièce ronde que je coupai . . . avait le nerf optique pour centre." 31 mars 1638, *ibid.,* pp. 216–217.

31. For a discussion of Descartes' indebtedness to others see Adam, *Vie,* pp. 195–196 and Scott, *The Scientific Work of René Descartes,* pp. 36–38.

32. "Celui qui m'accuse d'avoir emprunté de Kepler les ellipses et les hyperboles de ma *Dioptrique,* doit être ignorant ou malicieux; car pour l'ellipse, je n'ai pas de mémoire que Kepler en parle, ou s'il en parle, c'est assurément pour dire qu'elle n'est pas l'anaclastique qu'il cherche; et pour l'hyperbole, je me souviens fort bien qu'il prétend démontrer expressément qu'elle ne l'est pas. . . . Or je vous laisse à penser si je dois avoir emprunté une chose d'un homme qui a tâché de prouver qu'elle était fausse." Lettre à Mersenne, 31 mars 1638, *Corr.,* II:215–216.

33. "Pour Ferrier, laissez-le faire; il y a grande apparence qu'il n'achèvera rien, et je crois que le moindre petit tourneur ou serrurier serait plus capable que lui de faire voir l'effet des lunettes." *Ibid.*, p. 215.

34. ". . . un philanthrope devant une humanité dont il veut le bonheur, et qui refuse de le recevoir de ses mains." Étienne Gilson, *Discours*, Comm. X. ". . . moins soucieux d'assurer à l'humanité la maîtrise du monde que d'acquérir la claire conscience de ce qu'est l'homme." Ferdinand Alquié, *Oeuvres philosophiques*, I:565.

Chapter 5

1. Cohen, *Écrivains français en Hollande*, p. 483.

2. "Véritablement c'est un homme qui est au delà de toute l'estime qu'on en saurait faire. . . . Il y a des qualités qui font qu'on estime ceux qui les ont sans faire pour cela qu'on les aime, et d'autres qui font qu'on les aime sans qu'on les en estime beaucoup davantage; mais je trouve qu'il possède en perfection celles qui font ensemble l'un et l'autre." Lettre à Golius, 16 avril 1635, *Corr.*, I:276–277.

3. Cohen, *Écrivains français en Hollande*, p. 485.

4. "Toutes choses vont ici le mieux que nous saurions souhaiter. Je parlai hier à mon hôtesse pour savoir si elle voulait avoir ici ma nièce, et combien elle désirait que je lui donnasse pour cela; elle, sans délibérer, me dit que je la fisse venir quand je voudrais, et que nous nous accorderions aisément du prix, parce qu'il lui était indifférent si elle avait un enfant de plus ou de moins à gouverner." 30 août 1637, *Corr.*, I:378.

5. "En effet, il faut faire qu'Hélène vienne ici le plus tôt qu'il se pourra; et même, s'il se pouvait honnêtement avant la Saint-Victor et qu'elle en mît quelque autre en sa place, ce serait le meilleur." *Ibid.*, p. 379.

6. "La lettre que j'écris à Hel. n'est point pressée, et j'aime mieux que vous la gardiez jusques à ce qu'Hel. vous aille trouver, ce qu'elle fera, je crois, vers la fin de cette semaine, pour vous donner les lettres qu'elle m'écrira, que de lui faire porter par votre servante." *Ibid.*

7. "Il est vrai que je ne fus jamais moins en humeur d'écrire que maintenant. . . . Les poils blancs qui se hâtent de me venir m'avertissent que je ne dois plus étudier à autre chose qu'aux moyens de les retarder. C'est maintenant à quoi je m'occupe, et je tâche à suppléer par industrie le défaut des expériences qui me manquent. . . ." 5 octobre 1637, *Corr.*, II:32.

8. "Je n'ai jamais eu plus de soin de me conserver que maintenant, et au lieu que je pensais autrefois que la mort ne me pût ôter que trente ou quarante ans tout au plus, elle ne saurait désormais me surprendre qu'elle ne m'ôte l'espérance de plus d'un siècle. Car il me

semble voir très évidemment que, si nous nous gardions seulement de certaines fautes que nous avons coutume de commettre au régime de notre vie, nous pourrions sans autre invention parvenir à une vieillesse beaucoup plus longue et plus heureuse que nous ne faisons; mais, parce que j'ai besoin de beaucoup de temps et d'expériences pour examiner tout ce qui sert à ce sujet, je travaille maintenant à composer un Abrégé de Médecine, que je tire en partie des livres et en partie de mes raisonnements, et que j'espère me pouvoir servir par provision à obtenir quelque délai de la Nature et à poursuivre mieux ci-après en mon dessein." 4 décembre 1637, *ibid.*, pp. 59–60.

9. "Il faudrait que je fusse fort las de vivre si je négligeais de me conserver après avoir lu vos dernières, où vous me mandez que vous, et quelques autres personnes de très grand mérite, avez tel soin de moi que vous craignez que je ne sois malade, lorsque vous êtes plus de 15 jours sans recevoir de mes lettres. Mais il y a 30 ans que je n'ai eu, grâces à Dieu, aucun mal qui méritât d'être appelé mal. Et pour ce que l'âge m'a ôté cette chaleur de foie qui me faisait autrefois aimer les armes, et que je ne fais plus profession que de poltronnerie, et aussi que j'ai acquis quelque peu de connaissance de la médecine, et que je me sens vivre, et me tâte avec autant de soin qu'un riche goutteux, il me semble quasi que je suis maintenant plus loin de la mort que je n'étais en ma jeunesse. Et si Dieu ne me donne assez de science pour éviter les incommodités que l'âge apporte, j'espère qu'il me laissera au moins assez longtemps en cette vie pour me donner loisir de les souffrir. . . . L'un des points de ma morale est d'aimer la vie sans craindre la mort." 9 janvier 1639, *Corr.*, III:161.

10. "Mais je n'en sais pas encore tant pour cela, que je puisse seulement guérir une fievre. Car je pense connaître l'animal en général, lequel n'y est nullement sujet, et non pas encore l'homme en particulier, lequel y est sujet." 20 février 1639, *ibid.*, pp. 196–197.

11. Baillet, *Vie*, II:89–90.

12. 15 septembre 1640, *Corr.*, IV:159.

13. "Si je vous mesurais au pied des âmes vulgaires, la tristesse que vous avez témoignée dès le commencement de la maladie de feu Mme de Zuylichem me ferait craindre que son décès ne vous fût du tout insupportable; mais, ne doutant point que vous ne vous gouverniez entièrement selon la raison, je me persuade qu'il vous est beaucoup plus aisé de vous consoler et de reprendre votre tranquillité d'esprit accoutumée, maintenant qu'il n'y a plus du tout de remède, que lorsque vous aviez encore occasion de craindre et d'espérer. Car il est certain que, l'espérance étant ôtée, le désir cesse ou du moins s'affaiblit et se relâche; et que, lorsqu'on n'a que peu ou point de désir de ravoir

ce qu'on a perdu, le regret n'en peut être fort sensible. . . . Mais une âme forte et généreuse, comme la vôtre, sait trop bien à quelle condition Dieu nous a fait naître, pour vouloir par des souhaits inefficaces résister à la nécessité de sa loi. Et bien qu'on ne s'y puisse soumettre sans quelque peine, j'estime si fort l'amitié, que je crois que tout ce qu'on souffre à son occasion est agréable, en sorte que ceux mêmes qui vont à la mort pour le bien des personnes qu'ils affectionnent, me semblent heureux jusques au dernier moment de leur vie." 20 mai 1637, *Corr.*, I:346–347.

14. "Ce serait être barbare que de ne se point affliger du tout, lorsqu'on en a du sujet, aussi serait-ce être trop lâche de s'abandonner entièrement au déplaisir." Mi-janvier 1641, *Corr.*, IV:247.

15. "Au reste, la dernière lettre que vous m'avez envoyée m'apprend la mort de mon Père, dont je suis fort triste, et j'ai bien du regret de n'avoir pu aller cet été en France, afin de le voir avant qu'il mourût; mais puisque Dieu ne l'a pas permis, je ne crois point partir d'ici que ma *Philosophie* ne soit faite." 3 décembre 1640, *ibid.*, p. 215.

16. Clerselier's account as recorded by Baillet is given in *Oeuvres*, XII:576–577.

17. Mahaffy, *Descartes*, p. 63.

18. "Je ne suis pas de ceux qui estiment que les larmes et la tristesse n'appartiennent qu'aux femmes, et que, pour paraître homme de coeur, on se doive contraindre à montrer toujours un visage tranquille." Lettre à Pollot, mi-janvier 1641, *Corr.*, IV:247.

19. "À la fin de la page 8, je trouve encore mon nom: ce que peut-être je puis plus honnêtement laisser passer dans un titre, pourvu, un honnête homme peut bien, s'il vous plaît, que vous m'épargniez davantage les épithètes. Et j'aimerais mieux aussi qu'on m'appelât de mon vrai nom Descartes, que de celui qu'on a forgé Cartesius." 24 mai 1640, *ibid.*, p. 65.

20. "S'il y a quelque chose dont vous désiriez une plus ample explication, vous me trouverez toujours prêt à vout servir soit par lettre ou de vive voix. Et même, pour la soutenance de ces Thèses, j'irai, si vous voulez, faire un tour à Utrecht; mais que personne ne le sache, et que je puisse me tenir caché dans l'écoute, où la demoiselle de Schurmann a coutume de venir entendre vos leçons." *Ibid.*, pp. 68–69.

21. A summary of *The Learned Maid* is given by Godfrey in *A Sister of Prince Rupert*, pp. 109–113.

22. This incident is related in Samuel Desmarets' *Vie de Jean Labadie* (1670) and quoted in *Oeuvres*, IV:700–701.

23. Gustave Cohen suggests that Mademoiselle Schurmann might have been secretly in love with Descartes, a supposition which Cornelia Ser-

rurier finds untenable. The latter also doubts that Descartes would have spoken so disrespectfully of a Biblical text. *Cf.* Cohen, *Écrivains français en Hollande*, p. 536, and Serrurier, *Descartes*, pp. 144–145.

24. "Ce Voëtius a gâté aussi la Demoiselle de Schurmann; car au lieu qu'elle avait l'esprit excellent pour la Poésie, la Peinture et autres telles gentillesses, il y a déjà cinq ou six ans qu'il la possède si entièrement, qu'elle ne s'occupe plus qu'aux controverses de la Théologie, ce qui lui fait perdre la conversation de tous les honnêtes gens." 11 novembre 1640, *Corr.*, IV:198.

25. "Dieu a éloigné mon coeur de l'homme profane et il s'est servi de lui comme d'un aiguillon pour ranimer en moi la piété et pour me faire me donner entièrement à Lui." Quoted by Cohen, *Écrivains français en Hollande*, p. 537.

26. "Je vous remercie des nouvelles du sieur Voëtius, je n'y trouve rien d'étrange, sinon qu'il ait ignoré ce que je vous suis; car il n'y a personne ici, qui me connaisse tant soit peu, qui ne le sache. C'est le plus franc pédant de la terre, et il crève de dépit, de ce qu'il y a un Professeur en Médecine en leur Académie d'Utrecht, qui fait profession ouverte de ma Philosophie, et fait même des leçons particulières de Physique, et en peu de mois rend ses disciples capables de se moquer entièrement de la vieille Philosophie. Voëtius et les autres Professeurs ont fait tout leur possible pour lui fair défendre par le Magistrat de l'enseigner; mais, tout au contraire, le Magistrat lui a permis malgré eux." 11 novembre 1640, *Corr.*, IV:198.

27. "J'ai lu (et j'ai bien ri) à la fois les Thèses du jeune Voet, le fils de l'autre, et qui n'est qu'un enfant, le Jugement de votre Académie, qui peut-être mérite bien qu'on dise aussi d'elle qu'elle est en enfance. . . . Mais je suis un peu fâché contre vous: vous semblez prendre à coeur pareille chose; vous devriez vous réjouir extrêmement, de voir vos adversaires se juguler avec leurs propres armes. Certainement personne d'une intelligence moyenne ne lira jusqu'au bout ces écrits-là, sans remarquer aisément que les raisons manquent à vos adversaires pour vous réfuter, et qu'ils n'ont pas non plus la sagesse de cacher leur sottise. . . . Ne faites qu'en rire, et tranquillisez-vous, je vous prie; n'ayez crainte, vos adversaires seront assez vite punis. Enfin vous l'emportez, si veulement vous savez vous taire." Avril 1642, *Corr.*, V:186–188.

28. "En effet, je ne demande que la paix des uns et des autres, mais je vois bien que pour l'obtenir il me faut un peu faire la guerre." 26 avril 1642, *ibid.*, p. 191.

29. "Il passe pour théologien, orateur, disputateur; il s'est concilié les petites gens en étalant une piété fervente et un zèle indomptable pour la religion, en attaquant les gouvernants, l'Église Romaine et toute opi-

nion différente de la sienne propre, en chatouillant les oreilles de la populace par ces brocards de bouffon. Il édite chaque jour des pamphlets qui ne sont lus de personne, citant des auteurs qu'il ne connaît peut-être que par leur table des matières et qui plaident plus souvent contre lui que pour lui, parlant avec autant de présomption que de maladresse de toutes les sciences, comme s'il les savait et, par là, ne passant pour savant qu'auprès des ignorants." *Oeuvres*, VII:584.

30. "Je respecte tous les théologiens, comme étant les serviteurs de Dieu, même ceux qui sont d'une autre religion que la mienne, parce que nous adorons tous le même Dieu." *Ibid.*, VIII:180.

31. "Si quelqu'un se donne pour théologien mais que je le sais menteur insigne et calomniateur et que ses vices sont tels qu'ils constituent, à mon sens, un danger pour la chose publique, ce titre de théologien ne m'empêchera pas de les dévoiler." *Ibid.*, p. 179.

32. "Et je n'ai pas besoin non plus d'invoquer la liberté de religion qui nous est accordée dans cette république. Je me borne à affirmer que votre livre contient des mensonges si criminels, des injures si bouffonnes, des calomnies si abominables qu'aucun ennemi n'en pourrait proférer de semblables contre son ennemi, aucun chrétien contre un infidèle, sans se dénoncer lui-même comme un malhonnête homme et un scélerat. . . . Engin je connais assez le tempérament des Hollandais pour savoir que leurs gouvernants imitent le souverain Dieu en ceci qu'ils tardent souvent et hésitent à punir les coupables, mais que, lorsque la hardiesse des méchants a dépassé la limite où ils jugent une répression nécessaire, ils l'appliquent sans miséricorde et sans se laisser tromper par de fallacieuses paroles. Et vous qui, en publiant des livres, vides de charité et de preuves et remplis seulement de calmonies, avez déshonoré votre Profession et votre Religion, prenez garde qu'ils ne jugent que la seule satisfaction qui convienne à celles-ci soit votre châtiment. Adieu!" *Ibid.*, pp. 110–111.

33. "Un homme étourdi me fit un jour une plaisante comparaison, disant que les Théologiens étaient semblables aux pourceaux, que quand on en tire un par la queue, tous crient." 6 juin 1643, *Corr.*, V:302.

34. "J'ai écrit une longue lettre aux Curateurs de l'Académie de Leyde, pour demander justice contre les calomnies de ces deux Théologiens. Je ne sais point encore la réponse que j'en aurai; mais, selon que je connais l'humeur des personnes de ce pays, et combien ils révèrent, non pas la probité et la vertu, mais la barbe, la voix et le sourcil des Théologiens, en sorte que ceux qui sont les plus effrontés, et qui savent crier le plus haut, ont ici le plus de pouvoir . . . encore qu'ils aient le moins de raison, je n'en attends que quelques emplâtres, qui, n'ôtant point la cause du mal, ne serviront qu'à le rendre plus long et plus importun. . . .

Et en cas que je ne puisse obtenir justice (comme je prévois qu'il sera très malaise que je l'obtienne), de me retirer tout à fait de ces Provinces." 10 mai 1647, *Corr.*, VII:308.

Chapter 6

1. Both Borel and Haldane state that Descartes took part in the battle, but Adam gives more convincing arguments to the contrary. *Oeuvres*, XII:60.

2. This description is given by her sister in *Memoiren der Herzogin Sophie* (Leipzig, Adolf Koecher, 1879), quoted in *Oeuvres*, XII:403, Note a.

3. Godfrey, *A Sister of Prince Rupert*, p. 75.

4. ". . . d'un corps si semblable à ceux que les peintres donnent aux anges. . . ." 21 mai 1643, *Corr.*, V:289.

5. Most of the details of Endegeest come from Godfrey, *A Sister of Prince Rupert*, pp. 95 *et seq.*, which contains a photograph.

6. Cohen, *Écrivains français en Hollande*, p. 607.

7. "Et je puis dire, avec vérité, que la principale règle que j'ai toujours observée en mes études, et celle que je crois m'avoir le plus servi pour acquérir quelque connaissance, a été que je n'ai jamais employé que fort peu d'heures, par jour, aux pensées qui occupent l'imagination, et fort peu d'heures, par an, à celles qui occupent l'entendement seul, et que j'ai donné tout le reste de mon temps au relâche des sens et au repos de l'esprit. . . ." Lettre à Elisabeth, 28 juin 1643, *Corr.*, V:323.

8. *Briefe der Kinder des Winter Königs* (Heidelberger Historisches Taschenbuch), quoted by Godfrey, *A Sister of Prince Rupert*, p. 65.

9. "Il y a quelque chose de surprenant dans les malheurs, quoique prévus, dont je ne suis maîtresse qu'après un certain temps, auquel mon corps se désordonne si fort qu'il me faut plusieurs mois pour le remettre, qui ne se passent guère sans quelque nouveau sujet de trouble." 22 juin 1645, *Corr.*, VI:248.

10. ". . . et je désespérai de trouver de la certitude en chose du monde, si vous ne m'en donnez, qui m'avez seul empêchée d'être sceptique. . . ." 1 juillet 1643, *ibid*, p. 2.

11. "J'ai peur que vous n'avez pas reçu ma dernière . . . parce que vous n'en faites pas mention. Je serais fâchée qu'elle venait entre les mains de quelqu'un de ces critiques qui condamnent pour hérésies tous les doutes qu'on fait des opinions reçues." 27 décembre 1645, *ibid*., p. 339.

12. ". . . mais je me promets que votre Altesse, étant accoutumée aux disgrâces de la Fortune, et s'étant vue soi-même depuis peu en grand

péril de sa vie, ne sera pas si surprise, ni si troublée, d'apprendre la mort d'un de ses proches, que si elle n'avait point reçu auparavant d'autres afflictions." Lettre à Elisabeth, 22 février 1649, *Corr.*, VIII:142–143.

13. "Et bien que cette mort si violente semble avoir quelque chose de plus affreux que celle qu'on attend en son lit, toutefois, à le bien prendre, elle est plus glorieuse, plus heureuse et plus douce, en sorte que ce qui afflige particulièrement en ceci le commun des hommes, doit servir de consolation à v. A. . . . Et il est certain que, sans cette épreuve, la clémence et les autres vertus du Roi dernier mort n'auraient jamais été tant remarquées ni tant estimées qu'elles sont et seront à l'avenir par tous ceux qui liront son histoire. . . . Et pour ce qui est de la douleur, je ne la mets nullement en compte; car elle est si courte, que, si les meurtriers pouvaient employer la fièvre ou quelque autre des maladies dont la nature a coutume de se servir pour ôter les hommes du monde, on aurait sujet de les estimer plus cruels qu'ils ne sont, lorsqu'ils les tuent d'un coup de hache. Mais je n'ose m'arrêter longtemps sur un sujet si funeste; j'ajoute seulement qu'il vaut beaucoup mieux être entièrement délivré d'une fausse espérance que d'y être inutilement entretenu." *Ibid.*, p. 143.

14. "De quoi je ne puis deviner autre chose, sinon que, les conditions de la paix d'Allemagne n'étant pas si avantageuses à votre maison qu'elles auraient pu être, ceux qui ont contribué à cela sont en doute si vous ne leur en voulez point de mal, et se retiennent, pour ce sujet, de vous témoigner de l'amitié." *Ibid.*, p. 144.

15. Descartes puts certain restrictions upon self-sacrifice, however, which are discussed by Serrurier, *Descartes*, p. 211, and are found in the *Oeuvres*, IV:293.

16. "L'expérience m'avait fait connaître que la plupart des esprits qui ont de la facilité à entendre les raisonnements de la Métaphysique, ne peuvent pas concevoir ceux de l'Algèbre. . . ." Lettre à Elisabeth, novembre 1643, *Corr.*, VI:70.

17. "Sur ce que vous m'écriviez dernièrement de Mme la Princesse de Bohême, j'ai pensé être obligé de lui envoyer la solution de la question qu'elle croit avoir trouvée, et la raison pourquoi je ne crois pas qu'on en puisse bien venir à bout, en en supposant qu'une racine. Ce que je ne fais néanmoins avec scrupule, car peut-être qu'elle aimera mieux la chercher encore, que de voir ce que je lui écris. . . ." Lettre à Pollot, *ibid.*, p. 57.

18. "La solution qu'il a plu à votre Altesse me faire l'honneur de m'envoyer, est si juste, qu'il ne s'y peut rien désirer davantage; et je n'ai pas seulement été surpris d'étonnement, en la voyant, mais je ne puis m'abstenir d'ajouter que j'ai été aussi ravi de joie, et ai pris de la vanité de voir que le calcul, dont se sert votre Altesse, est entièrement

semblable à celui que j'ai proposé dans ma *Géométrie*." Lettre à Elisabeth, *ibid.*, p. 7.

19. "La rencontre de quatre ou cinq visages Français, qui descendaient de chez la Reine, au même moment que je sortais de chez Mme la Princesse de B(ohême), fut cause que je ne n'eus pas dernièrement l'honneur de vous revoir, et que je m'en allai sans dire adieu. Car ayant ouï de loin qu'ils me nommaient, et craignant que ces éveillés ne m'arrêtassent avec leurs discours, à une heure que j'avais envie de dormir, je me retirai le plus vite qu'il me fut possible. . . ." Lettre à Pollot, 8 avril 1644, *ibid.*, p. 137.

20. Consult Adam and Tannery's comparative study of the two works in *Oeuvres*, XI:698–706 and XII:146, 358.

21. These examples are cited by Adam, *Oeuvres*, XII:378.

22. ". . . philosophie signifie l'étude de la sagesse, et que par la sagesse on n'entend pas seulement la prudence dans les affaires, mais une parfaite connaissance de toutes les choses que l'homme peut savoir, tant pour la conduite de sa vie que pour la conversation de sa santé et l'invention de tous les arts. . . ." *Ibid.*, IX:2.

23. "C'est proprement avoir les yeux fermés, sans tâcher jamais de les ouvrir, que de vivre sans philosopher; et le plaisir de voir toutes les choses que notre vue découvre n'est point comparable à la satisfaction que donne la connaissance de celles qu'on trouve par la philosophie; et, enfin, cette étude est plus nécessaire pour régler nos moeurs et nous conduire en cette vie, que n'est l'usage de nos yeux pour guider nos pas." *Ibid.*, p. 3.

24. "Ainsi toute la philosophie est comme un arbre, dont les racines sont la métaphysique, le tronc est la physique, et les branches qui sortent de ce tronc sont toutes les autres sciences, qui se réduisent à trois principales, à savoir la médecine, la mécanique et la morale." *Ibid.*, p. 14.

25. "Premièrement, un homme . . . doit, avant tout, tâcher de se former une morale qui puisse suffire pour régler les actions de sa vie, à cause que cela ne souffre point de délai, et que nous devons surtout tâcher de bien vivre. Après cela, il doit aussi étudier la logique, non pas celle de l'École, car elle n'est, à proprement parler, qu'une dialectique qui enseigne les moyens de faire entendre à autrui les choses qu'on sait, ou même aussi de dire sans jugement plusieurs paroles touchant celles qu'on ne sait pas, et ainsi elle corrompt le bon sens plutôt qu'elle ne l'augmente; mais celle qui apprend à bien conduire sa raison pour découvrir les vérités qu'on ignore; et, parce qu'elle dépend beaucoup de l'usage, il est bon qu'il s'exerce longtemps à en pratiquer les règles touchant des questions faciles et simples, comme sont celles des mathématiques. Puis, lorsqu'il s'est acquis quelque habitude à trouver la vérité en ces questions, il doit commencer tout de bon à s'appliquer à la vraie

philosophie, dont la première partie est la métaphysique, qui contient les principes de la connaissance, entre lesquels est l'explication des principaux attributs de Dieu, de l'immatérialité de nos âmes. . . ." *Ibid.*, p. 13.

26. "Mais ce qui augmente le plus mon admiration, c'est qu'une si parfaite et si diverse connaissance de toutes les sciences n'est point en quelque vieux docteur qui ait employé beaucoup d'années à s'instruire, mais en une princesse encore jeune et dont le visage représente mieux celui que les poètes attribuent aux Grâces que celui qu'ils attribuent aux Muses ou à la savante Minerve." *Ibid.*, p. 23.

27. Et il faut que je vous avoue que, depuis mon voyage de France, je suis devenu plus vieux de vingt ans que je n'étais l'année passée, en sorte que ce m'est maintenant un plus grand voyage d'aller jusques à Rome. Ce n'est pas pourtant que j'aie aucune indisposition, grâces à Dieu; mais je me sens plus faible, et pense avoir davantage besoin de rechercher mes commodités et mon repos." Lettre à Pollot, 18 mai 1645, *Corr.*, VI:227.

28. There is some confusion about Rembrantsz' occupation. Some believe that he was a pilot. Most of the details given here come from Serrurier, *Descartes*, pp. 145–148.

29. "Car elle m'a plus troublée la santé du corps et la tranquillité de l'âme, que tous les malheurs qui me sont encore arrivés. Si vous prenez la peine de lire la gazette, vous ne sauriez ignorer qu'il est tombé entre les mains d'une certaine sorte de gens, qui ont plus de haine pour notre maison que d'affection pour leur culte, et s'est laissé prendre dans leurs pièges, jusqu'à changer de religion pour se rendre catholique romain. . . . Il faut que je voie une personne, que j'aimais avec autant de tendresse que j'en saurais avoir, abandonnée au mépris du monde et à la perte de son âme (selon ma croyance). Si vous n'aviez pas plus de charité que de bigoterie, ce serait une impertinence de vous entretenir de cette matière, et ceci ne m'en garantirait pas, si je n'étais en possession de vous dire tous mes défauts, comme à la personne du monde la plus capable de m'en corriger." 30 novembre 1645, *Corr.*, VI: 334–345.

30. "Car tous ceux de la Religion dont je suis (qui sont sans doute le plus grand nombre dans l'Europe) sont obligés de l'approuver, encore même qu'ils y vissent des circonstances et des motifs apparents qui fussent blâmables; car nous croyons que Dieu se sert de divers moyens pour attirer les âmes à soi, et que tel est entré dans le Cloître, avec une mauvaise intention lequel y a mené, par après, une vie fort sainte. . . . S'ils considèrent qu'ils ne seraient pas de la Religion dont ils sont, si eux, ou leur pères, ou leurs aïeux n'avaient quitté la Romaine, ils n'auront pas sujet de se moquer, ni de nommer inconstants ceux qui

quittent la leur. . . . Ce qui m'empêche de pouvoir imaginer que ceux qui ont été auteurs de ce conseil aient en cela voulu nuire à votre Maison. Mais je ne prétends point que mes raisons puissent empêcher le ressentiment de votre Altesse; j'espère seulement que le temps l'aura diminué, avant que cette lettre vous soit présentée. . . ." Janvier 1646, *Corr.*, VII:2–3.

31. See Tallemant des Réaux, *Historiettes* (Paris, Techener, 1854), Vol. II, pp. 287–289. Gustave Cohen in his *Écrivains français en Hollande* draws heavily upon this source.

32. "Mais il me serait encore trop long, si je ne m'assurais que vous y continuerez la charité de me faire profiter de vos Méditations par vos lettres, puisque, sans leur assistance, les froideurs du nord et le calibre des gens avec qui je pourrais converser, éteindrait ce petit rayon de sens commun que je tiens de la nature, et dont je reconnais l'usage par votre méthode. On me promet en Allemagne assez de loisir et de tranquillité pour la pouvoir étudier, et je n'y amène de plus grand trésors, d'où je prétends tirer plus de satisfaction, que vos écrits. J'espère que vous me permettrez d'emporter celui des passions, encore qu'il n'a été capable de calmer ceux que notre dernier malheur avait excités. Il fallait que votre présence y apportât la cure, que vos maximes ni mon raisonnement n'avaient pu appliquer." Août 1646, *Corr.*, VII: 140–142.

33. ". . . et il semble qu'en ces rencontres Dieu donne le droit à ceux auxquels il donne la force. . . . Car, au regard des ces derniers, on a quasi permission de tout faire, pourvu qu'on en tire quelque advantage pour soi ou pour ses sujets; et je ne désapprouve pas, en cette occasion, qu'on accouple le renard avec le lion, et qu'on joigne l'artifice à la force." Septembre 1646, *ibid.*, pp. 164–165.

34. ". . . ces maximes qui enseignent que la félicité d'un chacun dépend de lui-même, et qu'il faut tellement se tenir hors de l'empire de la Fortune, que, bien qu'on ne perde pas les occasions de retenir les avantages qu'elle peut donner, on ne pense pas toutefois être malheureux, lorsqu'elle les refuse; et pour ce qu'en toutes les affaires du monde il y a quantité de raisons pour et contre, qu'on s'arrête principalement à considérer celles qui servent à faire qu'on approuve les choses qu'on voit arriver." *Ibid.*, p. 168.

35. "Ici je n'y rencontre point beaucoup de difficulté, étant en une maison où j'ai été chérie depuis mon enfance et où tout le monde conspire à me faire des caresses. Encore que ceux-là me détournent quelquefois d'occupations plus utiles, je supporte aisément cette incommodité, par le plaisir qu'il y a d'être aimé de ses proches." 10 octobre 1646, *ibid.*, pp. 189–190.

36. ". . . quoique je sois engagée de promesse à ce vieux duc . . .

de les lui faire avoir, pour orner sa bibliothèque. Je ne crois point qu'ils lui serviront pour orner sa cervelle catarrheuse, déjà tout occupée du pédantisme." 29 novembre 1646, *ibid.*, p. 230.

37. "Je n'ai point regretté mon absence de La Haye, que depuis que vous me mandez y avoir été, et que je me sens privée de la satisfaction que je voulais avoir en votre conversation, pendant le séjour que vous y faisiez; il me semblait que . . . le repos que je trouve ici . . . surpasse tous les biens que je puisse avoir ailleurs . . . que je ne me saurais néanmoins promettre en quelque mois, ni en prédire le nombre, puisque je ne vois point que Madame l'Électrice, ma Tante, soit en humeur de permettre mon retour, et que je n'ai point sujet de l'en presser, avant que M. son fils soit auprès d'elle, ce qui . . . ne sera qu'au mois de septembre. . . . Je souhaite que vous puissiez rencontrer en ce voyage le succès que vous y demandez, et que, si je n'avais expérimenté la confiance de vos résolutions, je craindrais encore que vos amis ne vous obligeront d'y demeurer." 11 avril 1646, *ibid.*, pp. 277–278.

38. The details of this first meeting with Pascal are related by his sister Jacqueline. See Cohen, *Écrivains français en Hollande*, pp. 637–638.

39. Frédérix, *Monsieur René Descartes et son temps*, pp. 275–281.

40. Lettre à Chanut, mai 1648, *Corr.*, VIII:32.

41. "Je les ai considérés comme des amis qui m'avaient convié à dîner chez eux; et lorsque j'y suis arrivé, j'ai trouvé que leur cuisine était en désordre, et leur marmite renversée; c'est pourquoi je m'en suis revenu sans dire un mot, afin de n'augmenter point leur fâcherie." Lettre à Chanut, 26 février 1649, *ibid.*, p. 148.

42. Godfrey, *A Sister of Prince Rupert*, pp. 194–195.

Chapter 7

1. This anecdote is related by Taylor, *Christina of Sweden*, p. 1.

2. "Et j'ai ouï faire tant d'estime de cette Reine, qu'au lieu que je me suis souvent plaint de ceux qui m'ont voulu donner la connaissance de quelque grand, je ne puis m'abstenir de vous remercier de ce qu'il vous a plu lui parler de moi. J'ai vu ici Monsieur de la Thuillerie, depuis son retour de Suède, lequel m'a décrit ses qualités d'une façon si avantageuse, que celle d'être reine me semble l'une des moindres; et je n'en aurais osé croire la moitié, si je n'avais vu par expérience, en la Princesse à qui j'ai dédié mes *Principes de Philosophie*, que les personnes de grande naissance, de quelque sexe qu'elles soient, n'ont pas besoin d'avoir beaucoup d'âge pour pouvoir surpasser de beaucoup en érudition et en vertu les autres hommes. Mais j'ai bien peur que les écrits que j'ai publiés ne

méritent pas qu'elle s'arrête à les lire, et ainsi qu'elle ne vous sache point de gré de les lui avoir recommandés. Peut-être que, si j'y avais traité de la morale, j'aurais occasion d'espérer qu'ils lui pourront être plus agréables; mais c'est de quoi je ne dois pas me mêler d'écrire." Lettre à Chanut, 1 novembre 1646, *Corr.*, VII:199.

3. "On peut dire beaucoup de choses en peu de temps, et je trouve que la longue fréquentation n'est pas nécessaire pour lier d'étroites amitiés, lorsqu'elles sont fondées sur la vertu. Dès la première heure que j'ai eu l'honneur de vous voir, j'ai été entièrement à vous, et comme j'ai osé dès lors m'assurer de votre bienveillance, aussi je vous supplie de croire que je ne vous pourrais être plus acquis que je suis, si j'avais passé avec vous toute ma vie." *Ibid.*, p. 200.

4. "Il est vrai que la colère est une de celles dont j'estime qu'il se faut garder, en tant qu'elle a pour objet une offense reçue; et pour cela nous devons tâcher d'élever si haut notre esprit, que les offenses que les autres nous peuvent faire, ne parviennent jamais jusques à nous. Mais je crois qu'au lieu de colère, il est juste d'avoir de l'indignation, et j'avoue que j'en ai souvent contre l'ignorance de ceux qui veulent être pris pour doctes, lorsque je la vois jointe à la malice." *Ibid.*, p. 201.

5. "Et on voit tous les jours des exemples de cette amour, même en des personnes de basse condition, qui donnent leur vie de bon coeur pour le bien de leur pays, ou pour la défense d'un grand qu'ils affectionnent. En suite de quoi il est évident que notre amour envers Dieu doit être sans comparaison la plus grande et la plus parfaite de toutes." Lettre à Chanut, 1 février 1647, *ibid.*, p. 257.

6. "Et si je vous demandais, en conscience, si vous n'aimez point cette grande Reine, auprès de laquelle vous êtes à présent, vous auriez beau dire que vous n'avez pour elle que du respect, de la vénération et de l'étonnement, je ne laisserais pas de juger que vous avez aussi une très ardente affection. Car votre style coule si bien, quand vous parlez d'elle, que, bien que je croie tout ce que vous en dites, parce que je sais que vous êtes très véritable et que j'en ai aussi ouï parler à d'autres, je ne crois pas néanmoins que vous la pussiez décrire comme vous faites, si vous n'aviez beaucoup de zèle, ni que vous pussiez être auprès d'une si grande lumière sans en recevoir de la chaleur." *Ibid.*, p. 255.

7. "Je préfère le bonheur de M. Descartes à toutes le couronnes de la terre." Lettre de Chanut à M. de Saint-Romain, *Bibliothèque Nationale* MS. fr. 17963, p. 315. Quoted by Adam, *Vie*, p. 522.

8. See Lettre à Chanut, 6 juin 1647, *Corr.*, VII:345 *et seq.*

9. "Et je ne vois point qu'il soit possible d'en disposer mieux, que si l'on a toujours une ferme et constante résolution de faire exactement toutes les choses que l'on jugera être les meilleures, et d'employer toutes

les forces de son esprit à les bien connaître." Lettre à Christine, 20 novembre 1647, *ibid.*, p. 369.

10. Lettre à Descartes, 12 décembre 1648, *Corr.*, VIII:109–110.

11. "... j'ose ici protester à votre Majesté qu'elle ne me saurait rien commander de si difficile, que je ne sois toujours prêt de faire tout mon possible pour l'exécuter; et que si j'étais né Suédois ou Finlandais, je ne pourrais être, avec de zèle, ni plus parfaitement que je suis. ..." Lettre à Christine de Suède, 26 février 1649, *ibid.*, p. 150.

12. "Mais ce qui m'a le plus dégoûté, c'est qu'aucun d'eux n'a témoigné vouloir connaître autre chose de moi que mon visage; en sorte que j'ai sujet de croire qu'ils me voulaient seulement avoir en France comme un Eléphant ou une Panthère, à cause de la rareté, et non point pour y être utile à quelque chose." Lettre à Chanut, 31 mars 1649, *ibid.*, p. 195.

13. *Cf.* Lettre à Freinshemius, juin 1649, *ibid.*, pp. 229–231.

14. "... s'il n'y a pas tant de miel qu'en celle que Dieu avait promise aux Israélites, il est croyable qu'il y a plus de lait." Lettre à Brasset, 23 avril 1649, *ibid.*, p. 218.

15. "Etant sur le point de partir pour aller à Stockholm, et considérant que je puis mourir dans le voyage ..." Lettre à l'Abbé Picot, 30 août 1649, *ibid.*, p. 270.

16. *Oeuvres*, V:411.

17. *Cf.* Adam, *Vie*, XII:200.

18. Baillet, *Vie*, II:387–388, quoted in *Corr.*, VIII:285.

19. Lettre à l'Abbé Picot, 9 octobre 1649, *Corr.*, VIII:289.

20. Lettre à Elisabeth, *ibid.*, p. 286.

21. "Lettres et Discours de M. de Sorbière," quoted in *Oeuvres*, V:460.

22. Lettre à Elisabeth, 9 octobre 1649, *Corr.*, VIII:287.

23. Lettre à l'Abbé Picot, *ibid.*

24. *Oeuvres*, V:468.

25. Lettre à Brégy, 15 janvier 1650, *Corr.*, VIII:313–314.

26. The anecdote of the savant of Dijon is recounted both in the *Oeuvres*, V:462–463 and in the *Corr.*, VIII:309–310.

27. Thibaudet, "Un Ballet de Descartes," août 1920.

28. Baillet, *Vie*, II:484.

29. De la Mare, Philibert, *Mélanges historiques et littéraires*, MS. 493, Bibliothèque de Dijon, pp. 128–129, quoted in *Oeuvres*, V:468.

30. "La plus grande de toutes les sciences est celle de savoir bien vivre et bien mourir; toutes les autres sont inutiles, si elles n'y contribuent pas." Quoted by Cassirer, *Descartes*, p. 48.

31. *Ibid.*, p. 95. Chapter IV gives a detailed account of the doctrine of the passions.

32. Most of the details of Descartes' illness come from Baillet's *Vie*, II:414–423.

33. *Oeuvres*, V:490.

34. "C'a, mon âme," disait-il, "il y a longtemps que tu és captive; voici l'heure que tu dois sortir de prison, et quitter l'embaras de ce cors; il faut souffrir cette des-union avec joye et courage." Quoted from Clerselier's account in *Oeuvres*, V:482.

35. "Ah! mon cher Schluter, c'est pour le coup qu'il faut partir." Quoted from Baillet's account in *Oeuvres*, V:493.

36. Ainsi par la vertu et non par la durée
Notre vie icy-bas doit estre mesurée;
Eh, j'aurois donc vescu bien inutilement,
Si je n'avois appris à mourir un moment.
From Catherine Descartes' account of her uncle's death. *Ibid.*, p. 499.

Notes to the Epilogue

1. In a letter to his older brother Christian Huygens wrote: "Pour la plus importante (nouvelle), je vous raconterai ce que j'ai leu dans la Gazette. Il y avait dedans celle d'Anvers le dimanche passé: *Dat in Suede een geck gestorven was, die seyde dat hy soo langh leven kon als hy wilde.* Notez que c'est ici M. des Cartes." *Oeuvres*, X:630.

2. "Je ne doute point, madame, qu'il ne fût avantageux à votre réputation que l'on connût que vous avez eu des entretiens sérieux avec le plus habile homme qui ait vécu depuis plusieurs siècles; et j'ai su de Monsieur Descartes même que vos lettres étaient si pleines de lumière et d'esprit, qu'il ne vous peut être que glorieux qu'elles soient vues. Et néanmoins j'ai pensé qu'il était de mon respect envers votre Altesse Royale, et de ma félicité envers mon ami défunct, de n'en lire aucune, et ne permettre pas qu'elles tombent entre les mains de qui que ce soit, que par l'ordre et la permission de votre Altesse Royale. . . ." Chanut à Madame la Princesse Elisabeth Palatine, 19 février 1650, *ibid.*, V:471.

3. "Je crois, madame, que s'il eut pensé le jour précédent être si proche de sa fin, ayant encore la parole libre, il m'eut recommandé plusieurs choses de ses dernières volontés, et m'eut en particulier ordonné de faire savoir à votre Altesse Royale qu'il mourrait dans le même respect qu'il a eu pour elle pendant sa vie; et qu'il m'a souvent témoigné par des paroles pleines de révérence et d'admiration." Chanut à Madame la Princesse Elisabeth de Bohême, 16 avril 1650, *ibid.*, p. 474.

4. Foucher de Careil was the first to edit them in 1879.

5. I have borrowed the term *nécrologie burlesque* from Sacy, *Descartes par lui-même*, p. 178.

6. *Oeuvres*, XII:599.

7. The parallel is taken from Serrurier, *Descartes*, p. 297.

8. Godfrey, *A Sister of Prince Rupert*, p. 349.

9. For Clerselier's judgment of Descartes, see *Oeuvres*, V:484.

10. For detailed accounts of Descartes' debt to previous thinkers, see Gilson, *Études sur le rôle de la pensée médiévale dans la formation du système cartésien* (Paris, Vrin, 1930).

11. "Chaque homme est obligé de procurer, autant qu'il est en lui, le bien des autres, et c'est proprement ne valoir rien que de n'être utile à personne." Quoted by Adam, *Vie*, p. 172.

12. Much of the foregoing summary of Descartes' contribution to science is based upon Frederick Purser's statement quoted by Mahaffy, *Descartes*, pp. 207–211.

13. The preceding quotes from Montesquieu and Voltaire are taken from Fataud's edition of the *Discours*, p. 182.

14. D'Alembert, *Discours préliminaire de l'encyclopédie,* quoted by Fataud, *op. cit.*, p. 182.

15. *Ibid.*, p. 184.

16. The two quotes from Sartre are taken from his *Descartes*, Paris, Trois collines, 1946, pp. 20, 31.

17. A. Koyré in *Entretiens sur Descartes*, New York and Paris, Brentano, 1944, quoted by Fataud, *op. cit.*, p. 189.

18. Péguy, *Note sur M. Bergson et la philosophie bergsonienne,* quoted by Fataud, *op. cit.*, p. 189.

Bibliography

Editions of Descartes' Works

Correspondance, Charles Adam and Gérard Milhaud, eds. Paris, Félix Alcan (Vol. 1–2); Presses Universitaires de France (Vol. 3–8), 1936–1963.

Discours de la méthode, J. M. Fataud, ed. Paris, Bordas, 1965.

Discours, de la méthode, Gilbert Gadoffre, ed. Manchester, Manchester University Press, 1941.

Discours de la méthode, Étienne Gilson, ed. Paris, Librarie Philosophique, J. Vrin, 1930.

Discours de la méthode, Louis Liard, ed. Paris, Garnier Frères, 1950.

Lettres sur la morale, Jacques Chevalier, ed. Paris, Boivin, 1935.

Oeuvres, 13 vols., Charles Adam and Paul Tannery, eds. Paris, Cerf, 1897–1913.

Oeuvres et lettres, André Bridoux, ed. Paris, Bibliothèque de la Pléiade, 1952.

Oeuvres philosophiques, Ferdinand Alquié, ed. Paris, Garnier Frères, 1963.

Les Passions de l'âme, Geneviève Rodis-Lewis, ed. Paris, Librairie Philosophique, J. Vrin, 1964.

The Philosophical Works of Descartes, trans. by Elizabeth S. Haldane and G. R. T. Ross, Cambridge, Cambridge University Press, 1931.

Critical Works and Studies

Adam, Charles, *Descartes, ses amitiés féminines*. Paris, Boivin, 1937.

———, "Descartes et sa correspondance féminine." *Revue internationale de l'enseignement* (janvier 1937), pp. 5–16.

———, *Descartes, sa vie et son oeuvre*. Paris, Boivin, 1937.

Alquié, Ferdinand, *La Découverte métaphysique de l'homme chez Descartes*. Paris, Presses Universitaires de France, 1950.

———, *Descartes*. Paris, Librairie Hatier, 1956.

———, *Descartes, l'homme et l'oeuvre.* Paris, Librairie Hatier-Boivin, 1956.

Arckenholtz, Johan, *Mémoires concernant Christine Reine de Suède,* Vol. I, Amsterdam, Pierre Mortier, 1751.

Baillet, Adrien, *La Vie de Monsieur Des-Cartes.* Paris, Chez D. Horthemels, 1691.

Balz, Albert G. A., *Descartes and the Modern Mind.* New Haven, Yale University Press, 1952.

Beck, L. J., *The Method of Descartes.* Oxford, The Clarendon Press, 1952.

Bertrand, Joseph, "Une Amie de Descartes—Elisabeth, Princesse de Bohême." *Revue des deux mondes,* Tome 102 (1890), 93–122.

Boorsch, Jean, *État présent des études sur Descartes.* Les Belles Lettres. Paris, Société d'Édition, 1937.

Brunschvicg, Léon, *René Descartes.* Paris, Rieder, 1937.

Cantecor, G., "L'Oisive adolescence de Descartes." *Revue d'histoire de la philosophie* (1930), pp. 1–38.

———, "La Vocation de Descartes." *Revue philosophique,* Vol. 96 (juillet–août 1923), pp. 372–400.

Cassirer, Ernest, *Descartes, Corneille, Christine de Suède.* Librairie Philosophique. Paris, J. Vrin, 1942.

Chevalier, Jacques, *Descartes.* Paris, Plon-Nourrit, 1921.

———, "La Méthode de connaître d'après Pascal." *Revue de métaphysique et de morale,* Vol. 30 (1923), pp. 181–214.

Cohen, Gustave, *Écrivains français en Hollande dans la première moitié du 17e siècle.* Paris, E. Champion, 1920.

Cresson, André, *Descartes, sa vie, son oeuvre.* Paris, Presses Universitaires de France, 1957.

De Corte, Marcel, "Les Sources cartésiennes et kantiennes de l'idéalisme français." *Revue de philosophie* (mars–avril 1937), pp. 149–56.

Descartes, A Collection of Critical Essays, Willis Doney, ed. Anchor Books. Garden City, New York, Doubleday & Company, 1967.

Dimier, Louis, *La Vie raisonnable de Descartes.* Paris, Librairie Plon, 1926.

Dugas, L., "Une Amitié intellectuelle: Descartes et la princesse Elisabeth." *Annales de Bretagne* (janvier 1891), pp. 223–263.

Espinas, A., "Descartes de seize à vingt-neuf ans." *Revue bleue,* Vol. 45 (23 mars 1907), pp. 353–356, 389–392.

———, "Le Point de départ de Descartes." *Revue bleue,* Vol. 3 (10 mars 1906).

Faguet, Émile, *Dix-septième siècle—études littéraires.* Paris, Société Française d'Imprimerie, 1903.

Fischer, Kuno, *History of Modern Philosophy: Descartes and His School.* New York, Charles Scribner's Sons, 1887.

Foucher de Careil, Louis Alexandre comte de, *Descartes, la princesse Elisabeth, et la reine Christine.* Paris, Félix Alcan, 1909.

———, *Descartes et la princesse palatine ou de l'influence du cartésianisme sur les femmes au XVIIᵉ siècle.* Paris, Auguste Durand, 1862.

Fouillée, Alfred, *Descartes.* Paris, Librairie Hachette, 1893.

Frédérix, Pierre, *Monsieur René Descartes et son temps.* Paris, Gallimard, 1959.

Galston, Iago, "Descartes and Modern Psychiatric Thought." *Isis,* Vol. XXXV (Spring, 1944), pp. 118–128.

Gibson, A. Boyce, *The Philosophy of Descartes.* London, Methuen & Co., 1932.

Gilson, Etienne, *Etudes sur le rôle de la pensée médiévale dans la formation du système cartésien.* Paris, Vrin, 1951.

Godfrey, Elizabeth (pseud. Jessie Bedford), *A Sister of Prince Rupert.* New York, John Lane Co., 1909.

Gouhier, Henri, *Essais sur Descartes.* Librairie Philosophique. Paris, J. Vrin, 1937.

———, "Le Malin génie dans l'itinéraire cartésien." *Revue de philosophie* (janvier–février 1937), pp. 1–21.

———, *Les Premières Pensées de Descartes.* Librairie Philosophique. Paris, J. Vrin, 1958.

Gullace, Giovanni, "Sartre et Descartes: le problème de la liberté." *La Revue de l'Université Laval,* Vol. XXI (octobre 1966), pp. 107–125.

Haldane, Elizabeth, *Descartes, His Life and Times.* London, John Murray (Publishers), 1905.

Hamelin, Octave, *Le Système de Descartes.* Paris, Félix Alcan, 1911.

Itard, Jean, *La Géométrie de Descartes.* Université de Paris, Conférences du Palais de la Découverte, série D, No. 39 (1956).

Janet, Paul, "Descartes, son caractère et son génie." *Revue des deux mondes,* Vol. 73 (1868), pp. 345–69.

———, *Les maîtres de la pensée moderne.* Paris, Calmann-Lévy, 1883.

Keeling, S.-V., *Descartes.* London, Ernest Benn, 1934.

Laporte, Jean, "La Liberté selon Descartes." *Revue de métaphysique et de morale,* Vol. 44 (janvier 1937), pp. 101–164.

Lefèvre, Roger, *La Vocation de Descartes.* Paris, Presses Universitaires de France, 1956.

Leroy, Maxime, *Descartes, le philosophe au masque,* 2 vols. Paris, Rieder, 1929.

Lewis, Geneviève, "Bilan de cinquante ans d'études cartésiennes." *Revue philosophique* (avril–juin 1951), pp. 249–267.

——, *René Descartes, français, philosophe.* Paris, Maison Mame, 1953.

Liard, Louis, *Descartes.* Paris, Librairie Germer Bailière, 1882.

Mahaffy, J. P., *Descartes.* London, William Blackwood and Sons, 1880.

Maritain, Jacques. *The Dream of Descartes.* London, Editions Poetry, 1946.

——, *Le Songe de Descartes.* Paris, Corrêa, 1932.

——, *Three Reformers: Luther, Descartes, Rousseau.* London, Sheed and Ward, 1928.

Mesnard, Pierre, *Descartes ou le combat pour la vérité.* Paris, Éditions Seghers, 1966.

——, *Essai sur la morale de Descartes.* Paris, Boivin, 1936.

Milhaud, Gérard, "Sur les obscurités de la géométrie de Descartes." *Congrès Descartes,* Vol. 2 (1937), pp. 21–26.

Milhaud, Gaston, *Descartes savant.* Paris, Félix Alcan, 1921.

Millet, Joseph, *Descartes, sa vie, ses travaux, ses découvertes avant 1637.* Paris, Didier, 1867.

Néel, Marguerite, *Descartes et la princesse Elisabeth.* Paris, Éditions Elzevir, 1946.

Péguy, Charles, *Note sur M. Bergson et la philosophie bergsonienne. Note conjointe sur M. Descartes et la philosophie cartésienne.* Paris, Éditions Gallimard, 1935.

Poulet, Georges, *Études sur le temps humain.* Paris, Éditions Plon, 1950.

Rochemonteix, P. Camille de, *Un Collège de Jésuites aux XVIIe et XVIIIe siècles—Le Collège Henri IV de la Flèche,* Vol. I. Le Mans, Leguicheux et Cie., 1889.

Sacy, Samuel S. de, *Descartes par lui-même.* Ecrivains de toujours. Paris, Éditions du Seuil, 1956.

——, "Monsieur René Descartes." *Mercure de France* (septembre 1956), pp. 99–113.

Sartre, Jean-Paul, "La Liberté cartésienne," in *Descartes,* Paris, Trois collines, 1946.

Schönberger, Stephen, "A Dream of Descartes: Reflections on the Unconscious Determinants of the Sciences." *International Journal of Psychology,* Vol. XX (January, 1939), pp. 43–57.

Scott, Joseph F., *The Scientific Work of René Descartes.* London, Taylor and Francis, 1952.

Sebba, Gregor, *Bibliographia Cartesiana: A Critical Guide to the Descartes Literature 1800–1960.* The Hague, Martinus Nijhoff, 1964.

Serrurier, Cornelia, *Descartes, l'homme et le penseur.* Paris, Presses Universitaires de France, 1951.

Sirven, J., *Les Années d'apprentissage de Descartes (1596–1628).* Paris, Vrin, 1930.

300 BIBLIOGRAPHY

Smith, Norman Kemp, *New Studies in the Philosophy of Descartes*. New York, Russell and Russell, Inc., 1963.

Stolpe, Sven, *Christina of Sweden*. London, Burns & Oates, 1966.

Taylor, I. A., *Christina of Sweden*. London, Hutchinson & Co., 1909.

Thibaudet, Albert, "Un Ballet de Descartes." *Revue de Genève*, Vol. I (juillet–décembre 1920).

——, "Préface à la naissance de paix." *Revue de Genève* (août 1920).

Valéry, Paul, "Descartes." *Revue de métaphysique et de morale*, Vol. 44 (octobre 1937), pp. 693–710.

——, "Fragment d'un Descartes." Reprinted in his *Variété II*. Paris, Éditions Gallinard, 1930.

Vuillemin, Jules, *Mathématiques et métaphysique chez Descartes*. Paris, Presses Universitaires de France, 1960.

Wang, Leonard, "A Controversial Biography: Baillet's *La Vie de Monsieur Des-Cartes*." *Romanische Forschungen*, Vol. 75 (1963), pp. 316–331.

Index